JACKSON C. FRANK
The Clear, Hard Light of Genius

A Memoir by Jim Abbott

Ba Da Bing Records • *Brooklyn, NY*

Ba Da Bing Records
181 Clermont Ave. Suite 403, Brooklyn, NY 11205

ISBN: 978-0-9909164-0-6

Design by Katie Von Schleicher
Copy Edit by Mara Connor and Karen Millar

www.badabingrecords.com
www.twitter.com/badabingrecords

Dedication

This book is dedicated to the memory of Sean Body. Sean was the driving force and main man behind Helter Skelter Publishing, a company that brought a new definition to the word "class." It was Sean who encouraged me to write this book and then, almost immediately after reading and liking the first few chapters I sent him, died from leukemia. Due to the distance between us, and the fact that he had not been in touch for a few months, I had no idea that he had passed until a friend in the UK sent me his obituary. His estate was a tangled affair and with Sean no longer running the show, I put my manuscript away for a bit, waiting for a sign, I guess. And I got one. In 2011, some long-lost studio recordings finally surfaced, and word got to the attention of Ben Goldberg, owner of Ba Da Bing Records in Brooklyn, New York. You are holding in your hands one part of Ben's faith in this project, and my gratitude knows no bounds..

I also want to dedicate this to the memory of my own friend and mentor, Jim Lemyre. Jim was my English teacher in high school and after that was so much more, until kidney disease took him too soon at 59 years of age. Thank you for your wisdom and support, old friend. You are missed every single day.
Also, a huge debt is owed to Mark Anderson, who was instrumental in making my first meeting with Jackson C. Frank come to pass. Who knows what would have happened if he had not...?

I also want to mention several people whose help was invaluable to me. Thank you to Al Stewart, Curtis Delisle, whose failed documentary efforts were my gain, the late Marilyn and Elmer Frank, Jackson's parents, and his ex-wife, Elaine Frank, who spoke openly and honestly about her years of pain, John Ren-

bourn, who took the time to write to me about the old days, a big thank you to Richard Stanley, whose own recollections added some much appreciated humor to Jackson's early story. Also, thank you to Katherine Henry Wright, John Kay, the late Bert Jansch, John Boylan, Jerry Raven, Diana J. Stern, Norm Boggs, Marianne Collins, Alf Storrud, Charles Reynolds, Geoff Sullivan for his wonderful tribute page to Jackson, Marlene Cook and Kathleen Nealy, whose memories of her foster sister Marlene Du-Pont were touching and fresh. Also, huge thanks to T. J. McGrath and Pamela Murray Winters for the use of their interviews with Jackson. And a big "thank you" to Philip Ward for allowing me to use his words about Sandy Denny's wonderful tribute to Jackson. And lastly, my gratitude to Chris Jones, whose memory of the brilliance of Jackson's return performance in 1968, and his subsequent locating of the Telegraph's review actually led me to change the title of this book.

And to the many people out there who have appreciated his music. This is his story. I hope you like it.

Foreword

It started with a song that seemingly came out of nowhere, but that is still with us, years after its creator has departed. The blues, as it says, do run the game, every time.

I was perusing an internet blogger's list of what he called the "top five hundred songs of all time." As is the case with all lists of this sort (and I have seen many of them), it was very subjective, but most of the greats were on there, including the Who, Beatles, Stones, Dylan, Simon and Garfunkel, even some that I would question and some that just don't make the cut (Foreigner???). All in all, though, it was a decent roster, and I have been fortunate to live my half century of life right in the middle of almost all of the great music on it, with the exceptions of the 1950's rock and roll. It's been a good time to be alive, especially from a musical standpoint.

My musical awareness began very early, thanks to a babysitter who would often bring her portable record player over along with a stack of 45-rpm records, including Peter, Paul and Mary, Dylan, and more. I watched the Beatles on Ed Sullivan and fell into a love of music without a struggle. Little did I realize while I was growing up in upstate New York, a five-year-old in 1965, that thousands of miles away from my sandbox a story was unfolding that someday would take over a good part of my own life. It would take almost twenty years, but that story eventually became entwined with my own and would stay that way for over fifteen years. That story was Jackson C. Frank's. His name didn't appear on that tally of the five hundred greatest songs, making the list suspect in hindsight. In fact, his name is barely seen anywhere, which is a crime, because he could have been, and maybe still was, one of the greats. But, as John Lennon wrote, "Life is what happens while you're busy making other plans."

Jackson C. Frank, who had lived a lonely life, died an equally lonely death of pneumonia and a heart attack on March 3, 1999. Much of his fifty-six years were spent in a constant state of severe pain and severe confusion, so when the end came his spirit likely rose from his body and breathed a sigh of relief. As songwriter Dan Bern wrote about the day that Elvis Presley died, it "was like a mercy killing" when Jackson C. Frank's soul finally left this planet.

What was over was a life that saw incredible heights of creativity, and incredible lows of homelessness, mental illness, and moments of cruelty that no human being should have to suffer. But, such is the world we live in.

What is striking about his story isn't just the incredible music that he gave us, but the fact that he did it while at various times deep into paranoid schizophrenia, and in a drone of aching bones and muscles and general pain.

Rolling Stone Magazine Editor David Fricke has called Jackson C. Frank "one of the best forgotten songwriters of the 1960s." He came of age in a time when there weren't cameras in every phone or mounted in every corner, and as a result there is almost no evidence on film or video of his very existence. He did exist though. And Fricke knew what he was talking about, because Jackson C. Frank really was that good. There are those who make their mark in this world. They create, compose, build—whatever their special talent is, and then fade into the background to live out their lives in relative obscurity. There are also people who accomplish nothing—the Kardashians of the world who have little if any discernible skills but through relentless self-promotion become famous for...being famous. In the "cult of celebrity" world where reality TV rules and celebrities are created just by someone putting their dirty laundry out there for the world to see, true talent and a compelling story too often fall through the cracks of history. Nick Drake, Jackson Frank, Jimi Hendrix, and others were barely in the spotlight long enough to work up a sweat, but look at what they created. What the hell has Kim Kardashian ever done???

Coincidence, or maybe fate, put me on the trail of the obscure, and as Bert Jansch's biographer Colin Harper once described him, near-apocryphal folk singer, and after years of near misses (or near meets, to paraphrase the late, great George Carlin) I finally located him. This is his story, and due to the circumstances that steered us to meeting in Queens, New York, one hot summer day in 1993, it is also in part my story, although I have tried to keep myself out of the text as much as possible except for one long chapter detailing how we met and what happened to him in the last seven years of his life.

If ever there was a man destined to travel through life with a dark cloud over his head it was Jackson C. Frank. Bad luck and misfortune followed him like a shadow. The reasons why aren't clear—they just did. Some of his problems were the man himself. A line from the Alan Parker film *Midnight Express* might sum it up: "The bad machine doesn't know it's a bad machine." Injuries from the fire that almost killed him were certainly a factor, but events that happened later in his life had absolutely nothing to do with those injuries. Mental illness, almost certainly a residual effect of the fire, was another factor. Jamaicans have a word for people who constantly have misfortune and can never shake it—"salt" they call it. Jackson Frank was "salt," to be sure.

The idea of writing a book about Jackson had been in the back burner of my mind for many years, but I wasn't confident that I had enough material. It wasn't for lack of encouragement by people to whom I told the nutshell version of his story, that much is certain. They all said "Book!" but I was hesitant. Because my association with him went a long way towards costing me a home and a marriage, it actually became a part of my life that I had needed to, wanted to, and managed to put behind me for a while. However, rummaging through the collection of documents, letters, photos and more that I had accumulated, and by actually reading them, I was amazed to discover how much information there was about Jackson, his ailments and his injuries. There was even a rough chronology of sorts. What was left for someone to do was to piece the puzzle together and dig around for the parts that were missing, to make the picture as complete as possible. His mother, Marilyn Frank, was a big help, unwittingly. She had saved everything he ever wrote to her and made copies of everything she ever wrote to him and for him: to doctors, legal professionals, even landlords, trying to help her son's cause. At one point before Jackson's death she sent him a large, representative packet of these letters and other ephemera from his past. Her stated purpose was to basically browbeat him into quitting smoking and to keep up with his medications, which he was wont to quit taking on occasion (whenever he felt better). The letters and a few old photos were to show him what he used to be like and what she thought he could be once again. It was not to be, and after he died I called her with the intention of giving them back to her but she told me to hold on to them. Later on I called her for more, if she had any, for the purposes of an article, which eventually became this book. She did send me a box full of letters and photos, among other things, but I had already moved on from the article. I put them away and only recently had the inclination to look through them.

Some people shine through adversity, making something positive out of their misfortune. Some turn the wrong way and make matters worse for themselves and everyone around them. Jackson was by most accounts a good man, an injured human being who did the best he could with the hand he was dealt. Severe burns are one thing, but when hidden forces like mental illness are lurking in the shadows, life becomes a twisted trail, full of traps and hazards. How we deal with them is how we build character. Woody Guthrie is a good example. Unwittingly doomed to suffer the ravages of the hereditary and fatal Huntington's Disease, he didn't know what was afflicting him for a long time, although he had borne witness to what it could do when it had previously afflicted and then killed his mother. He tried to live a normal life but the tics and flailing arms that inevitably come with Huntington's were too much for him and eventually he was forced into institutionalization. He legendarily was arrested in New Jersey for public drunkenness due to the flailing arms and muted responses associated with the ailment. When his manager Harold Leventhal was summoned to bail him out, he was informed by the police that the man must be delusional—he claimed to have written books and a thousand songs, to which Leventhal replied, "He has."

Jackson coped as well as he could, but also ended up institutionalized, many times. The stigma attached to mental illness is very powerful and there are some who would rather be labeled a criminal than carry the shame of being called "mentally ill." Jackson and his mother both fought that label for his entire life, even when the evidence was overwhelming. Those who knew him all say this: the man didn't have an evil bone in his body, but his psychological problems caused him to say and do things that were hurtful to some of his closest friends and family. While they would always forgive him, it still hurt.

He was an extremely complicated human being—stubborn, temperamental and unyielding at times. He did some things that made people angry with him, and he seemed to lack empathy, the ability to place himself in someone else's shoes, which caused him to say some things that were deeply hurtful. Yet, his scarred body housed a beautiful soul, and I found him to be a lovely and decent man, one of the most inherently good people I have ever known.

And he made music as beautiful as his soul, complicated and enduring music that belied the terrible tragedies through which he had suffered, singing in a voice that others could only envy, with real passion and power. The lucky few who saw him play never forgot him. In recent years, with the surge in popularity of the internet, his back story, to use a phrase in vogue at the moment, has become more notable than his music, and that in itself is another tragedy, because his musical gifts were prodigious. His good friend Richard Stanley, an accomplished classically trained musician himself, has noted of Jackson's music that while bits of it sound somewhat derivative in nature, most of the songs and their elements are original and unique to Jackson. That is the sign of true genius...take one part of this, another part of that, and presto! Something new and unique. Woody Guthrie did it. Dylan did it. Jackson Frank did it.

Stanley, who contributed generously to this book, also struggled with being able to describe the effect that Jackson had on him. Although their friendship was intense and very close, it was relatively short, and to this day Stanley, usually very eloquent, is hard-pressed to come up with words to explain why something so limited in scope has so strongly affected him to this day. It shouldn't, but it has.

I discovered a strange paradox—the people who knew Jackson for any real length of time were often relieved when he would drop out of their lives, but almost every person loved him and would not say a negative word about him. They knew his demons were not him. He might have been abrasive and overly blunt, but to a great degree it wasn't his fault. Still, Jackson in small doses seems to have been the successful prescription.

He wasn't alone in this world. He had a mother and father who loved him. He had been married and fathered two children, losing one shortly after birth, and losing his wife and daughter to his own mental illness when it began to take over his personality. He had friends who cared deeply but could only stand by helplessly as his demons had their way with him.

The word tragedy is a heavy one but somehow it fits Jackson's story. I don't want the reader to be put off by the heaviness of Jackson's burden, but to admire the way that he managed to shine through the clouds when he was able. I also want the reader to then listen to the music that the man created and try to make sense of it all. Beauty comes from the ugliest places sometimes.

About Jackson's mother, Marilyn: I have no doubt that without her lifelong support, financially and spiritually, Jackson's story, as sad as it is, would have been much worse. For four decades she watched the trials and tribulations her only child was put through. To see a happy normal child wake up one morning and go to school, only to return home eight months later as a scarred, crippled and tortured soul is a tragedy. That he would later be plagued by voices in his head and yet still be gifted with a rare talent he could never take full advantage of, except for one bright shining moment in 1965, is another tragedy.

She certainly was overly protective and overbearing and couldn't or wouldn't let him make a move without a critical word, but she was his mother. She also was at times his worst enabler. That she outlived him is against the ways of nature, but that she was there for him in all of his times of need is exactly the way it should be.

Prologue

Levy's Recording Studio, located at 103 New Bond Street in London was a small and intimate place, and a room favored by Columbia Records as a place for many of their artists to record. The singer, a newcomer to professional recording studios, hated closed-in spaces. On this day, just a couple months after Bob Dylan had recorded some tracks in the very same room, he also hated having anyone watching him. He was nervous about the entire recording process, and the microphone in front of him seemed to be staring him down, taunting him, challenging him to open his mouth and sing. So too, it seemed, were the men and women, friends all, who were seated behind the glass walls of the control room.

"I can't play. You're watching me," he said. So, screens were set up in the room to give the singer a place to hide, and he used them to full advantage. The producer, a diminutive young New Yorker named Paul Simon, had an idea. He said, "Jackson, just run through the song while I work on getting the levels right."

Of course Jackson C. Frank knew that it was a trick but he went along with it, swilling a lot of tea, probably spiked with whiskey, until the recording was finished. Six hours after the tape began rolling, a masterpiece was "in the can" and the pressure was off.

The place was London and it was July of 1965. Jackson Frank had just recorded his first album for Columbia-EMI. His friend and fellow American Paul Simon had taken money, around fifty pounds, from his own pocket to pay for the session. Others present at the session were Sandy Denny, Jackson's girlfriend, and Judith Piepe, his de facto landlady and a gregarious woman who looked out for his best interests in her role as his unofficial manager. The record would sell less than 5,000 copies, but the impact it and its creator would have on the burgeoning folk scene in England would be huge and lasting.

Jackson had not come to England to make a record. His running story was that he had come to buy fancy cars and the music had happened almost by chance. As we shall later find out, the truth is often less glamorous, but still, England wasn't America, where nothing had gone right for him for years. Maybe his luck was changing. He was talented, some would even call him a genius, and he was as focused as he would ever be. He had an album on the way, had made a lot of new friends, had an equally talented girlfriend in Sandy Denny. Later, she would be called "the finest female singer to come out of England," but for the moment she was just a girlfriend watching her man make some magic. Given the quality of what found its way onto the tape that day, Jackson C. Frank's future was looking very bright indeed.

The future superstars assembled in that small room could not possibly know that Jackson C. Frank would never make another record again.

The World Did Explode

On the morning of March 31, 1954, recently turned 11-years-old Jackson C. Frank awoke from a good night's sleep. It would be the last good night's sleep he would have for a long time. Sleeping is difficult when half of the skin has been roasted off your body.

Around the snowy Buffalo, New York suburb of Cheektowaga, hundreds of other children also awoke to face the day. It would be a fateful one for all of them, tragic, filled with stories of heroism and loss. The events of that day ultimately would be responsible for sweeping safety regulations and changes in the schools of the nation.

What came to be known as the "Cleveland Hill School Fire" began on that day in the basement boiler room. The school's old furnace was roaring away, keeping the students and teachers warm inside the school while outside everyone endured the often brutally harsh Buffalo winter (an unfortunate result of the city's being located right in the path of weather formations as they crossed the Great Lakes that cluster the western New York and Ohio borders, often bringing so-called "lake effect" snowfalls of over twenty feet during the course of the winter season). You had to be tough to live in Buffalo after October blew through, and though it was technically springtime on March 31, winter in Buffalo often overstays its welcome.

Unbeknownst to anyone, (or possibly ignored?) multiple holes, some the size of a child's hand, had formed on the side of the ancient furnace, allowing gases and coal dust fumes to leak out, and slowly but steadily build up in the hollow areas of the school, in the rafters and near the ceiling. There had been complaints about odd odors around the school for a while but nothing had been done. The music room was in a new but temporary wooden annex, which had been hastily built to accommodate the increased student population that resulted from the large influx of new families as people were hired to work for several growing local companies. It was connected to the rest of the school by a long tunnel, into which the long lines from the food serving area of the cafeteria would sometimes spill. There were no exits save for the classroom doors and the long corridor leading to the connecting tunnel. In effect, the annex was the silent bomb at the end of a long fuse.

In the music room of the annex, Mr. Thomas Griffin's class of sixth graders, including young Jackson Frank, were having their music lesson. They had walked as a group from their classroom in the main building, and were having fun practicing their rhythm sticks. They were probably happy for a couple of reasons. For one, Mr. Griffin was out sick that day, which is always fun for the students because substitute teachers are easy prey for good-natured ribbing from their charges. The other cause for happiness was that it was the last day for student teacher June Muhaney, who was moving on in her career in music education. There are usually little class celebrations when a student teacher is ready to move onward.

School officials have reported that there were thirty-one students in class that day, along with Mrs. Muhaney and the music teacher, Mrs. Melba Siebold. There was also a choir gown salesman named Robert Winters present in the room taking measurements when the accumulated fumes and coal dust exploded, sending a line of fire down the hallway toward the music room. It was 11:22 a.m. Like mice in a maze the students could only react to the fast and furious smoke and flames by running to the exits available.

The rest of the school, away from the fire, knew something was happening. Administrators and teachers moved quickly, announcing over the public address system that everyone was to leave their classrooms and follow their teachers' instructions. They had all heard the explosion when the boiler blew. They were then systematically herded to another school building and were assembled there while music (one student remembers that Blue Moon was played) and other distractions were employed to divert their attention from the carnage in the annex. Plans were made for them to go home, and they were dismissed a short time later.

In the tunnel, where the lunch line had spilled out from the main building, fourth grader Ed Marek had just gotten his food. He recalled what happened next.

"At the time of the explosion," he says, "black smoke started coming down the line from [behind me] and I moved quickly to the lunch room...the alarms were sounding and the teachers were moving us all in good order to an exit door."

Tension began to build when the teachers either could not open the doors or saw smoke outside in the hallway and elected not to send the students out through them. Marek recalls the feeling of frustration.

"All I remember is," he said, "I was close to those doors and now I couldn't use them. A moderate amount of panic then set in and we all ran for the doors at the other end of the room."

Thankfully for Marek and the others, the school staff were well trained and acted appropriately. What was already a bad situation could have been much worse had they not kept their composure.

'The teachers slowed us down and whipped us into shape" he said. "By the time we got to the exit we were marching out in an orderly way." Years later, in recalling the story for Talking Proud: A Magazine About Service And Sacrifice, a very gracious and thankful Marek is careful to remember the gift he and many others were given that day.

"To my knowledge, we all got out of that lunchroom, through the grace of God and the discipline of those teachers who forced us to slow down, make way and exit in good order. They saved our lives," he said.

Unlike Marek's situation, for Mrs. Siebold's music class things couldn't have been much worse. For one thing, there were no exits. With the fire blazing outside and smoke working its way through the wooden structure there was not much time to do anything but panic.

In the Cheektowaga Times the next day, Mrs. Muhaney described the scene as follows: "There was a loud noise, very sudden. I guess it was an explosion...the door to the hallway was open at the time and I suddenly saw smoke pour down the hall. Then the whole hall was in flames." As can be expected, many children, all around 11-years-old and inexperienced in fire safety, ran toward the door, just as the flames burst through the doorway. "I think it was the children who rushed through the door who were burned most seriously," said Mrs. Muhaney.

Mrs. Siebold, seeing the flames, shouted loudly, "Break the windows!" and she, Mrs. Muhaney, and the gown salesman, Robert Winters, all rushed to the windows, using their hands in frantic attempts to smash the small window panes which were held in place by a sturdy metal frame. The class was, in effect, in a cage. At first the teachers and the salesman started to pound the panes with their fists, breaking the glass but cutting their hands and arms. Students began using chairs to break more panes. Once the glass was out, the smaller children were lifted and pushed through the tiny openings. The ground outside was wet and covered with snow. This may have helped save a life or two. As Jackson Frank would recall many years later, "I don't remember it but was told that someone managed to throw me out a window and into the snow and that the snow helped put out the flames that were on my back."

Jackson, who was one of several young heroes that day, pushing several children through the small window panes before collapsing from the heat and smoke, later recalled, "Someone flagged down a car...I think it was a station wagon driven by a stranger, and I was loaded into it and taken to the hospital." Along with four other children, Jackson was taken by the station wagon driver to Meyer Memorial Hospital in Buffalo. Years later it would still be fresh in his mind, as he complained that emergency procedures were not in place to take the burn victims to the hospital. For many years he was bitterly angry at the powers that be for their poor planning and lack of foresight where the safety of the children inside the school was concerned.

Mrs. Siebold, who was credited with saving the lives of twenty-four of the children, decided to head to the office to get help. She managed to get out through one of the windows and jumped. She was already suffering from severe burns and smoke inhalation. The fall from the window, despite being a short one, broke her back in three places.

Mrs. Muhaney, amid all of the fire and smoke didn't see any more children in the room, and, assuming they were all safe, herself jumped to safety. She later was treated for several bad burns and cuts from the broken glass. The gown salesman, Robert Winters, also managed to get out in one piece, suffering only minor injuries.

Ten children didn't make it out. They died right there in the annex, inches from safety, helping their classmates to escape the inferno. The ten who ignored their own well-being and as a result sacrificed their own lives, and who will forever be 11 years old, and whose names respectfully warrant mention here were Bruce Brand, Verna Bagley, Michael Hause, Elizabeth Lies, John Mendofik, Patricia Steger, Marlene Dupont, Barbara Watkins, Blaine Poss and Reba Smith. Tragically, witnesses at the scene said later that they saw Blaine Poss push three children out of the window after he had already escaped. When he realized that his girlfriend, Reba Smith was still inside, he turned around and went back into the flames for her. He was just beginning to push her out the window when the walls collapsed on both of them.

Mrs. Mary Lies, a second grade teacher, left the area with bloodstains on her blouse. She had rushed down the tunnel to try to help, and succeeded in carrying two children out to safety, all the while knowing that her own daughter Elizabeth was still inside and was likely not coming out. This was true and selfless courage in human form.

The other eight children's bodies were later discovered huddled by the window walls as they apparently sought relief from the smoke and heat. Five more children, Patricia Blendowski, Donald Kelleher, Marlene Miller, Suzanne Jors and George Hoffman would die of their injuries over the course of the next eight days, bringing the final total of fatalities to fifteen.

Identification of the dead children was a difficult task. One of the children's bodies was burned so badly that the feet were missing. Some were identified by bits of clothing that were still intact. Blain Poss' steer-shaped belt buckle was instrumental in letting his family know which victim was their son. Marlene Dupont was identified by her foster parents, William and Ceil Axford. Her biological father Joseph Dupont, who had given up custody of Marlene temporarily, collapsed upon hearing the news of the fire and had to be hospitalized. The moment was captured by *LIFE* magazines cameras and appeared in a poignant tribute to the fallen children in the April 10, 1954 edition of that publication. What *LIFE* didn't relate in their brief, photo-filled story was how angry the parents of the injured and dead children were because of the fact that photographers were so intrusive at the local hospitals, pushing and sneaking around trying to get photos for their magazine, with no respect for their privacy.

§

The summer of 1954 was a long one for the victims and their families. Besides *LIFE* Magazine, then the leading weekly in the country, many other publications covered the story with touching photos and great sympathy. Local newspapers kept the public updated about the recovery process of the injured on a daily basis. Looking at photos of the school as it burned, and seeing the impossibly small window panes brings not only sadness but a touch of anger when one realizes that if the windows were of the type that are used in schools today, it is likely no one would have been killed. The time it took to break out the panes and squeeze small children through smaller spaces was too great. It only took thirty minutes for the annex to burn completely down to the ground. The amount of time that the children and teachers would have been able to withstand the heat was far less. The windows, as much as the fire, were the reason so many were killed and maimed.

The Cleveland Hill School fire was not, by far, the worst school fire in the history of the United States. That dubious distinction goes to the Consolidated High School in New London, Texas, where 294 children and teachers were killed on March 18, 1937 when there was a massive gas explosion caused by incorrectly installed gas pipes.

The tragedy of the Cleveland Hill fire did have a tarnished silver lining of sorts. As a result of the fire, and after an analysis of the deficiencies in the area of safety, massive reforms in school fire safety were enacted, leading to fire alarms, minimum window sizes, sprinkler systems and more. And although there have been tens of thousands of fires in schools or on school properties (in 2002 alone there were over 6,000 structure fires in non-adult schools) since 1954, there has not been a single fatality. It was a tough lesson well-learned on that fateful day over 55 years ago.

Over the years there have been many memorials and tributes to the fallen students and the heroic rescuers. Many accolades have also gone to Mrs. Melba Siebold, who allowed self-doubt to slip into her thoughts occasionally, wondering if she should have closed the door to the room to slow the fire since the breaking of the windows caused a draft that may have pulled the fire in more quickly. Though there are many scenarios to consider, a fire burning through a building as fast as the one in the annex isn't going to be deterred for long by a door. Had modern, fire-rated doors been the norm, the outcome of that day might well have been a different one. It is, however, pointless to speculate this many years after the fact.

Mrs. Siebold was out of work for two years, recovering from her broken back, as well as burns and severe smoke inhalation, which damaged her vocal chords, an injury that would make teaching vocal music a real challenge. She returned and taught for a few more years, retiring in 1960 so she could focus on a related passion—the teaching of difficult stringed instruments to small children, in an era when such a concept wasn't considered realistic. She persevered, however, and founded the Cleveland Hill Elementary School Orchestra, and taught hundreds of children how to play violin, viola and cello.

It was eight months before all of the injured were out of the hospital. For many the worst was yet to come. Burns are among the worst types of injuries even today, in an era of superior medical treatment, and the suffering and pain they cause is often unbearable, and the effect they have on other parts of the body and its functions is unpredictable. To suffer such injuries in the mid-1950's was often a death sentence, or a fate worse than death.

For Jackson C. Frank, the rest of his life was just beginning.

Before the Fire

Jackson Carey Jones was born on March 2nd, 1943, in Buffalo, New York, the only child of Marilyn Rochefort Jones and her husband Jack Jones. Jack Jones was a test pilot. Indeed, he was almost the stereotypical test pilot straight out of The Right Stuff. Photos show him as a handsome man, gallant in his leather bomber jacket, flying for the Boeing Aircraft Company, and looking not unlike another contemporary flyboy of renown, Chuck Yeager. There even exists a picture of him standing next to his plane, a la Yeager and his Bell X-1.

Yeager took his plane to Mach 1, the speed of sound, before anyone else. Jack Jones was no Chuck Yeager, however. He lacked character, and he may well have been an alcoholic. He also seemed to have a dislike for income-producing activity, other than flying, and justly earned his reputation as a philanderer. This lousy combination of character flaws tore his family apart. Jones' son would, years later, prove that the fruit doesn't fall far from the tree, and would be accused by his wife of "trying to re-enact Jack Jones, and destroy himself and his family."

Acquaintances would later recall that even though Jack Jones was a poor role model, his son maintained a high level of admiration for the man, and would often tell fanciful stories about his flying exploits for years after they faded from everyone else's memory. One such tale involved young Jackson's belief that Jack Jones was the model for the book God is My Co-Pilot, by retired United States Air Force General Robert Scott, but a quick examination of the book reveals the story to be all that of General Scott and none of Jack Jones. Was it a father's exaggeration of his resume to his son? A son's fantasy of his wayward father? Who can say?

It isn't known why the boy came to be called Jackson, except by virtue of being Jack's son. Many years later, Sandy Denny would use that reference to great advantage in "Next Time Around," her powerful song about her relationship with Jackson.

"Then came the question and it was about time
The answer came back and it was long
The house, it was built by some man in a rhyme
But whatever came of his talented son?

Who wrote me a dialogue set to a tune?
Always, you told me of being alone
Except for the stories about God and you

And do you still live there in Buffalo?

"Next Time Around," by Sandy Denny © 1971

At any rate, he wouldn't be a Jones for long. His mother divorced Jack Jones and his self-destructive bent. She was on her own for a while, bravely and gamely working her way through secretarial school with the help of her mother, while also working typing jobs and other clerical duties. It was the middle of World War II and there were many jobs in the secretarial pools for capable women, so Marilyn excelled. They moved to Elyria, Ohio, to a "wartime world with chickens in the front yard," as Jackson would describe it many years later, before returning to the Buffalo area, settling in Cheektowaga, on Kensington Road.

Shortly after the war ended, Marilyn met Elmer Frank. He was a military man, one who had done time as an officer on duty during the Nuremberg Trials and had retired to a civilian position as a cereal chemist. She fell in love for all the right reasons. Elmer Frank was a good man, straight out of the "good man" mold. He immediately knew what he wanted out of life—a wife as good as he was a man, and a family. It was a simple "I do" away. As he recalled in 2007, "When I got married, my wife was divorced and Jack came from that marriage, and naturally when I got married my first thought was adoption, which I did right away."

Adopting another man's child indicates Elmer's good grace, despite pressures from his family. "As I recall my folks said, 'When are you going to have a baby of your own?' and I told them that if I had my own baby I would probably care more for it whether it was a boy or a girl than I would for my adopted son, and I don't want to be in that position. So we held off, and we held off to the point where we no longer thought about it that way."

Jackson's name was legally changed to Jackson Carey Frank,

and the family went about their living and growing together. Jackson and Elmer got along just fine. There were some "you're not my real father" kind of conflicts, but Marilyn was happy to dote on her only child. Everything was going fine and the picture was a happy one, until that one fateful spring morning in late March of 1954.

... The Damage Done...

In a letter some years later, Marilyn Frank described the devastation that had been wrought upon her son to yet another doctor who would be evaluating Jackson. It was as horrible a letter as any mother has ever had to put on paper.
She wrote:

"Dear Dr. Weiss,
...I think it's important that you be aware of some extenuating circumstances concerning what resembles arthritis in Jack's hip joint. As was explained to me in laymen's terms, Jack had first, second and third degree burns over 58% of his body after the school fire. All burns are considered extremely toxic. The first hurdle they had to get over was cleansing and containing the burned areas. Pressure bandages were applied, treatment for traumatic shock started with intravenous fluids etc. The next thing was the body's reaction in the form of swelling which caused his face to swell so much his eyes were swollen shut, nose flat and lips like a split in a melon...the neck and air passages had to be kept clear and they had closed causing a buildup of fluids in the chest cavity or lungs. An emergency tracheotomy was performed in the hospital room. Jack was considered exceptional the way he mastered the art of speaking with the trach tube in his throat. He was completely cooperative and fighting hard to stay alive.

And then we descended into the valley. Jack's body temperature rose to 108 degrees and stayed there for a long period of time. He was not alone in this. Most of the other children had the same or similar problems."

Indeed, though the situation was dire, lives were saved utilizing the methods that were in place for Jackson and the other children. Most of the injured were gathered together in one large ward with two nurses standing by each child. They were packed in ice beds and given ice water enemas to help bring down their fevers, which had risen to dangerous levels. Brain damage can occur after a sustained period of high temperature and the ice treatments, which must have been excruciating, were used with the hopes of preventing that from happening. When one child died during the procedure, Marilyn and Elmer Frank were told to prepare themselves for the very real probability that Jackson would be the next to go. Prayers and a strong fight from their son apparently did the trick, and Jackson's fever broke.

The letter continues, "…If this were a movie the next scene would be where a miraculously restored child was wheeled out of the hospital to live happily ever after. But this was real life and the months and years that followed would try our faith greatly."

Sadly, it was not a movie. The fever finally did break but the damage that it caused would not be understood until some time later. Located in the neck is a pair of glands called the parathyroids, whose job is to tell the body where to send the calcium that it receives through food intake or other means. If the leg bones need it, calcium gets sent there, and so on. Excess calcium in a healthy person is then sent out of the body through the body's waste disposal system. Jackson wasn't healthy. The high fever had completely shut down his parathyroid glands. The intravenous fluids that were being given to him contained levels of calcium that were considered normal for a growing eleven-year-old boy, but now, unregulated by the damaged or non-functioning parathyroids, the calcium was floating around freely in Jackson's body. It eventually began to settle in his elbows, shoulders and hip joints, much the same way that silt and sand build up at bends in a river. And those joints began to fuse together, which was extremely painful for Jackson. In an attempt to ease the suffering he was given Demerol, but in his discombobulated system, it actually excited the pain, worsening matters. Also of no help: some of the staff at the hospital, who were, according to Marilyn Frank, used to dealing with welfare patients and not a large group of severely injured children. One nurse in particular, known as Miss Dee, thought Jackson to be a spoiled child and made his life difficult, as if things weren't already tough, over what Marilyn Frank referred to as "regulations and trifles." As a result, the family decided to hire a private nurse and a private doctor to care for their son.

It was not an easy added expense. Marilyn Frank, in another letter years later, wrote, "Our income was cut almost in half because I could not return to work. Our expenses didn't decrease by half, in fact they increased…when the hospital called us in for a discussion about ' who?', and 'how much?', and 'when?' they (the burned victims) would get paid we (all the parents of the fire victims) decided to hire a lawyer."

The attorney idea was a good one and would result in insurance payouts that netted each burn victim the equivalent of close to a half million dollars today. With the proper investments and a little care, the beneficiaries would be set for life. At least that was the plan.

Jackson started a rigorous course of physical therapy once his burns began healing. His long list of surgeries already included the insertion of a metal plate in his head, to reinforce areas that had been burned severely, as well as skin grafts and removal of dead or charred tissue, and now several more would be necessary to free up his joints. The problem in his joints was diagnosed when Jackson, who was by most accounts (except, apparently, that of nurse "Miss Dee") an extremely good patient, began to scream loudly when asked, and then forced, to do some activities that were causing him severe discomfort. The nurses at the hospital were convinced that he was "acting out" but his mother, who knew her son well, was steadfast in her belief that he was in severe pain. Her persistence convinced the doctors to have another look at him. After a fresh set of x-rays was taken and the parathyroid/calcium problem identified, the forced therapy was halted and new surgeries were scheduled. Doctors decided to not touch his hips in the hopes that through regular walking, Jackson might keep them limber enough to avoid having them surgically fused. That procedure would have prevented him from either sitting or standing, depending on how they were set, but the doctors' gambit paid off, and although his hips were never fused together, they would forever be a constant source of discomfort, and he walked with a pronounced limp for the rest of his life.

His arms were another matter. There was no way he could use them that would prevent the calcium from doing its damage, so it was decided that, since he had to eat, his right arm would be fused in a ninety degree angle, a position that would enable him to reach his mouth to eat. His left arm would be more or less straight. While he would retain bits of motion in each arm, he'd be severely limited and that range of motion would decrease as he got older. Coincidently and fortuitously though, these positions were also conducive to being able to play a guitar.

The fire had garnered national attention in *LIFE* and other publications. Actor Kirk Douglas had heard about the fire and decided to make a trip to the hospital to visit Jackson and the other patients. A newspaper photo was published of Douglas, along with a swollen Jackson and his beaming mother all looking at a wallet that Douglas presented to Jackson, with an inscription in gold leaf pen, "To Jackie, A swell guy! Kirk Douglas." Jackson, bless his heart, was smiling.

While it was a fifties version of a photo-op, Douglas, who proved himself to be a class act, maintained a correspondence with Jackson for several years, exchanging notes and cards on holidays.

Another celebrity also got in touch. Although he wasn't a big name when the fire did its damage, as Jackson described it years later, "Elvis wrote me, saying 'I wish I could meet you, you're a brave little boy', and he sent me a letter and an autographed photo.' Decades later, Jackson would sadly sell his Elvis letter and photo for food money.

New York State requires all children to have an equal chance to have an education, regardless of their situation, so an instructor was assigned to work with the hospital-bound Jackson to keep him up on his studies. Charlie Castelli, the teacher assigned, brought his guitar and, accompanying a slide presentation of various historical eras, sang songs pertinent to each era, and to the lesson. It was a learning aid that Jackson would later adapt for his own purposes when presenting some of his research papers for history class. Jackson took to the instrument quickly and learned to play some basic finger-style accompaniment to old folk songs, which were his favorite type of music.

"I liked guitar so much when I heard him play it that I decided I would buy one for myself and I would teach myself how to play," recalled Jackson. "When I was about thirteen I got about thirteen dollars together and bought a Montgomery Ward guitar and from then on went about picking up things from various people who I'd meet...." Later his mother would give him a Gretsch Streamliner, his first electric guitar. Jackson spent eight-and-a-half months in the hospital. His case made medical history, as it gave doctors an opportunity to see the effects of fire on the inner workings of the body, and what can go wrong when a patient experiences a fever of the degree of the one that Jackson suffered. Most people who are burned as badly as Jackson die within a few days, as infections set in and the body is unable to fight them due to the havoc wrought on the immune system. Jackson's age, as well as his youthful spirit and support from his parents, kept him alive. He returned home in mid-December, with a long road of healing ahead of him. In the meantime, he kept at the guitar, read voraciously, and picked up an interest in writing and history.

§

As often happens in a good story, at some point a character is introduced who will help the protagonist to move forward in his life. Jackson had several of these characters play this role, starting with a fellow guitar neophyte named Richard Stanley. Jackson's impact on Stanley is still being felt today, more than thirty-five years after they last saw each other. They met, as might be expected, at a music store. Stanley's memories are precise and evoke both the time and their friendship perfectly.

Stanley: "Nyhart's Music Center was run by Charlie Nyhart out of the ground floor of his house, located behind the East Aurora movie theater in 'uptown' East Aurora. The front of the building looked out on the backs of various Main Street businesses, to one side a large parking lot, on the other an auto collision repair shop. The street, parking lot and area behind the stores seemed always to be full of potholes, accumulated refuse lined the backs of the buildings across the narrow street and the typical racket of the auto body shop filled the air much of the time.

The front room of the ground floor of Nyhart's was made to somewhat resemble a real store with a glass counter containing stuff like clarinet reeds, guitar picks and the like, a few feet inside the door. In the afternoon of a warm spring day, I stood at one end of this counter and looked up to see a person standing at the other end regarding me with a curious, friendly and somewhat whimsical air that was instantly attractive despite his somewhat strange appearance. I could not understand what it was about his appearance that seemed unusual. With fine blondish hair and skin that seemed almost translucent he rather had the effect of a semi-spirit as he stood there illuminated by the soft, late afternoon light. He had a guitar case next to him, I was there to buy strings and we exchanged greetings and names quite directly as I rather grappled with the effect of the person I had just met. He was decidedly not a normal person. A boyish smile flickered about the corners of his mouth and he spoke in a soft voice that seemed slightly hoarse and somehow enhanced his visual attractiveness which was overwhelming despite the strangeness about him.

For one thing, he seemed sort of crooked and oddly bent in his posture. His upper body leaned a bit to one side, his head cocked naturally to the other, a leg did not seem to quite straighten all the way, one arm was stiff and did not seem to flex past a right angle. In short, he gave the impression of being a little crumpled up like one of the wrecks in the yard of the body shop next door. And yet the entire effect was at once absolutely attractive, even irresistible with the warm magnetic glow of some kind of aura about him.

We both took a few lessons from Charlie Nyhart using the Nick Manoloff Guitar Method, first published in the mid-30's and unrevised at that time (late-50's). The book came with Nick Manoloff's Modern Accompaniment Guide, a sort of chord finding and transposing guide in the form of a circle with little windows that showed chord names and diagrams for all the keys as the second layer was rotated. On the back the mysteries of key signatures, major and relative minor were illuminated. The book was a dreadful bore, but this was the start for me of eventually learning to read music. Jackson had little use for this sort of thing and I don't think that he ever really learned notation. We both lasted but a few months although Charlie was an amiable enough teacher."

Jackson and Richard would remain friends for several years, and Richard even played the lute at Jackson's wedding in Elma, New York many years later. He would also be invited to appear with his band Time, at the 1968 Woodstock Sound Festival. Though their friendship eventually came to an unexpected end, Stanley still calls his bond with Jackson one of the two or three most important and closest relationships he has had to this day.

§

It is likely that because his hands were so delicate and sensitive, Jackson's guitar playing was affected in a unique way—it was, for the most part a gentle and clean fingerstyle, with very precise notes and was very melodic. Later, his British (and American) peers would all note how flawless and smooth his playing was. His hands had been badly burned and the resulting scar tissue threatened to tighten them up into a useless claw unless he did regular activity to keep the skin loose and the joints freely moving. The guitar exercises that he learned in the Manoloff method went a long way towards achieving that goal, as we now know, since his guitar playing would later be praised by all who were fortunate enough to hear it. It was difficult to copy his playing because he had learned to play with severe scar tissue connecting his right thumb and forefinger, the result of which led to a subtle but effective variance in syncopation when he played fingerstyle. Later, that flap of skin would be removed, but the style remained.

It took Jackson almost nine months in the hospital before he was deemed healthy enough to be discharged, and he returned home in mid-December. He still had a long road ahead of him but was healed enough to recuperate where he was comfortable, surrounded by family and his own things. In the meantime he kept working at the guitar and soon became quite proficient.

Young Mr. Frank Goes to Memphis

An Elvis performance in Buffalo and a "meet and greet" with the children who were injured in the fire had been tentatively scheduled. Unfortunately, it never came off as planned as Elvis' star rose ever higher, and the children of Cleveland Hill Elementary never got the chance to meet him.

That is, most of them didn't.

In the summer of 1957, Jackson and his mother took a trip down to the American south. Mrs. Frank had always been a Civil War buff, and subsequently young Jackson became fascinated with the subject as well. They had decided to spend the summer visiting some of the historic Civil War battlefields, which are, with one exception, Gettysburg, all located below the Mason-Dixon Line. While Elmer stayed home to work, Marilyn and Jackson headed out in the family's new Ford. Following a visit to one particular locale near Memphis, they realized that they were close to the big new house that the newspapers had reported had been recently purchased by Elvis Presley. They decided to make a pass by to see it. As fate would have it, Elvis's father, Vernon Presley, was out near the front gate, and they said hello to him. Marilyn Frank explained who Jackson was and told him about the correspondence that Elvis had exchanged with young Jackson following the fire. Within minutes Jackson and his mother were being escorted into Graceland and introduced to Gladys, Elvis's mother. Jackson was taken out back to the swimming pool for a private meeting with Elvis himself, and Vernon Presley took two photos of the young men standing by the pool. Elvis is wearing a bathing suit and has a towel around his shoulders. There is a jukebox behind them. Jackson looks uncomfortable and has his hand buried, Napoleon-like, in his shirt, which was hand sewn by his mother and modeled after one worn by Elvis on one of his album covers. It could be argued that it was not mere coincidence that he was wearing the shirt on the day they just happened to be near Graceland, but who knows?

The impromptu visit to Graceland stimulated something in Jackson. A few months later he and two buddies visited the Howell Recording Studio at 2703 Delaware Avenue in Buffalo, intent on making a record, ostensibly as a gift. His friends' names were Beau, or Bo, and Dave and the three of them ran through an instrumental and then Jackson performed solo on a two song medley. Before the instrumental, there is a quaint, somewhat formal introduction from Jackson to his grandparents, for whom the record was intended as a gift at Christmas. "Hi, Gram and Gramp. . . . We're sending you this record to wish you a Happy New Year's and a Merry Christmas. We hope that it's finding you well and in the best of health. As you know, the trio, Beau (or Bo-ed.), Dave and I played out at the Hamburg Fair this year and had quite a good time. We are sending you this record so that you may hear the trio as they were before Beau went to Tabor which is the Naval Academy training school. It's very good. . . he's on strings, Dave is on drums and I'm on background guitar. It's just a take-off and an exercise on 'Heartbeak Hotel,' so I think without further introduction we'll let you have the record. . ."

The recording sounds like what might have been heard in any garage in any neighborhood at the time—the early Elvis Presley years; a bunch of teenagers amateurishly plowing through the basic R&B chord progressions that make up "Heartbreak Hotel" lots of reverb and the volume up to ten.

The flip side of the 78 rpm disc contains some of Jackson's first recorded vocals, on a rather strange, two song medley comprised of "Santa Bring My Baby Back to Me," with a segue into the old gospel tune by Thomas Dorsey called "Precious Lord Take My Hand." The two songs are both from the Elvis canon, and tries his best to sound like him, not really succeeding but revealing a fine voice of his own with good control and pitch. His electric guitar playing is still in its formative stages, just basic strumming with very little nuance, just straight up and down on the strings. Jackson would record at Howell again several times, making records with songs related to school subjects he was learning. Unfortunately none of the school-related discs seem to have survived the years.

Marilyn Frank would write years later that she and Jackson were both fans of Elvis Presley, but for two very different reasons. Jackson, because his music inspired him to want to play and make his own way in the music world, and Marilyn, because a national icon had taken the time out to both write to her son and to treat him with kindness at his own home. It's unlikely that Elvis ever knew what had become of the young man with scars who visited him at Graceland. A little kindness goes a long way, though, and the young Elvis knew that in the years before the madness of fame took over. In 1957 though, there were no histrionics, no entourage or "Memphis Mafia," nothing to stop a young man from Buffalo from spending a few moments with his hero.

§

Jackson returned to school and continued to heal. Because he was a good student, and because of the large amount of down time he had experienced, and by virtue of having had more study time than even he probably wanted, he accumulated enough credits and graduated in 1960 from Iroquois Central High School, a year earlier than his classmates.

He spent the summer before college working as a copy boy at the Buffalo Evening News, the biggest newspaper in the Buffalo region. He would eventually work his way up to the position of dictation clerk before taking his leave for England in 1964. It was a way for him to acclimate himself to a real work environment and to be close to the writers, whose work was something that he strove to emulate. He had to choose a college, and could have easily made the decision to stay at home and take classes at the State University of New York at Buffalo. Being a teenager, it was natural to not want to be so close to home and his mother, whose raison d'etre at times seemed to be to make his life miserable with her truckload of good intentions colliding with Jackson's real ones.

He chose Gettysburg College, in the Civil War battlefield city of the same name in Pennsylvania, a 300-mile trip from Buffalo. His goal, of course, was to major in English and develop his skills in writing, his new-found passion, and to secure a future job as a big time reporter for a newspaper. Oddly, Gettysburg is not a school known for producing journalists, but something about it must have appealed to Jackson. Maybe it was the historical setting of the school, located in a Civil War battleground.

A career in music wasn't on his mind at that time, but he had spent a lot of time perfecting his playing and one of the things he made sure to bring along when his family packed up the car with his clothing, books and other belongings was his guitar. Music has the ability to connect people almost immediately, and one sunny fall day in 1961, as Jackson sat with his guitar under a tree on the peaceful campus at Gettysburg College, Mark Anderson and his banjo walked by.

Mark and Jackson... Talkin' and Signifyin'

All of our lives have someone who is a catalyst, a role model, someone who gives us the impetus to move forward, even when we think we know it all. Jackson had Mark Anderson, a man whose importance in the life and career of Jackson C. Frank cannot be overstated. While Jackson quickly found his own path in just about every venture he would embark upon, Anderson played an important part in Jackson's story later on by handing me a letter which sparked a chain of events that brought a few more good years to someone who hadn't known many. In fact, if Mark's involvement with Jackson had ended in 1961, the thread of Jackson's life would have been changed dramatically and his last years, while sad in their own way, almost undoubtedly would have ended in real tragedy. A lifelong folk music aficionado, Anderson credits his mother with cultivating his interest in the genre.

"My mother had been raised in the border towns in south Texas," he explains, "and she would sing us to sleep when we were children with old hymns, ballads and a little remnant of a Mexican tune that I still remember. Her family had known the Lomax family and my uncle John had a great collection of Burl Ives songs on the new-fangled 45 rpm records. While in high school I began a serious collection of the books like those of the Lomaxes and Carl Sandburg. I also played some piano, sang in the choir, played trumpet and took the music theory classes that were offered in my big city high school. Because of my older brother, I developed an interest in playing 5-string banjo (young Pete Seeger was one of his heroes), and by my third year in high school began singing Weavers songs."

Their friendship began on the Gettysburg campus. "It was a nice warm, autumn day in 1961," Mark recalls. "I was walking across the campus with a 5-string banjo over my shoulder. A voice called out: 'Hey you! With the banjo! Come over here!' Sitting under a tree with a guitar was Jackson. When I got to him he said, 'Can you play that thing?' 'Nope,' I replied, 'I just carry it to impress the girls.' He laughed and I sat down and we began to play."

"We were about 18 and 19 years old. I was in my first year, as was Jackson. He had worked summers for The Buffalo Evening News and I had worked for The New York Daily News. We became fast friends and, along with guitarist Tim Parsons, a trio singing everywhere we could, on and off campus."

They called themselves the D'Juray Singers. Jackson coined the name, apropos of nothing. "No meaning. He just liked the way it sounded," explains Anderson. A photo from the Gettysburg College yearbook captures the group mid-song, with Jackson and Parsons on guitar, and Anderson on banjo. One doesn't have to look hard to see the scars on Jackson's face.

Anderson provided Jackson with an outlet for his music. Comfortable facing a microphone both onstage and behind a console, Anderson gave radio a try. Having musical friends didn't hurt either when you needed something different to fill up the airtime.

"I began doing a folk music program for the college radio station (then WWGC)," says Anderson, "We listened to endless new recordings during the folk music boom. Twice a month, I would try and have all live talent on the show. Jackson, Tim and a girl from a nearby college were my most trustworthy performers." Evidence of this is found on an old reel of tape that Anderson's son discovered in 2008 while rummaging through some old stuff. Labeled *Mark and Jackson Talking and Signifyin'*, the tape contains over twenty "live on the radio" performances, at least 11 of them featuring Jackson solo or as lead vocal on a host of traditional numbers like "Frankie and Johnnie" and "John Henry."

Jackson's musical background was nowhere near as extensive or as varied as Anderson's. "He had no background in music other than a few guitar lessons and lots of listening," says Anderson. "I introduced him to a lot of the literature and spent time working out chord progressions with him. As I mentioned, we also had the advantage of listening to all of the folk music records that were being sent out to the radio stations at that time."

Jackson C. Frank was a sponge, soaking up all that he heard.

When college broke for Christmas, Jackson headed home to Buffalo. He didn't sit around his parents' house, though, returning to the Howell Recording Studio and recording seven tracks onto a 33&1/3 rpm acetate. He had at least four copies of the record pressed, and with a magic marker he scrawled a title—*Peaches and Crust* by Jack Frank—on at least two white generic album covers.

"The songs," Mark Anderson says, "include one ('Jesse James') that Jackson learned from me, which I had learned from my mother, one that he picked up from both the Lead Belly & Lightnin' Hopkins recordings ('Borrow Love and Go' or 'Bottle Up and Go'), and one from an Odetta recording ('On My Way to the Canaan Land')." The record also has a strong version of "Last Month of the Year," about the birth of Jesus, which has been recorded by everyone from the Kingston Trio and the Anita Kerr Singers to the Fairfield Four and the Blind Boys of Alabama, "Ananias," "Black Girl (In the Pines)" and "Washington Jail." The records that survive, although in bad shape, reveal a mature voice from a young man who had done his musical homework. While it isn't known exactly when, it is likely that the record was made in the weeks before Christmas, explaining the inclusion of "Last Month of the Year." Jackson had Christian beliefs which were carried from youth and were strengthened by his religious mother. Later, as his misfortunes mounted his faith not only waned but reversed itself completely and by the time of his death in 1999 he was a vehement iconoclast and atheist, often complaining that no God would ever do the things that had been done to him.

§

After winter break, Jackson returned to Gettysburg College to continue his work towards his journalism degree. Maybe it was the freshness of the experience of having gone into the recording studio and making a record, though more likely it was the knowledge that he would soon be rich, but Jackson's discipline at school was gone and his academic performance there was in a constant state of underachievement. He was smart, but Jackson was also very stubborn. That trait helped him survive through the years but it finally cost him a college education in the spring of 1962. A surviving research paper from his time in school is well written and intelligent but veers from the stated instructions and proper format, and as a result bears the following, and telling hand-written critique: "D+...you succeed fairly well...the grade results mainly from your flouting of standard practices on research papers."

Jackson flunked out at the end of the semester, his academic career at an end. The next time he would enter an institute of higher learning would be 32 years later when he once again crossed paths with Mark Anderson.

In 1962, however, Anderson stepped out of the picture. He lived in Alaska for a time, performed at coffeehouses around the country and even worked at a commercial radio station on Long Island for a while before finally finishing his degree. Around 1966, as Jackson was making a name for himself in England, Anderson joined the army and lost touch with his old friend.

In the Limelight

Returning to Buffalo in September of 1962, Jackson landed the same job, but full time, as a copy boy at the Buffalo Evening News. His abbreviated college career notwithstanding, he was still a journalism fanatic. Jackson loved writing, even more than singing, and tried his hand at everything from poetry to novels, as he stated in a letter to British music critic Karl Dallas years later. By his own admission, in that same letter, he was not someone who would be seen working if he could avoid it.

"I do what I want to," he said, echoing the philosophy that earlier had failed to get him through college. He did, however, stick with the paper for close to two years, and was there in November of 1963 when John F. Kennedy was killed and the nation was plunged into despair. His friend D. J. Boggs was at Alfred University in rural Allegany County, two hours away from Buffalo. She recalls, "Jack had a job at the Buffalo Evening News. When Kennedy was shot, I immediately got on the bus and went to Buffalo. I was met by my brother Norman and Jack. Jack had the ticker tapes that had come in at the newspaper. We watched Ruby shoot Oswald at my brother's place. What a time!"

The place to hang out in Buffalo in those days was a little coffeehouse and art gallery called the Limelight, where many of the finest folksingers and songwriters from Buffalo got their first public exposure. It would be there that Jackson cut his musical teeth in earnest and began to make a name for himself as a performer and musician.

Jackson was no stranger to the Limelight. Located on Edwards Street in Buffalo's hip bohemian area (every city has one) called Allentown, it was the premiere coffeehouse in town. It was started by a man named Jerry Revzin, whose professional name was Jerry Raven, and who was himself a singer with partner Don Hackett in the duo Hackett and Raven. The Limelight Gallery had a stage setup while also featuring paintings and artwork. It wasn't the first coffeehouse in town, (that honor went to Coffee Encores) but it was the best known. Having performed at Coffee Encores, Raven liked the experience so much that he opened his own place. He recalls a young Jackson C. Frank coming into his club:

"I can't put a date on it but I think he was about sixteen or seventeen when he first showed up. There was the very obvious physical distress he had been through. His attitude was really cool but a little cynical for a guy that age. The impression of Jack that I had at that time was that here was a kid with a lot of demons that he was working with as well as a lot of talent that he had and he was getting into playing music a little heavier than he had earlier. You might imagine what it was like around my coffeehouse at the time. There were some pretty wild people hanging out there. The local scene was pretty heavy, where you would see the types of people like John Boylan and John Kay and Eric Andersen. They were very talented young guys and girls, and the stage gave them a place to play."

John Boylan, a longtime, well-respected record producer who worked with, among others, Linda Ronstadt, The Eagles, and Charlie Daniels, got his start in Buffalo. He recalls the heyday of the club as an important part of his own story as well as that of Jackson C. Frank:

Boylan: "We used to have open mic nights. We're talking early sixties. I was trying to be a folk performer then, and I performed around town. I occasionally performed at the Limelight when Hackett and Raven were on the road."

Boylan would emcee some of the open mic nights. He would

get up onstage, do a short two or three song set, then introduce others as they came up. The benefit of that was that you
always got seen first, in case the crowd was small or left early.
Boylan remembers Jackson C. Frank: "I remember him coming in hauling a dreadnought sized guitar—I don't remember
what it was. He said 'Can anyone sit in here?' and I said sure,
and he told me his name was Jack Frank—I don't think he
was using the name 'Jackson.' He had a limp, and he had
some scar tissue, but apart from some scars he did not look
like your classic burn victim that people go, 'Whoa!' He was
not a jaw-droppingly injured looking guy."

Boylan became good friends with Jackson, and got to know
his foibles and his disarming sense of humor. "He was pretty
stoic, not a big old whiner. He had some sarcasm going, and
he was very protective of his privacy."

Jackson never forced himself on an audience. He tried, as if
such a thing was possible, to blend in while being alone, stage
center. Boylan got to see him as a work in progress, noting
that the injuries and trauma from the fire had a big effect on
him.

Says Boylan, "He obviously had PTSD (Post Traumatic
Stress Disorder, a diagnosis popularized through the various
testimonies of Vietnam War veterans). Maybe he was shy
about his appearance. That kind of injury is totally life alter-
ing and changes almost everything."

Jackson soldiered on, putting in his time and gaining experience being onstage in front of friendly crowds. Boylan
describes Jackson as "kind of a nervous performer. He was a
little bit mic shy and it would manifest itself in his voice. He
didn't seem like a natural performer in a normal sense. Most
of us were big old hams who couldn't wait to get up there. I
think he was less of that style."

The mic shyness never left him. His performances always
incorporated a bit of humor about his predicament; he would
act like the microphone was an adversary, and talk to it. It

helped to hide his stage fright and added comic relief to his performances.

Hanging out at the Limelight provided the opportunity to meet other musicians, and Jackson encountered a few people who would become part of his musical and personal life. Two musicians were Norm Boggs and Marianne Welch, and with Jackson they would form a trio, later a quartet called the Grosvenor Singers, named after a now-defunct library across from the Limelight Gallery. Norm Boggs was the acting bouncer for the club, as though such a thing was really necessary in a folk venue. Boggs and Jackson formed a friendship around their shared love of music.

Boggs recalls: "Jackson was working with the Buffalo Evening News as a copy boy, hoping to get a byline or two. He was a blues singer at the time, and he really never changed his vocal style. 'Hair ball,' I think he called it. One thing that provided a mutual hook was our interest in history. He had a pistol, a brass frame Colt, small caliber, .31, I think, that he said was by serial number one away from one owned by Wade Hampton, an American Civil War soldier and politician. Whether or not that was true I do not know, but he was proud of it. Marianne, Jack and I began singing together soon after our meeting. I can't recall all the gigs we did, but they certainly included local coffee houses. I know that we did the following songs: "Plane Wreck at Los Gatos," "Wild Bill Jones" and "3:10 to Yuma" and maybe "The Bold Fisherman." I threw away a collection of cheat sheets 10 years ago. We had an interesting sound. I think Marianne's low and loud voice along with Jack's really husky voice were the keys. I sang mainly high harmonies."

The group collaborated frequently, playing their largest show at Glen Casino in Buffalo. The show, which contained a number of acts, featured John Boylan, who did triple duty by playing, promoting and emceeing the show, which also featured a folkie from Toronto named Doug Brown, Hackett and Raven. a trio featuring future star Eric Andersen, and the Grosvenor Singers, who had now added a bass player named Ev Nienhouse.

The Grosvenors were one of the most intellectually brilliant groups of people ever to play music. Boggs and Nienhouse become experts in the field of chemical biology. Marianne Welch, who would later marry and divorce Boggs, went into the education field and serves as a college dean. Jackson C. Frank had the tragic markings of a natural genius whose multiple abilities never came to fruition.

During his time with the Grosvenors, one incident in particular gives insight to what was going on in his head. Injured as he was, Jackson was non-physical, unable to do much to protect himself. He was, however, very assertive. That staunchness worked well in intellectual debates, but not as much in physical challenges, The group had a show booked in Toronto, at a well-known coffeehouse called the Bell, Book and Candle. During their performance, a motorcycle group had lined up nearby. They revved their engines loudly, probably for no other reason than that is what bikers do when bored. The noise infuriated Jackson, who took it upon himself to step outside and confront them. Instead of being tactful, he told them in no uncertain terms to halt the racket immediately. Jackson C. Frank got the beating of his life that night. He was picked up by the legs and his head was slammed into the ground multiple times. Fortunately, the plate in his head did not get damaged, and there was no serious injury. On that night the spirit forgot that the body wasn't able and he came away an intact and lucky man.

§

The Limelight wasn't the only coffeehouse in town that Jackson frequented. The Boar's Head was just around the corner on Pearl Street. It was there that Jackson met another musician who would make a name for himself, although not in folk music. John Kay would go on to become the vocalist for Steppenwolf, whose biggest song, "Born to Be Wild" was featured prominently in the quintessential sixties countercultural film *Easy Rider*. At the time, he was just another Buffalo-based folk and blues singer looking for his big break.

Born in Germany, Kay came to Toronto in 1958 and spent his high school years there while his parents attempted to get an import-export business off the ground. He moved to Buffalo in 1963, and left for California a little over a year later, but in that year he wandered around wondering what there was to do around Buffalo. He discovered the coffeehouse circuit and soon heard about Jackson C. Frank.

Kay, who now lives in Vancouver, British Columbia, recalls his first encounter with Jackson. It was in one of those casual settings where a lot of people are mingling, enjoying the atmosphere. Says Kay: "I first met him at the Boars Head, or the Golden Boar, as the owner called it for a while. I remember him performing at those kind of hootenanny things where a variety of people got up to play."

Kay came late to the city and was not aware of the Cleveland Hill School Fire until someone related to him that Jackson had been injured in it. Kay remembers:

"It disfigured him. He dealt with that physically, and he always had a limp, but he had this great voice. When he was playing, one of the things he always did was "John Henry" and things along those lines…a lot of those great ballads." He had an option of sitting on a stool which usually had a rung to rest your foot on the bottom, and he had a habit of really accenting in a very heavy, almost stomping manner of keeping time when he was playing, his foot pounding on the rung. He would heavily accent his performances with this heavy thumping sound which some of the old fashioned blues singers I saw like Son House and other people like that often did. He played a Martin. He sure played it well; his voice and his intensity with which he sang. His singing was bluesy, but it wasn't blues in the way I myself kinda got into, which was more or less a mish mosh of Delta blues and Texas blues. His thing was more melodic. It was intense like the blues, but he had, not a high pitched voice, but a soaring voice."

The fire wasn't something that Jackson was likely to talk about on his own but if asked he would make jokes, keeping it light, but people could see that underneath the humor there was a darkness. Kay drew an apt comparison with another tragic figure in the American music pantheon—the equally talented yet self-destructive Townes Van Zandt. Van Zandt, whose songs, like "Pancho and Lefty," "Tecumseh Valley," "Lungs," "To Live is to Fly" and "If I Needed You", rivaled Dylan's best work in their perfection and timeless appeal. Yet, he was a severe alcoholic and drug abuser. Once commenting when he heard the name of a group from Canada, Van Zandt said "Cowboy Junkies? Have you ever shot up while riding a horse? I have...whooooeeeee!!" Like Van Zandt, Kay says that Jackson's sense of humor "was really on the sardonic side and he would say something that was fairly acerbic and then he'd kind of poo-poo it a little with a joke."

Flunking out of college had not been an earth-shattering experience for Jackson. Besides the experience of playing with the D'Juray Singers, he was learning how to be a journalist, He liked working at the Buffalo Evening News, and his musical performances were reaching professional levels of quality. Still, he had other things on his mind, his 21st birthday foremost among them. March 2, 1964 was approaching, and he knew what was in store on that date: money, and lots of it. The insurance claim from his injuries had been settled years earlier. He was to receive $110,500 upon reaching his majority—a kid with a trust fund who actually deserved it. Minus the fees for the attorney, Jackson received $80,000.00, just over a half million dollars in today's currency.

Mark Anderson knew the money was coming, as did

anyone who knew Jackson. "He spoke about it almost daily during the year at Gettysburg. He was both very excited about getting it and tremendously unhappy about where it came from ...blood money for his crippled body." When the settlement did come, he went on a spree, having decided that if he had the money, then he would advantage of the opportunity to piss off his mother by squandering it as quickly as possible. Such was the love-hate relationship he shared with her. Mark Anderson is convinced that the next stage in Jackson's life, his trip to England, was all just a cover and a means to spend his windfall down. Intentionally or otherwise, Jackson would prove Mark Anderson to be a very intuitive man.

To say that Jackson took the money and ran would be an understatement. It only took him until April 9, 1964, just a little over a month after his ship came in, to quit his job at the Buffalo Evening News. His level of irresponsibility seemed to increase tenfold when it came to the impending cash, and the amount he received in 1964 must have brought orgasmic levels of ecstasy in a young man without a plan. Unfortunately, or fortunately, his mother and father had plans of their own, all for his benefit. His mother had consulted an accountant who crunched the numbers and determined if he invested "this much in that manner," as Jackson described it, and only spent a certain amount a year, his interest would accrue at a goodly rate, and he would be a millionaire by the time he was thirty-four. She also looked into real estate, finding a large parcel in rural Aurora, a few miles from Buffalo, that would have been an excellent investment. Jackson, after visiting the parcel, declared that he had other ideas. He never stated his ideas out loud, but once he started spending his future, he never looked back. He probably didn't realize it at the time, but he was afflicted with a pretty horrific case of "survivor's guilt." By the time he was twenty-three, let alone thirty-four, he had nothing left but the lint in his pocket. John Kay was an unfortunate accessory at the beginning of the spree.

"He had access to his settlement for what he went through in the school fire," says Kay, whose frugal, working-class European background would never let him approve of Jackson's wanton spending. "He went out and got himself a [Jaguar] XKE." As Jackson proudly put it later, "I bought it right out of the showroom." He bought several Jags, each one different from the others. He was proud of the cars but was either unwilling or too lazy to care for them properly. One particular Jaguar, with few miles on it, fell victim to simply having no oil in the pan. He apparently had removed the oil without replacing it. He drove it until the engine seized up, which is death for a car.

Kay continues, "There was a Native American girl named Tanis, and the three of us went to Toronto in that XKE once or a couple of times. And we went to Niagara Falls. He wound up buying these Mexican wedding shirts, the kind that are linen white—they have these embroidered panels up front on each side. I remember wearing that thing shortly thereafter during my little folk ethnic period." Caught up in the times, and probably because of his relationship with Tanis, and subsequent friendship with Jackson's Mohawk/Irish girlfriend Kathy Henry, Kay, from eastern Europe, began proclaiming himself at least part Native American. If Bob Dylan could lay claim to having run off with the circus, then John Kay could be an Indian if he wanted to!

§

It almost seemed as if Jackson was trying to do all he could to get rid of the money, and certainly there were plenty of people who wanted it. Sudden close pals appeared out of nowhere at the sound of a cash drawer opening. On the one hand, he was spending freely, generously picking up tabs. On the other hand, he became increasingly irritated by the fact that there were barflies everywhere.

"He was going through his money with frightening speed," says Kay. "Once he got his car, it was like, 'Come on, let's go to Toronto!'"

"I used to take John up to Toronto when I got my money for the fire," said Jackson. "I tried not to be impressive—it's hard not to be impressive, being a young guy with a lot of money. I had a Jaguar and so forth, and when the Jaguar was in the shop, I had an old '59 Chevy from the dealership...it would hold four people in there."

Toronto had a burgeoning folk scene and a lot of well-known acts passed through there. One time, Jackson told Kay that Josh White Jr. was playing at a club in Toronto, so the two of them went to see the show. They met White afterwards and hung out with him at an all-night eatery, even going with White the following night to an all-black club to see Ahmad Jamal play. On another occasion, they saw Muddy Waters perform and once again got to hang out with a big name. One night, Kay looked around and realized that he and Jackson were the only white faces in the crowd. More lenient attitudes toward race in Canada made this type of fraternization not as big an issue as in the United States.

Jackson's cars were a blessing for Kay. "It wasn't like we were hanging around morning, noon and night drinking," says Kay. "I don't drive, I'm legally blind. So I would take a bus from my parents' house on Woodward Avenue. I was on the night shift at a factory for a while trying to scrape some money together, and we'd bump into each other at the Limelight or the Golden Boar."

In the summer of 1964, Kay headed out west for a ride and in the process fell in love with southern California. He returned to Buffalo a few weeks later, packed his belongings, and headed on to rock and roll stardom. Before leaving for good, he tried but he had no luck in locating Jackson, who was likely off on a tear somewhere.

"He was just one of these guys from Buffalo that I would

have said had as good a chance as anyone to get out of there, like Eric Andersen, or John or Terrence Boylan. He was one of those people who passed through my life. Our paths crossed for a relatively short period of time. But he was a very memorable guy, and I liked him a lot."

Kathy

Something else had been happening to Jackson in the early sixties. He was discovering that his good looks were not going unnoticed by members of the opposite sex. He briefly dated a pretty college girl named Linda, whose last name was Ffolkes, or Ffoulks. A photo survives of the two of them, dressed like they were going to church and looking not terribly comfortable about it. She was his first serious girlfriend, but it was his next passion, a beautiful Mohawk Indian/Irish lass named Kathy Henry, who would have the most profound impact on his life during the years 1963-1965, and would bring about a major rift between Jackson and his parents.

Kathy related years later: "It was very close to Christmas in December 1963. I'm an only child and my parents fought like cat and dog, and should have separated long before they did. They never did, as a matter of fact. It was one of those occasions when my mother was spending the holidays with relatives in Niagara Falls, which was 30 miles or something away from Buffalo, where we lived. I was gonna stay home and spend the holidays with my dad. We had a fight, and I flounced out the door and decided to take a bus to where my mother was. The bus station in Buffalo was close to a few coffee houses, and I was early, so I thought I'd stop in and see if anyone was there. There wasn't much going on. Just one other person. It was Jackson. I don't remember ever meeting him before then. The two of us being thrust together on what I think was Christmas Eve was unusual enough, and we sat around and talked for a while."

She had wandered into the Boar's Head. "I remember there was a fireplace and he was just there in the audience," says Kathy. He came over and we started talking, and he said, 'I'll drive you to Niagara Falls.'"

Which he did. Even today, Kathy is amazed that they ever met at all.

"He was very charming. He had a way of encompassing me in a sort of a big warm hug, and, at the same time, he had a sense of his own authority and superiority. I was a very different person as an 18-year-old freshman to the person I am now, and he would have been two and a half years older than me. He had an authority and a sense of being older, probably from what he'd been through. He felt somewhat apart from the normal. I'm sure he wanted to seem worldly and intelligent."

They met totally by chance, she figures. "I have no idea what Jackson was doing in an empty coffeehouse so close to a major holiday like Christmas, when he wasn't performing. I was only there because it was close, and I was just waiting for the bus. He just had nothing to do the same night I had nothing to do."

Kathy was dealing with the rift between her parents and the added pressure of her first year of college. Jackson was, as always, still affected by his injuries and the knowledge that his money, at that point in time, was only a few months away. He was getting a constant barrage of advice from his mother, among others, about what he should do with the money. Also, he was undoubtedly lonely. Something was needed to take his mind off everything, and the vivacious Kathy fit the bill. They spent every free moment together after the holidays. During the day, Jackson was at work at the newspaper, and Kathy was in school. Evenings, he would hit the coffeehouses and bring Kathy along. Or, they would hang out at each other's houses, until it was time for one or the other to go home. Staying over wasn't an option in 1964. Intimacy wasn't a problem for Kathy, but for Jackson it was difficult, given his strict Christian upbringing.

"There was very little sleeping together," she recalls, "and there was no such thing as living together. In Buffalo, we would have dinner together every night, drink a bottle of wine, he'd read his book, I'd read mine. Once in a while, we'd go to a motel, and then he would drop me off at home. The notion of Jackson as a sexual person is an interesting idea, because he was so conflicted. He'd want to sleep with women, but would be thinking that sleeping with women that he wasn't married to was wrong."

The relationship continued to grow, but major issues arose in unexpected places. Jackson's parents, who had warmed to Linda, did not like Kathy at all. She was decidedly different, outspoken, and a free thinker. On one particular occasion, Elmer Frank became very upset with her for leaving hairs in the bathroom sink. Marilyn Frank simply didn't like the competition for her son's attention.

In between the hair in the sink episode and the trips to motels, Jackson and Kathy spent a lot of time together. On some evenings, she watched him perform at the coffeehouses, by himself or with the Grosvenors. It was a good opportunity for Kathy to see the real Jackson C. Frank.

Or was it? His behaviors started changing. One minute, he was calm and the next minute, he would be, as Kathy described to me, "off the handle" upset.

Today, she realizes that he must have been bi-polar. The money probably facilitated the paranoia. As she told *MOJO Magazine*: "It's easy at this point to say that the money he came into was a door that he stepped through and he was a different person on one side than the other...I'd known him for four months before he'd had the money. We'd spent every day together - and I would say the paranoia, although that's probably the wrong word, the sense that people were taking advantage of him, started then. We were sitting in a coffee house, he was talking to someone else and I didn't even hear his conversation. He came storming over to my table and said, 'You're only taking advantage of me in this relationship! You heard me talking about the money I'm coming into.'

That was my first indication, not only that he had that kind of temper, but that it was absolutely tied up with the fact that he was gonna be pretty rich. I'm sure I denied it, and there was eye-rolling and arm-crossing and toe-tapping. I somehow talked him down from it. That was the arc of that kind of behavior all the time - he would explode and had to be cajoled back into another frame of mind."

As Jackson grew more erratic, Kathy realized the relationship wasn't a good idea. His behaviors escalated to the point where she knew that enough was enough. Tired of being the dishrag she felt he was treating her as, she left Jackson, and the country. She had read about the Queen Elizabeth, the Cunard Line luxury ship that sailed between New York City and Southampton, England and decided to go on a vacation. What she didn't expect was an uninvited guest.

"I was going to England in the first place," she says. "I told him, 'I am breaking up with you. I am leaving you. I am leaving this country. I am leaving my college. I am leaving.' I had gotten totally fed up. I had been with this guy for a while, and I really got my courage up and said, 'I'm not doing this anymore. You're just crazy.' It never occurred to me that Jackson would just cave. I could have done that the first time he was abusive and hostile and horrible to me, but I didn't. So after all that time, I was amazed he would attempt to put the relationship back together again. At the snap of a finger, Jackson recapitulated. He became charming and witty, and I guess that was all I needed. I couldn't believe it. I realized I could have put my foot down so long ago, and this could have been a different relationship."

Jackson booked a ticket for himself and they made the trip from Buffalo to New York Harbor, where the big ship was moored. Then, they headed to Europe.

Catch a Boat to England...

With what was still a large amount of his insurance money, a Martin guitar and Kathy Henry along, Jackson C. Frank boarded the Queen Elizabeth in New York City in February 1965. Always fascinated by expensive cars, he was stoked to purchase some of England's finest automobiles. Where else could one get one's money's worth than in England, where Aston-Martins, Rolls Royces and Bentleys awaited his arrival. Also waiting: a music scene that was ready for a new face.

The five-day trip was a leisurely one and he had time to kill. The ship, a luxury cruise liner, was carrying a large group of college students, and Kathy, being somewhat younger than Jackson, fell in with them. Jackson, for his part, made himself scarce. He stayed holed up in his cabin, coming out infrequently to look out at the ocean, often with a guitar in hand. Three years of playing folk clubs had honed his singing and guitar work and, relaxed by the big ship chugging onwards toward England, he decided to give songwriting a shot. He had previously toyed with the idea, but prose was his preferred style, and with the chaos in his life being what it was, he had never sat down to actually write an entire song. Now, he had time and privacy. "He was writing a lot of songs that turned up on that album," says Kathy. "He was playing around with them, noodling. He would play with several songs at the same time; he wouldn't stick with one until it emerged in its entirety. The music came before the words. 'Yellow Walls' was the only one I remember him talking about, it being a hallucinatory experience of his being in hospital, probably in tremendous pain."

There is skepticism as to whether "Blues Run The Game" was, as Jackson claims, the first song he ever wrote and if he actually wrote it on the ship. Jackson repeated the claim many times. Interviews with contemporaries at the folk clubs in Buffalo and Toronto yield no recollections of him performing anything but old folk, country and blues standards. If he was writing them, he wasn't singing them. Kathy isn't so sure. "He might have," she says, "although it seems to me you have to have the experience before you can write about it. It would be extraordinary if he actually wrote it while it was happening to him. We spent a great deal of time in the ship's observation bar where we would get blind drunk so it seems unlikely that there was a lot of songwriting going on."

As the song says, "Catch a boat to England, baby, maybe to Spain…wherever I have gone…wherever I've been and gone…the blues are all the same…" Whenever it was written. The arrival in Europe didn't go as planned. Being unaware of the rules about visas, Kathy had not brought nearly enough money to satisfy British customs officials.

"The Queen Elizabeth, as a courtesy, sent customs people out into the North Atlantic to check everybody's passport so you didn't have to stand in line," she says. "As it turns out Jackson had given the bursar all of his money. I had one hundred dollars and told the British customs officials that I planned to stay on indefinitely."

It was the wrong answer.

"They said, 'OK, here are your choices: You can stay on the boat, and take it back to New York City and we're gonna charge your parents [for the return trip] there, or you can get off in France,' which was much more liberal about admitting people without [visible] means of support. I got off in France and by the time the boat docked in Cherbourg, Jackson got hold of his money and had wired me some. I told them I was on spring break, and I have all this money. Of course, France welcomed me with open arms. I landed in France on the fifth of February, I left on the eleventh and landed in England on the twelfth." Later, he would give Kathy the credit for his being in the UK at all when he inscribed a copy of his album to her with the following: "To Kathy, who kicked me into England..."

Jackson, by virtue of having arrived first, found a room at the Strand Palace Hotel. Across the street was the more hip Savoy, where Bob Dylan and Joan Baez were staying (this was the tour that resulted in the D.A. Pennebaker film, *Don't Look Back*), while Buffy Sainte Marie, who Kathy was often mistaken for due to their similar Native American appearance, was at the Strand Palace.

Jackson and Kathy made the most of their early days in England, living, as Kathy called it, an "almost matrimonial" life. They traveled north to see Stonehenge with a fixture of the London cellar club scene, a big but gentle man named Theo Johnson, his Dutch girlfriend, Emmy, the American folksinger Tom Paxton and his wife Midge. On that trip, Johnson took the photo of Jackson and Kathy included in this book, one of the few photos of them together. Paxton would later recall that Jackson had acted as a de facto tour guide for he and his wife and had driven them all over the country.

However, old tensions between Jackson and Kathy remained, and were resurfacing, and it was obvious that the end was near. Jackson's behavior was volatile and he would go from normal to irate in a split second. Jackson never received a proper diagnosis, but his actions might be recognized as bipolar disorder (in the mid 1960's, it was called manic depression). Given his later problems, it is entirely possible. The sudden mood swings can be very disconcerting, even to those closest to the afflicted.

Jackson and Kathy didn't live together in Buffalo, for such

a thing would have been scandalous in those days and in that place. When they hit England, however, all bets were off, and inevitability reared its head. "I got pregnant," says Kathy. A baby was not part of her or Jackson's plan. After some discussion, it was decided that they would return to the United States. A sympathetic doctor was quietly contacted, referred by Jackson's old girlfriend Linda, and an illegal abortion was performed in Washington, D.C. Jackson soon returned, alone, to England, where his destiny awaited.

It was a traumatic event for them both, but especially for Kathy, but they both realized a child was not something either one of them was prepared to deal with, and thus the decision to terminate the pregnancy remains justifiable to Kathy over forty years later.

Saying goodbye to Jackson was another decision with which she is at peace. Two years of dealing with his unpredictable behavior, good and bad, were enough. One incident stands out for her even today. Before she left for England, Kathy's father had given her a beautiful string of pearls that had been in her family for years. She was wearing them one day when an argument broke out. Jackson, enraged, reached out and gave them a yank. The string didn't break, but the incident was a wake-up call. As abusive as he could be verbally, he had never been physical with her. This was new and scary ground. When they returned to the US from England to deal with the pregnancy, the pearls got left behind, but Jackson promised to return them when he came back later. When he did show up, it was without the pearls, and she never saw them again.

A year or so later, she saw Jackson again, when he returned from England. After clearing customs, he traveled to Buffalo, knocked on her door and told her he wanted to see her. "No thanks," she said, and shut the door. That bridge was burned forever.

A phone call Kathy made to him in the nineties was disappointing. "I called Woodstock information, and there he was. It must have been '95 or '96. It was a terrible conversation. He knew who I was, or claimed to. One of the first things he said was that the money was all gone. It wasn't like the old Jackson. I'd heard that he'd had a child. I thought we could establish some sort of camaraderie over the fact we had parenthood in common [but] there was no common ground that we could establish, because his daughter was not a part of his life. I felt there was no way to establish a relationship with him again."

Swinging England

Jackson, now single, and without Kathy as a constant presence, and intent on sticking to his plans of buying cars, headed back to London for the second time, this time on a plane. And the England to which he returned in June 1965 was alive with music. It was the height of "Beatlemania" and the British Invasion had exploded all over the airwaves. The era of "moon, June, spoon" pop lyricism was in high gear but was fast approaching a fatal intersection. Folk music's favorite son, Bob Dylan had plugged in, enraging the purists and casual fans alike, for whom electric guitars were anathema. Dylan's music was evolving at an incredible pace, and while the Beatles were still singing songs like "Eight Days a Week," Dylan had already been in the studio recording "Like a Rolling Stone," which, upon its release would turn the music world on its head. The Beatles were still over a year away from recording what was arguably their greatest achievement, the heavily Dylan-influenced Revolver. Never again would folk, or popular music for that matter, be simple and Jackson C. Frank knew it. As he reflected years later to music writer Karl

Dallas, when asked why he didn't stay in America. "Look at Dylan," Dallas said. Jackson responded, "The reason I didn't stay was that I looked at Dylan."

The folk scene, though, was intimate, and the places where acoustic music could be seen, especially in the mid-sixties London scene, were small in size and often little more than basements or attics in establishments that had seen better days, or had different uses. Musicians not well-known found it fairly easy to get up and play for a meal or for a few pounds, or even just for the chance to show their stuff.

John Renbourn was one such musician of the many young players who cut his creative teeth at a unique venue: the Folk Barge in Kingston-upon Thames, Surrey, which was often run, unofficially, by Theo Johnston.

Renbourn: "I used to hang around the Barge a lot. It was a big old hulk moored on the Thames near Kingston. I was supposed to be going to the Art School but the lure of the dockside bars was often too strong. As far as I remember, it was empty inside and damp and creaky. It was a place that scruffy types gathered, owned by a pleasantly odd old (or so they seemed then) couple who liked to drink some funny concoction that had an immediate effect."

What the Barge provided was a place for guitar playing types to congregate. The real folk scene was, according to Renbourn, "horribly snobbish and the scruffy types who liked blues and fingerpicking were kind of despised in those days. When Jackson arrived, he would have found himself squarely in that category. It was one of the few places that he would have fit right in."

Theo Johnson, says Renbourn, was encouraging to young players. The drawback was having to listen to him.

"He held court in a café in Richmond up river from Kingston. But he extended his domain to Kingston and "took over" the Barge some nights. I seem to remember he modeled himself on Theodore Bikel and sang terrible songs like "Donna

Donna." The characters I was friendly with would normally have avoided him but pretty much had no choice, as the Barge was one of the only places they could go. Most of the riverside pubs wouldn't admit them in those days."

As the name implied, The Barge was a converted Dutch sailing barge moored on the Thames River. Twice weekly, folk music aficionados saw a variety of performers. David Mercer was a regular visitor and gives a good account of the place, and of Jackson's role there. It is evident that Jackson was filled with conflicts that made it impossible for him to be comfortable in small spaces, as Mercer recounts:

"It (the Folk Barge) had previously been a jazz club before I started going there while still at school in the early sixties. The Barge was run by an old-ish guy called Geoff and his girlfriend Helen, and the music was played below deck by four regular performers, plus unpaid interval musicians and an occasional professional guest.... It was entirely acoustic, without microphones, and the audience sat on benches rubbing knees with the musicians.

"I remember Theo arriving to introduce Jackson for the first time in early '65. He thought it amusing that Jackson could write all these great songs but, according to Theo, had trouble deciding on titles for them. His voice was clear and strong, and he played his Martin guitars with gusto, so that within the close confines of the barge his impact was impressive."

This echoes what John Kay related about Jackson's performances. Despite his mic shyness, he was not a shy performer while singing, and put his all into performances.

"Much of what he played was his own composition " says Mercer. "Don't Look Back" was a favorite in those times of belief and hope, and he delivered it at volume. Similarly, he performed "Coal Tattoo" in a similar style; I liked this song so much that I bought the writer, Billy Edd Wheeler's album because Jackson never recorded it. I still prefer [Jackson's] version."

One gets the feeling that if Jackson had never written a song of his own, he could have carved out a successful career for himself as an interpreter of other's songs. Three years later, he appeared on John Peel's Nightride on the BBC and performed a cover of Patrick Sky's anti-war ballad, "Jimmy Clay," that is jarring and powerful.

Mercer also notes something that was different for Jackson from his days in the Limelight. He performed standing, in contrast to the seated regulars. Also, he didn't descend to the usual performance area below decks, preferring to play at an area just inside the entrance. The absence of amplification on the Barge meant that performers could sing where they stood. Tight spaces made Jackson very uncomfortable, and he would grow panic stricken if he was closed in for too long.

Mercer: "This may have had something to do with the warm and close atmosphere below deck. I understood at the time that it was due to his extensive burn scars. Possibly, it was an issue of nerves, I don't know. Whenever Jackson had finished his set, he used to go up the stairs to the open hatch and sit on the deck in the evening air. This enabled him to recover from whatever bothered him. Because I was a regular of the club, Theo used to get me to take cold drinks up to Jackson to aid his recovery. After a few months Jackson was no longer performing at the club, (I doubt that Theo paid him much, if anything) and he played more in central London."

He stopped playing at the Barge in part because his powerful performances had outgrown the tiny space. Word had gotten out about his talent and when that happens, you never know who, on any given night, might be in the crowd.

§

Among the audience at the Barge one evening were two people who would have profound and lasting effects on Jackson C. Frank's life and career. Nineteen-year-old Al Stewart, later to achieve superstar status in 1976 with his hit album and single "Year of the Cat," had heard from his landlady, Judith Piepe, of an amazing American singer who was performing at the Barge.

"I was staying at Judith Piepe's house," says Stewart, "and she told me about the Barge in Kingston. She'd met Jackson, and she told me about this American playing there. In those days, I used to go to a different folk club every night and would just get up and play. I was not really being booked, I was just trying to get exposure. Judith and I went to the Barge, and we listened to Jackson and we met him, and very shortly after that Jackson began spending quite a lot of time at Judith's."

The friendship between them was natural. Two young, literate guys with much, and little, in common. They were both gifted players and writers. Jackson had a boat load of cash, Al had none, but Jackson was very gregarious when it came to his fortune. In Stewart, Jackson saw a kindred spirit and a friend, which he had not had since Richard Stanley.

"Once I met him on the Barge, he was basically around all the time," Stewart says. "I saw him, if not every day, then a lot. We'd go to clubs and play, and do all that kind of thing."

Hanging around with an American was great fun, especially one with a lot of money. Folk singers were the steerage class of musicians in 1965 London, but no one bothered to tell Jackson C. Frank, automobile owner. Stewart is still in awe of Jackson's extravagance.

"He had all these exotic cars. It was amazing, going to a gig with Jackson. He had an Aston Martin. We'd just throw the guitars in the back and go to a folk club. In those days, folk singers didn't have cars, let alone those kind of cars. He had a

Bentley and a whole bunch of other things."

The late Bert Jansch also recalled seeing Stewart and Jackson show up at the Les Cousins club, with their guitars thrown casually in the back seat, exposed to the weather, while he didn't even own one, having lost his to thieves a year earlier. "I used to have to play on borrowed guitars," he told me, with a smile.

Some things never change, including Jackson's quirky nature. Stewart remembers him as a generous, sometimes eccentric figure who never failed to surprise his mates with odd behavior.

"Jackson would get passions about things, and for a little while, he would be very passionate about something," he laughs. "For a while, he had a very upper class English girlfriend called Caroline. One day, I'm upstairs over Cousins in the Greek restaurant, and in comes Jackson in the most incongruous outfit I've ever seen in my life. It was breathtaking." Jackson, a stocky American, was standing in front of him, his long scruffy blonde hair jutting out from underneath a bowler hat, dressed to the nines in a perfect image of a classic English gentleman, decked out in pinstripe suit. "I can't think of anyone who I've met in my life who was less born to wear a bowler hat than Jackson," Stewart laughs. "Of course, he was doing it because he was dating Caroline and had decided to join the British aristocracy."

The restaurant to which Stewart was referring was called the Dionysus, and was located over Les Cousins in 49 Greek Street in London's Soho district. Formerly known as the Soho Grill, the restaurant was owned and operated by Lucas (Papa) Matthews. His son Andy eventually ran the club in the basement after the original operator, Phil Phillips, allegedly disappeared with several paintings and other items of value. The actual family name was Matheou, but pronunciation difficulties led to the name change.

It wasn't the restaurant that brought the guys and gals with guitars, though. That was for late night eats. Nor was it the illegal gambling den in operation on the top floor. It was the club in the basement.

There were many other clubs in London and the surrounding area. There was Bunjies Folk Cellar, the aforementioned Folk Barge, the Darkroom, and more, but Les Cousins (pronounced "lay coo zan" by the French, but "lez cuzzins" by everyone else), located in the basement at 49 Greek street, was the hub of the British folk scene in the mid-sixties. A spawning ground, as regular Roy Harper once put it, the list of performers' names who stepped up on its tiny stage reads like a Who's Who of folk music. Among the young artists to tread upon the tiny stage were Bob Dylan, Paul Simon, Joni Mitchell, Tom Paxton, Davy Graham, Al Stewart, Nick Drake, Donovan, Bert Jansch, Long John Baldry, the Incredible String Band, and Cat Stevens, who went by the name of Steve Adams in those days and whose parents owned a restaurant called the Moulin Rouge, just a few blocks away.

A key difference between Les Cousins and other clubs was the all-night factor—Cousins stayed open until 5 a.m. or even later. At Cousins, one might walk in at 3:30 in the morning and catch Bert Jansch or Roy Harper working out new material. Or Jackson C. Frank, who had a hand in the look of the place. "I helped decorate it," he said. "I went out and got a couple of tin signs with an enamel on them, so you could advertise beer and so forth on them. We put those up on the back wall, and I put up curtains."

Not that everything always went as planned. "[One night] I broke the (Martin) D-28 on a microphone," Jackson says. "We nailed the microphones down so they wouldn't move, which was a stupid idea, and the microphone went right through the face of the guitar. I took it up to a music shop in Richmond across the bridge from Twickenham and traded it for another D-28 that he had and a little extra money."

John Renbourn was also a regular at Cousins. To him, the

place was a haven for those out of the mainstream.

"It became a meeting place for acoustic musicians who would not have been tolerated in the straight folk clubs at the time," he says. "One good thing about it was it stayed open all night, so it attracted plenty of characters who had nowhere else to go. That's where I first met Jackson. Oddly enough I still remember that clearly, possibly because he was a little different from the average Cousins clientele. He seemed reserved and even a bit cold. I found out later that he had a wonderful sense of humor but was pretty much the opposite of the 'loud American.'"

Like Al Stewart and Bert Jansch, Renbourn was as enthralled with Jackson's instruments as he was with his money. Renbourn: "He looked fairly well groomed and had a real Martin guitar. Bert Jansch and I used to play there a lot. My guitar was a funny old dance band instrument and Bert didn't even have one, so just the appearance of that guitar brought on a hush. Nobody I knew around the Cousins seemed to have any money and that was another thing that set Jackson apart."

Jackson's physical appearance must have been unusual to Renbourn. After all, most people burned as severely as Jackson don't survive, much less enter a profession that involves appearing in front of audiences. His facial scars were, as John Boylan has noted, "not jaw-droppingly bad," and Renbourn feels it only added to the overall effect of the man:

"He looked then as he does in the photo on the cover of the album, with lank hair and a goatee, which made me think of the musketeers. I have a feeling he always wore one glove which would have been to cover the burn marks on his hand. That and his general cool all contributed to a certain mystique. One of the first things he told me was the story of the fire. I guess it was almost a form of apology for his relative affluence. He explained that he had landed an insurance settlement and now liked to travel. He was staying in a hotel over on Store Street, which wasn't exactly up-market but still the type of area that the Soho types rarely frequented. When I asked him where he was from he told me, 'Buffalo, a good place to come from.'"

The musicians who got to know Jackson also had a bit of fun at his expense. He was very secretive about what the mysterious middle initial stood for, and during his time in England, he never let that middle name slip out.

Renbourn: "People used to speculate as to the 'C' in his name and add odd initials to their own for fun. When I found out what that 'C' stood for it was a letdown."

Renbourn particularly admired Jackson's performing style and knew a polished performer when he saw one. "Unlike a lot of characters down there, he never pushed himself forward to play," Renbourn recalls. "I think I only heard him do a full gig once, and it was right on the money. No pointless stage patter, just fine songs and accompaniments presented in a sequence that showed he knew what he was doing. The songs were a good mix of contemporary and traditional."

And then there was Judith Piepe....

Judith Piepe

One of the key people in the lives of many budding young singers who were drawn to the lights of London was Judith Piepe. A social worker and songwriter, she was a tough-as-nails protector of "outcasts and outsiders," although close friends privately said her attitude was all a show. On the inside, she had a soft spot for folksingers, because of all of the musicians in the world, she felt they actually had something to say. Her life story would make a great movie.

She was born Judith Maria Sternberg on February 22,

1920, in Silesia, Prussia, which is now part of Poland. Her father was noted economist Fritz Sternberg, who eventually emigrated to the United States and became part of Franklin Roosevelt's kitchen cabinet.

The stories about her are the stuff of legend, and they are mostly true: They say that as a young teenager in Berlin she was arrested by the Nazis...that she was held for three months before escaping... that she was tried in absentia and sentenced to death for high treason. During the Spanish Civil War, she was said to be an ambulance driver for the loyalists, carrying both medical supplies and a machine gun. There was also a lot of speculation that she worked for British political intelligence during the early days of World War II, resulting in a free pass when it came time to apply for British citizenship.

Judith died in 2003 after a long illness. I asked her third husband, guitar maker and repairer Simcha (nee Stephen) Delft about these tales.

"Judith did serve three terms in the Spanish Civil War," Delft confirms, "driving an ambulance, and she occasionally she had to deter Fascist forces bombing planes by firing an ancient machine gun on the roof." She was only sixteen and had been deserted by her father, leaving her adrift to wander around Europe, stateless and without a passport, until she was picked up by the Nazis. There was no escape, but rather she was released after three months. She was tortured during the incarceration. She got out of Germany, wandering around stateless, with no country to call home. She did work for "some secret squirrel group," as Delft puts it, during the second World War, but she never revealed which one. Two husbands fell by the wayside before Delft, but only the name of her second, Tony Piepe, is known, and she never talked to anyone about her first marriage. Tony and she had a daughter named Ariel, from whom she was estranged for many years, reconciling only during the last years of her life. Delft entered the picture in the mid-sixties and they married in 1981, moving to New Zealand. After Judith's death, Delft changed his name to Simcha and is currently living in New Zealand, and is a highly regarded luthier and guitar technician.

In 1966, the BBC broadcast a 25-minute feature on Piepe. The program was called "Meeting Point" and the segment, entitled "Outcasts and Outsiders" is a revealing look at a mystery. In the film, she comes across as a living, breathing contradiction; her speech is a dull monotone but her words are full of life. What she says is a fair description of what attracted her to the young people she made her life's work. Asked why she put so much effort into helping the drifters who came her way, she said, "A sick society produces sick children and then casts them out. This is the natural herd instinct. We see this in animals who will gang up and destroy the damaged animal. As human beings, we ought not to do the same."

Piepe took her passions to heart, including writing music. Heather Wood of The Young Tradition recalls the story of a folk purist who claimed he knew all about what she called the "English tradition." In notes accompanying a printed version of the song, Wood writes, "Judith wrote him a couple, which he averred were rural gems from the seventeen hundreds. When she told him the truth (that she had written them that week—ed) he went away and hasn't been heard from since. Splendid. So, we thought, was one of the songs. Judith called it 'The Procrastination Song:' we preferred to call it 'The Hungry Child.'"

A young child to its mother ran and
then it started crying,
Mother I'm hungry mother dear give me bread
or I'll be dying.
Wait my child, wait my child,
Tomorrow we'll be ploughing.
Now when the field it had been ploughed

the young child started crying,
Mother I'm hungry mother dear give me bread
or I'll be dying.
Wait my child wait my child,
Tomorrow we'll be sowing.
Now when the field it had been reaped t
he young child started crying,
Mother I'm hungry mother dear give me bread
or I'll be dying.
Wait my child wait my child,
Tomorrow we'll be threshing.
Now when the wheat it had been threshed
the young child started crying,
Mother I'm hungry mother dear give me bread
or I'll be dying.
Wait my child wait my child,
Tomorrow we'll be grinding.
Now when the wheat it had been ground
the young child started crying,
Mother I'm hungry mother dear give me bread
or I'll be dying.
Wait my child wait my child we'll be baking.
Now when the bread was warm in the oven
the child lay in his coffin.

© Judith Piepe

Meeting Point offers a glimpse into the era, and it contains footage of a young, snaggle-toothed Al Stewart playing a complete version of "Pretty Golden Hair," his song about a troubled young homosexual boy. The film also contributes to the story of Jackson C. Frank, in that it contains the only known existing footage of Jackson performing.

Possibly taken from a complete filmed show at Les Cousins, the footage was edited into the feature on Piepe, and only survived because it was stashed away in a desk when the BBC decided to make room on their shelves by destroying or erasing thousands of films and tapes, including the rest of the Cousins performance, if it existed. The first twelve seconds of Jackson performing "Just Like Anything" were used by filmmaker Jan Leman in his outstanding *Acoustic Routes* documentary. That film is about the acoustic musicians of the time, most specifically focusing on Bert Jansch. Those twelve seconds are now freely available for viewing on YouTube. In the original "Meeting Point" program, the audio runs for almost fifty seconds more, with Judith's voice-over continuing for most of the clip.

By opening up her Dellow Street flat, which she jokingly referred to as her "doss house for folksingers," Piepe employed her philosophy of "making someone your friend makes it easier to help them." which is how she describes it in the documentary.

The folk scene in London attracted young players from around the world, but the vast majority were from the United Kingdom. Besides Al Stewart, who was from Bournemouth, Scotland, there were guitar masters like John Renbourn, Davey Graham, Bert Jansch, and songwriters like Ralph McTell, Donovan, Wizz Jones and Sandy Denny. Some stuck around, others vanished. As Al Stewart recalls, "Weston Gavin was one. I don't think Weston stayed the course, as it were. He did very well in the short term, but I woke up one morning, and he was gone and never came back again." (Gavin did return eventually, and as recently as 2012 was holding down a residency at the Alleycat in Denmark Street, in the Louisiana Music shop.)

At Dellow Street, the first American to stay was also her favorite. Paul Simon traveled to England in 1964, following the disappointing failure of the Simon and Garfunkel album *Wednesday Morning, 3 AM*. He, like many other singer songwriters, was somewhat disillusioned by a lack of success in America. He already had much more experience in the music world than others on the scene, having achieved success as a rock and roller earlier in his life with his schoolmate and neighbor, Art Garfunkel. They were playing and recording together as Tom and Jerry when their song "Hey Schoolgirl" hit the charts in the late 1950's. Having the folksy *Wednesday Morning, 3 AM* album fail to impress the masses had to be a blow to a talented guy with an ego like Simon's, and he headed for England to save face and get out of sight for a while.

Judith saw Simon perform at a rhythm and blues club called the Flamingo in 1964 and was impressed with what she heard. She was the host of a radio program in the BBC's Five to Ten religious slot. In March of 1965, she lobbied the BBC to feature Paul's music on the program. She recognized the religious undertones and messages in many of his early works, like "Sparrow," "Sounds of Silence," "A Church is Burning," as well as a song that he wrote after visiting a church in Soho. As he recalled later to Karl Dallas, who was writing Judith's obituary, "One day I got caught in a downpour, and I stepped inside St. Anne's Cathedral [sic], which is in a little park in Soho. I was impressed with the sermon that I heard being delivered. What impressed me was that it didn't say anything, nothing. When you walked out of there, it didn't make any difference whether you walked in, unless you dug stained-glass windows, you know? Because the meek are inheriting nothing, nothing, and that's the basis of this song called 'Blessed.'"

§

Judith, of course, got her way, and the success of the radio spots resulted in CBS offering Simon a contract. Accordingly, he entered Levy's studio in May and recorded his first true solo album, the lovely *Paul Simon Songbook*, in barely an hour. It consisted of songs like "Sounds of Silence," "I Am a Rock," and other future classics that he later re-recorded with Art Garfunkel. One short song, "On the Side of a Hill," would see life later as the "Canticle" half of "Scarborough Fair/Canticle." The album did not see the light of day in the US for nearly forty years. When the *Paul Simon Songbook* album was finally released in America, it contained liner notes by Judith Piepe, written not long before her death.

In the year before making the *Songbook* album, Simon had been traveling the country performing at folk clubs and colleges. At one such show, he met a young woman named Kathy Chitty, who was the inspiration for "Kathy's Song" and who later reappeared as the Kathy in "America." By the time the album was released, they were living as boyfriend and girl-friend at Judith's flat, and they appear together on the cover of the album, sitting by water playing with small toys. Al Stewart was already living there, and that group increased by one with the arrival of Jackson C. Frank.

§

The sixties being the sixties, nobody can remember exactly who was where and when they were wherever they were, but it is certain that at one time or another, simultaneously or not, but within a few months either way, Jackson C. Frank, Al Stewart, Paul Simon, Art Garfunkel and Sandy Denny were all residents of Judith's three bedroom flat in Dellow Street. It was home, and Judith made them all feel cared for, cooking, doing laundry and generally taking care of her folk singers. Jackson would tell the story to friends that once, after Judith had done his laundry, she discovered several hundred pounds still in his jeans pocket, a small fortune in those days. She could have left it there to molder, but instead she separated the wet bills and hung each one separately on the line next to his pants to dry.

Early in his stay at Judith's, Jackson still had plenty of money, but he was careless with it, and with his possessions. As Simcha Delft relates, "At one time in England, I believe he owned a Jeep and a vintage Bentley. The Jeep was parked, unlocked outside Judith's apartment block in the east end of London for several weeks or months while he was back in the US, and miraculously was still there when he returned. This, in an area where local kids once stole the wheels off a parked police car!"

Trust was not an issue inside the house though, it was a given, and the atmosphere was friendly and casual, which is remarkable considering that many who passed through there were needy or had little to their name. Jackson, according to Delft, at one time had propped an old yellow construction worker's hat on a table behind the front door. "He used to fill it with English money to grab a handful when he went out." Judith Piepe's flat, however, was a safe haven for him and his cash. It also housed the world's smartest and most discerning feline, Judith's pet cat, a smart Siamese named Saturday, who had the run of the place and knew quality when she heard it. Simcha Delft: "Saturday apparently had an ear for music and used to nip Jackson if he played a guitar other than his usual one. Another time, Jackson imitated one of Paul's songs while Paul was away from the house. The cat went around the house looking for Paul, then sulked for days when she couldn't find him." Saturday also performed an early version of a "stupid pet trick" for Jackson. When no one was around to unlock a door, Saturday jumped up and swung from the handle on the inside of the door, pulling it down enough to unlock it. Local television cameras tried to capture the act on film, but Saturday, of course, played dumb.

Into this scene came an eighteen year old nursing student named Sandy Denny. A quick bit of info on her: She was born Alexandra Elene MacLean Denny in 1947, four years before Jackson. Blessed with a memorable voice and a boisterous personality, she captured the fancy of not only the folk scene but the rock world as well. Immensely talented, and with wide self-destructive streak, she was dead by age 31, a victim of a possible brain hemorrhage brought on by a fall a month previous to her last breath.. Heavy drinking and substance abuse, coupled with smoking and general hard living, were taking their toll on her voice and her career was already in a downward spiral.

But what a career it was. She sang lead vocals with not only Fairport Convention but also her own group, Fotheringay, and had done several solo albums as well. She wrote one of the finest songs to come out of England, the beautiful "Who Knows Where the Time Goes?" voted "Favorite Folk Track of All Time" by the BBC's Radio 2 in 2007. She dueted with Robert Plant on "Battle of Evermore" from Led Zeppelin's classic fourth album, and she made a brief cameo in the film version of The Who's rock opera, *Tommy*.

At the beginning, though, she was a nursing student at the Brompton Chest Hospital, and singing on the side, making appearances during the intervals at the Folk Barge in Kingston. What better than to go where the music was and where she felt comfortable among peers? She ended up, as so many did, at Judith Piepe's flat on the east end. It was there she got to know Jackson C. Frank, whom she had met before at a small club.

Jackson recalled their initial meeting in a 1994 interview with Dirty Linen's T. J. McGrath: "I went to a club called Bunjies with Theo Johnson and a bunch of other people. The Young Tradition, a very good group, were appearing and Sandy just showed up there and did a few songs. Everybody liked her so much that she was sort of a character there. I remember the first time I saw her, she was walking around saying, 'But hairy elephant I am afraid of you!' for some reason that cracked everybody up in the place. I got to know her and I got to like her very much."

Jackson, who later, intentionally or not, wrongly claimed full credit for Sandy's embracing of a music career, was more upfront with McGrath, allowing that other people in Sandy's life were also pushing her to go the musical route. "I wanted to mention that I helped her to become a singer because she was a nurse at the time and she didn't know what to do with her career. She was 'tired of seeing old men die,' that's what she said. We talked her into being a full time singer, her friends and I. She had a lot of promise, and she was very, very good, excellent voice. I never heard her play guitar that much. It was adequate at best but of course she was just starting. Living with her was a lot of fun. There was always a joke of some kind going on—she was a very hip young lady, very into it and would make us laugh."

Often there would be gatherings in Dellow Street similar to Nashville guitar pulls, where everyone would pass the guitar around and have a go at a song. The players were all welcome to stay the night if they weren't already living there. One night Judith, organizing as usual in the small flat, and thinking that Jackson and Sandy were a couple, gave them a room and bed together. They weren't in fact a couple, but that didn't last long. She and Jackson quickly got to know each other better, and she told him about an older suitor that she had met who had offered to put her up in a place of her own, at his expense. In exchange, she would be the man's mistress. "I said to her," recalled Jackson in a 1997 interview with Pamela Murray Winters, "'I'd like you to be my old lady for a while, if you want to. You don't have to but at least don't do that.'" It's likely the idea of being a kept woman wasn't appealing to the strong-willed Sandy either, although she allowed herself to fit, albeit loosely, under Jackson's protective wing for a time. They became a real couple, and it wasn't long before his musical influence began to show. "Sandy was a very shy person," he said of her onstage persona. "She was just getting her pins under her as far as being onstage was concerned.

She later founded a group called Fairport Convention and established herself as a very strong singer. People began to listen to her almost exclusively and I think that Fairport sort of sank to the background until it became on its own again." Jackson had most of his facts right, but Sandy was not a founder of the group, nor even the first female lead singer—that honor went to Judy Dyble. It was only when Sandy was fronting the group that the Fairport experiment really began to get results. Because of her unique voice, she began to draw most of the attention to herself, and the group did fade to the background, where they arguably stayed until Sandy left in 1969.

Her guitar playing became increasingly facile and, at least for a while early on, sounded much like Jackson's unique style. A few of his songs, namely "Blues Run the Game," "Milk and Honey" and "You Never Wanted Me" entered her repertoire of covers. Unfortunately, shades of Kathy Henry, other facets of Jackson's personality began to reveal themselves to her. Friends started noticing that the usually bubbly and outgoing Sandy appeared stifled when she was with Jackson, especially in public situations.

Al Stewart saw it one evening at Judith's house. "Jackson, I think, discouraged her from playing because she was his girlfriend," he says, "and I don't think he wanted her to play. Maybe she was shy. There was something going on where she wouldn't play around Jackson."

Stewart saw the difference, though, when Jackson wasn't around. "What would happen is that the next day Jackson would go off somewhere, and Sandy would pick up one of the guitars. I remember her playing 'The Ballad of Hollis Brown,' which is a Bob Dylan song. I didn't know she sang or played, and I said 'That's awfully good' and she said 'Well, don't tell Jackson. He doesn't like me to do it.' But I thought 'Wow, this girl's pretty good.'"

It's likely that Jackson was not keen to be upstaged by a young girl, one who actually used to show up in nurses uniform on occasion, and who was now known to be his "old lady." Their relationship, at least as intimates, wasn't a long one, and evidence seems to show that it wasn't entirely exclusive, as both Jackson and Sandy were known to have other people in and out of their lives. Sandy, especially, was vivacious and liked to have a good time, and the notion of her being monogamous is a stretch for any imagination. She offered a great counterpoint to the usually dour and serious Jackson. As Jackson would remember years later, "She was very funny. You're not supposed to drink and drive, but we would come home late at night from a gig and we'd be in my Land Rover and we'd have a bottle of Irish Mist. Every time we got a red light, it was time to take a drink (laughs), and we broke up completely all the way back, over those habits and the conversations we were having."

Given Sandy's outgoing nature and Jackson's controlling personality, it makes sense that their romance, such as it was, was a short one, lasting only a couple of months. You can't tame a wild horse in that short a time and Jackson couldn't fence Sandy in. After all, it was the 60's, and with the fact that Sandy was about as monogamous as Jackson was, it isn't likely they were ever that set on each other.

However, Jackson was the first suitor that, as Clinton Heylin put it in his Sandy Denny bio, No More Sad Refrains, "got under her skin." Their friendship would last longer, and for Sandy the memories of Jackson would linger in the depths of her creative sea for years, inspiring her to pen one of her most memorable and haunting songs, the cryptic ballad called "Next Time Around."

Then came the question and it was about time. The answer came back and it was long. The house it was built by some man in a rhyme, But whatever came of his talented son? Who wrote me a dialogue set to a tune? Always you told me of being alone, Except for the stories about God and you, And do you still live there in Buffalo? They put up the walls with no more to say, Nobody stopped to ask why it was done. The stream was too far and the rain was too high, So into the city the river did run. Because of the architect the buildings fell down, Smothered or drowned all the seeds which were sown. I wish I were somewhere, but not in this town. Maybe the ocean next time around. I seem to remember the face and the name, But if it's not you I won't care. I know of changes, but nothing would change you To Theo the sailor who sings in his lair. And then I'll turn and he won't be there, Dusky black windows to light the dark stair, Candles all gnarled in the musty air All without flames for many's the year.

"Next Time Around," by Sandy Denny © 1971

The song is the very definition of "haunting" and at first listen the only obvious connection to Jackson is the mention of his hometown. On his website, http://www.pemward. co.uk, writer and translator Philip Ward, from Cambridge, England, offers a thoughtful and detailed breakdown of the song, which is one of the highlights of Sandy Denny's catalogue.

One of the most striking numbers on The North Star Grassman and the Ravens, this, we are told (and it is all we are told), is 'about' Jackson C. Frank. From the obscure piano vamp that opens the song, circling around G minor, we detect no stylistic connection to the American troubadour who made such an impact on the London folk scene of the mid 'sixties and became Denny's first 'serious' boyfriend. But a close examination of the lyric reveals how Frank – and Denny herself – are firmly embedded in it. The first line introduces a 'question [...] about time': this may be the question posed in Denny's signature song, 'Who Knows Where the Time Goes?' or it may be some overdue question posed by one lover to the other (in the colloquial sense of 'about time too'). Lines

3 and 4 are a riddle: 'The house it was built by some man in a rhyme, / But whatever came of his talented son?' The 'man in a rhyme' is 'Jack' ('The House That Jack Built'); add the next line and we have 'Jack's son' or 'Jackson.' The next two lines allude to Frank's song 'Dialogue' and its first line, 'I want to be alone.' Frank did indeed come from Buffalo (mentioned in the last line of verse 1). The 'stories about God and you' may refer to Frank's nervous breakdown after he returned to the US, which was accompanied by delusional episodes. As a child Frank had been caught up in a serious fire at his school in which half of his classmates lost their lives. As well as carrying physical scars for the rest of his life, Frank was traumatized by the incident (which may have contributed to his later schizophrenia). Denny's second verse seems to allude to these events. An official US inquiry blamed the disaster on the bad design of the school buildings: in the song, the buildings fall down 'because of the architect' and the children ('seeds') are 'smothered or drowned.' In the final lines of verse two Denny wishes she were elsewhere, 'maybe the ocean next time around.' This not only links the song to the whole series of water metaphors in other lyrics but may also allegorize whatever differences led to their break-up. In the rather pretentious sleevenotes that Frank supplied for the sole LP of his career, he wrote: 'I am afraid of the ocean as much as the possibility it is really my mother.' The third verse, with its references to 'dusty black windows,' 'dark stairs' and 'candles all gnarled in the musty air,' surely takes us to The Barge, the Kingston folk club located on an old Dutch sailing barge, where both Frank and Denny performed in 1965. The performing space at The Barge was below decks, reached by a flight of stairs lit by the only windows in the place, where resident singers and guests were dependent on intermittent generator power and candlelight – a health and safety nightmare by modern standards and surely an ordeal for the fire-damaged Frank. One regular in the audience recalls that the barge had the smell of 'musty

air' common to all timber vessels. The club's driving force was one Theo Johnson, an ex-merchant seaman with a taste for bawdy, who appears in the song like some figure of folklore as 'Theo the sailor who sings in his lair.' Johnson, who played (or tried to play) an enabling role in the early careers of both Denny and her contemporary John Martyn, did indeed 'sing in his lair.'

EMI Columbia 33SX 1788 Is Born

Though he often would say that he wasn't serious about the musical side of his trip to England, Jackson belied those statements by working hard at the songs he was writing. A tape recorded by Judith Piepe's partner and future husband Steven Delft in the front parlor of Dellow House reveals three songs in completed form—"Here Come the Blues," "Dialogue," and "You Never Wanted Me." Although the quality of the recording is only fair—a small recorder over the back of a chair captured the session—it is easy to hear that the songs, although not polished, are of high quality and that Jackson is relaxed, joking at one point over some flubbed lyrics. Judith can also be heard, making some comments. It's a rare artifact from the time and one that stands in stark contrast to the official recordings, which, as we now know, were recorded under a huge amount of stress because of Jackson's shyness and a perceived pressure to perform.

At Dellow House, Paul Simon liked what he was hearing from his fellow Yankee. Although Jackson probably only had one completed composition when he landed in Dellow Street, the song was exquisite. During a conversation many years later with novelist Lilie Ferrari, Simon would repeatedly describe "Blues Run the Game" as "a jewel of a song."

Encouraged by its popularity in the clubs and other positive feedback, Jackson began writing more material. The other songs that Jackson composed and began performing around town and in the parlor of Dellow House were also jewels, perfectly polished. Simon, fresh from the studio himself, having just recorded the *Paul Simon Songbook*, made Jackson an offer he couldn't refuse. As Jackson recalled, Simon and Garfunkel had both gone out of town on separate excursions, and had recently returned to London and Dellow House.

Jackson: "Paul was a very nice guy—he'd get high on hashish a great deal, and laugh a lot—he had plans for me—he introduced me to Norrie Paramor, who was his publisher at Lorna Music. Paul returned from New York and Art returned from France and they came to Judith Piepe's place where they were staying, where I was too, and Paul walked up to me and said, 'You thought you could get away with it, huh?'" Jackson had no idea what Simon was talking about. "I had played 'Blues Run The Game' so much and it stuck in their minds so much that they thought that I had forgotten it. Paul said, 'I'd like to get you a record'—Art said the same thing—and they both thought they could get me a record in town. We went over to see Norrie Paramor at Lorna Music. They had Dusty Springfield for a while, I don't know what they did with her! (laughs)—and that got the record for me from EMI-Columbia—it was done at the recording studio for Columbia or CBS at New Bond Street."

Simon, not known for personal generosity (he would later demand a promissory note and the rights to Jackson's songs from a homeless Jackson when he lent him money) would pay the fifty pounds required for the session from his first advance for the *Songbook* album. It's not known exactly why Simon paid for the sessions, since Jackson had his own money, but he was also shy and perhaps did not have the self-confidence needed to just walk into a CBS Studio. After all, he had come to England to buy cars—so he had come a long way in a short time.

Still, the man had a gift and Simon, perhaps prodded by Judith Piepe, wanted to get it recorded. One theory advanced by Simcha Delft was that it was because Paul and the others knew of Jackson's physical condition—Jackson wasn't completely close-mouthed about the fact that he felt he would die very young, and Paul had a notion that since Jackson's time on earth might not be long, the recording needed to be done, and quickly, for posterity, if nothing else. Judith Piepe was also an early worrier for Jackson. He was never his own best friend—he took care of himself very little and his casual attitude toward things like health and hygiene did not go unnoticed by his friends and lovers alike.

Jackson, for his part, was equally impressed by Simon. As he put it in an interview later with T.J. McGrath:

"There was a time in which we were all working the same gigs, Paul, Art, and myself, or Paul and myself and so forth. We'd take the train out of London to upcountry and, get out at a place...they'd put us up for the night and we'd go to the club and play. I thought he was a bit wordy because I'd never heard his stuff done before but I got very much used to it because he was a very good poet as well. As for his guitar playing, I didn't pick anything up from him but he borrowed a guitar from me for a couple of sessions. I had a collection of guitars and we'd sit and play together once in a while."

In 2010 during performances by a reunited Simon and Garfunkel, Artie would tell the audiences stories about the early years and recalled busking with Paul in England. Paul would wait until Artie was done talking and then say that he never busked but that Artie did. However, recollections from both Jackson and Richard Stanley confirm that on at least a few occasions the three of them did indeed play on sidewalks for change.

It was after Simon returned from a trip to New York that things began to move forward for him. Unfortunately, Simon refused interview requests for this book. I wanted to ask him what compelled him to record Jackson, something he had never done before. The official statement from his office has constantly been that he is busy with other projects and is not granting interview requests now or in the near future.

Of all the singers and writers who had stayed at her place, Judith felt that Jackson by far had the gift that carried his message to the listener. It could be debated that Paul Simon was heavily influenced by Jackson, although Simon would never admit it himself and would probably claim the opposite—such is a powerful ego. The songs certainly seem to point to Jackson as the stronger writer at this stage, or at least on par with Simon. While Simon had begun to write songs that were deeper and introspective, they were few and far between, with his more or less topical material like "A Church is Burning" and "He Was My Brother" still in the fore. It wasn't until "I Am a Rock" that he really began to look inward. Give Dylan the credit for changing the way songs were written and performed, but Simon deserves equal due for his masterful crafting of the introspective, literary and thoughtful ballads that brought his greatest acclaim. Without him, it is likely that artists like James Taylor, Cat Stevens and their ilk would be very different performers. In the meantime, though, Jackson was at full force and had written some very powerful songs like "Dialogue," "Milk and Honey," "Here Come the Blues," "My Name Is Carnival" and "You Never Wanted Me," not to mention "Blues Run the Game," which, alongside Patrick Sky's "Many a Mile" is one of the greatest weary traveler songs ever written. In Jackson's case that road had truly been a hard one, and although it seemed the hard times were over, they were just beginning.

The session, held at Levy's Sound Studio at 103 New Bond Street, was actually two sessions, a three hour slot in the morning with a break before another three hours in the afternoon. Paul dragged Al Stewart along to play second guitar.

Stewart's memory of that day is still vivid. He recalls, "Paul decided to produce a record by Jackson and because I was there and I was 'Johnny on the spot' he wheeled me along to play some guitar on it. In the final analysis I only played on one track, which was Yellow Walls—I got to do my Duane Eddy impersonation." A sorely underrated guitarist, Stewart's accompaniment to the song does indeed sound like a Duane Eddy bottom-end riff, accented by some higher register descending two finger chords, adding some fine color to what is arguably the bleakest song on the record—a song that was, according to Jackson's girlfriend Kathy Henry, "about convalescing in a room after the fire." One can imagine the desolation of a young man, so badly burned and bedridden, staring at the walls, waiting and hoping his body will return to some semblance of health.

The album sessions were a study in contrasts. The morning session was almost a complete bust because of Jackson's shyness. Al Stewart again recalls, "Jackson just basically couldn't play if we looked at him but we couldn't not look at him because we were behind the glass booth and he was occupying the studio. So he basically said 'I can't do this.'"

It was up to Paul Simon to come up with a solution. Studios often have large sound mufflers or screens that block sound from one section of the room to another, to prevent the sound of one instrument "bleeding" onto the track of a different instrument. When Jackson said, "I can't sing—you're looking at me," Paul decided to use the mufflers to make a box around Jackson, and the gimmick worked. "When we put him in the homemade box he started singing away like a canary. In the afternoon session we just zipped through it. There were lots of first takes. We did that and then we all went out and ate Greek food."

Even so, boxed in and out of sight, at times there would be a full two minute pause, while the tapes were rolling, as Jackson steeled himself, and then, from the silence, his beautiful guitar sounded and his equally beautiful voice would emerge. Jackson would later remember the scenario a bit differently. In his version of the story, he was in control. "I had [Paul] sit up in the studio booth so I could see him. If we hit a boner I could get an okay or not by him nodding his head. We went right through it without a boner." The first three hours of boners and delays must have slipped his mind.

Even though he paid for the sessions, Simon's reputation for cheapness wasn't contradicted in the least. "I never got paid for the session, is the funny thing," says Al Stewart. "I think Paul promised me ten shillings or something and I never got it. But Jackson bought me lunch so that was really my payment for playing on his record."

Present that day in the studio, besides Jackson, Paul and Al, were Sandy Denny and Judith Piepe. A story still floats around about the session, and the real means of getting Jackson to relax. According to legend, when Jackson sang the line "Send out for whiskey, baby" from "Blues Run the Game," Judith winked at Sandy Denny, who slipped out, returning a short time thereafter with a bottle of whiskey. This seems likely to be a good sounding tall tale, since Art Garfunkel has acknowledged running out more than once for a different beverage. Al Stewart still laughs at the irony of that day. "The most notable thing for me from those sessions apart from having to box Jackson up was that Artie Garfunkel was the tea boy—we kept sending him out for tea. Jackson needed lots of tea and it just seems incredible to me that given what happened to them in their careers that Jackson was able to say, 'I need some tea. Art, would you get me some tea?' and Artie said 'sure' and trotted off and came back with tea for everyone. It's such a concept!"

§

Most of the songs on the *Jackson C. Frank* LP bear that timeless quality that makes them as relevant today as they were at the time of their creation. Only one song, "Don't Look Back" comes across as dated, and then only because of the subject matter—the civil rights movement, which is still, for better or worse, associated with the time between 1960 and 1965 in the American consciousness. The album's liner notes, often described fairly accurately as "pretentious," were written by Jackson himself. The identity of the author of a separate set of notes, initialed C.J.G on the right side of the back cover, were a mystery for years, until Jackson revealed to me in 1994 that he had written them himself. He felt that if people knew he had written them he would have come across as obnoxious and, yes, pretentious.

Years later, while talking to Dirty Linen's T. J. McGrath, Jackson would give further insight into the songs. "Blues Run the Game" has previously been discussed but Jackson elaborated further:

"I wrote 'Blues Run The Game' on the Queen Elizabeth on the way over to London. It was the first song I wrote for myself, or ever tried to write. What inspired it was the way I was living. I had a black coat and a black Stetson hat and I wore that to London—it was sort of a performance image. When Kathy and I wanted to go somewhere we'd have to go to a hotel, and we'd live off of ordering from downstairs—room service—(that's included in the song), and I thought that would be appropriate. So, I was writing about what I was doing. I wasn't depressed. I was a little nervous because I didn't know what I was doing, but I guessed I'd find out when I got there."

Jackson seemed almost ignorant about the quality of his creation. "I am very happy that people like it—I wasn't aware it was so big. People tell me they like the song but I don't know what it is about it that they like."

Besides "Blues Run the Game," the album is full of classic songs; Jackson claimed to T. J. McGrath that when he got word from Paul Simon that he was going to produce a record for him, he went home and wrote the rest of the songs in one long session that evening. While this is not likely (later in his life, after finding out about his lofty status as a cult icon, Jackson developed a tendency toward exaggeration on matters of the past) he probably did polish the songs that he had written. It is worth noting that two other songs, "She's Just Gone Again" and "You Don't Know My Mind" (listed in correspondence with Paul Simon) didn't make the album, for reasons unknown, and nothing more is known about them.

Commenting on his only protest song, he said, "'Don't Look Back' came out of reading an article in the paper that a murderer had gone free in the south. He had killed somebody during the demonstrations and was released on no bail and so forth—the law turned their back on him. I don't know who it was but I began to think about killing in those terms and how some people get away with it. It wasn't fair—no matter how many difficulties there are with the colored people, no matter how many times, they are always in the front to get the crunch every time somebody wants to lay it on them. When they did that in Selma it was a pipe bomb and that made me sit up and take a look at writing a song about it. Everybody else was writing protest songs so I thought I'd write one and see what would happen."

The second song on the album was "Kimbie," the only non-original song on the disc.

Jackson: "'Kimbie' is a traditional song you hear a lot in Canada. Like Paul [Simon] not having enough [songs] on the album, I put on a folk song that someone had written a long time ago. He put in 'Scarborough Fair' and Ewan MacColl [sic—he meant Martin Carthy] was really [pissed off] with him for putting it on his record [*Parsley, Sage, Rosemary and Thyme*] and claiming credit for it."

The song, "Kimbie" was based on an old recording of a song called "I Wish I Was a Mole in the Ground," author unknown, but most well-known is a version by Bascom Lamar Lunsford, and included in the seminal Anthology of American Folk Music collection by archivist Harry Smith, in the early 1950s. There is no doubt that Jackson, like almost every folksinger of his era, had listened to that collection many times.

Back to the album, where there were two explanations for "Yellow Walls...."

"'Yellow Walls' is about an old house I used to live in on Rugby Road in Buffalo and it's about leaving home and running around in the middle of view, where it's dark and there are lots of colored lights and so forth and not going home. I really felt happy when Al Stewart was able to do some guitar on that. It was a little guitar but he never got credit for it."

Jackson told a different story about "Yellow Walls" to his friend Richard Stanley, however. To Stanley, he reported that the song was a description of the hospital room at Meyer Memorial where he spent months recovering from his burns after the fire. One can only imagine the loneliness of a young boy, burned over half of his body, staring at the bland yellow walls of a hospital room when he would rather be out living his life. I suspect that the story he told Richard Stanley was much more truthful than the jumbled bit of fiction he reported to T.J. McGrath.

Continuing: "'Here Come The Blues' is from my blues background of listening to blues and then trying to write one...and it came out that way." Upon being told in 1994 shortly after his return to Woodstock that Nick Drake had recorded the song, which is arguably as fine as anything he ever wrote, Jackson humbly said, "My goodness. I didn't know I was covered this much. I'm just learning now." Like a sleeping Rip Van Winkle, it was as if after a couple decades he had awakened to a brand new world that suddenly revered his music. It had to be an especially great feeling for him.

"'Milk and Honey' is supposed to be a ballad. Other than

making the mistake of saying there were three seasons when there are four, I suppose I am happy with it. There was an old song called '3:10 to Yuma', which was in a cowboy movie. One of my girlfriends came by and was singing it for the folk group we had about three years previous to this time period. I started realizing there were songs about the seasons that could as well fit into English tradition as they have already and decided to do one like that because it would fit."

A listen to "3:10 to Yuma," by Frankie Laine, reveals not a lyrical similarity, but a musical one, a slow ballad style in a minor key, that just works on every level. The song would be used perfectly by director and fellow Buffalo native Vincent Gallo in his 2005 film *The Brown Bunny*, where the beautifully haunting guitar and singing evoke powerful emotions of yearning while split screen images of travel through the heartland unfold onscreen. The trailer for the film shows the scene from the movie with the song featured prominently and can still be seen on YouTube. It's a startlingly beautiful juxtaposition. YouTube is a fascinating tool. On it can be found various musicians performing several of Jackson's tunes, specifically "Milk and Honey," including a very accurate guitar tutorial demonstrating how to play the song on guitar.

Jackson continues: "'My Name is Carnival'—that one I am proud of. I like that song very much. I wish I had gotten more covers on it. I don't know of anybody who has ever done it [Bert Jansch finally covered it—in his own inimitable style, on his *Toy Balloon* album in 2002, and in 2008 Erland Cooper and the Carnival recorded a very inventive version] but it's about when I was a kid. I used to go to the Hamburg Fair, which was the biggest fair in the world at one point but had reduced itself to being the biggest fair in Erie County. I'd be walking down the sideshows—you know what the sideshows are like with skeletons out in front? And the scariness and the spookiness and the fat lady and the freaks—they aren't freaks but they are different, and I wrote that for that period of time. It sort of inspired me to consider the carnival as not always happy. And after I saw the film Carnival, that really made it stick to my ribs."

Jackson recalled Jansch trying to play the song: "…he couldn't play it—he tried…a couple of times—he was very impressed with that song, I know that much. Bert is a much better guitar player than I am in a certain form, there's no getting around that. I remember first meeting him by stepping over his body while he was lying down at the Cousins club trying to get some sleep, until it was time for him to go up. The first time I met him he had a little bottle of bourbon with him—he needed it to sleep." It was common for performers, and the audience to bring sleeping bags to the all-nighters at Cousins.

Jackson: "'Dialogue' was my first attempt at a serious song, for people who wanted to be entertained in a café or cabaret. I like European songs that do that—they are small, short and have interesting piano like the tune 'The Moon Was Yellow.'" The song, it should be noted, was also the "dialogue set to a tune…" that Sandy Denny referred to in "Next Time Around."

"Just Like Anything" is, ironically, the only song of which there exists a portion of a filmed live recording, in the excerpt from the Meeting Point program about Judith Piepe. "'Just Like Anything' is an attempt at a nonsense song. There were a lot of nonsense songs—'Hey Noni Noni' is just a perfect example of what they mean when they say 'nonsense song.' That was an attempt to write one like that."

"You Never Wanted Me" is probably the most well-known of his songs, after "Blues Run the Game," but he had nothing much to say about it, seemingly not considering it the major work that many see it to be. It has been covered by Sandy Denny, both solo and with Fairport Convention, as well as Derek Brimstone and Bonnie Dobson, among others.

Jackson: "'You Never Wanted Me'—that was sort of peeled

down too, because it was taking up space. It was the type of song I'd write later on too. It's about disappointment to a certain extent with a relationship—nothing very serious."

The album was released in December of 1965, to some acclaim. Writer Karl Dallas, of the popular weekly, the Melody Maker, wrote the following:

"On the face of it, …he sounds superficially out of the Jansch-Simon-Dylan mould, with a nice guitar and pathos as his main hallmarks. And yet there's more than that. Certainly, at least one of the original songs on this album, 'Blues Run the Game,' is all set to become a standard….partly it may be because Jackson isn't just putting on a mask of self-pity to win sympathy. He has had a pretty tough time and the songs are genuine communications of what it felt like. At the same time he can produce a little gem like the jaunty Jabberwocky of 'Just Like Anything,' which is one of the happiest songs I have heard."

§

Mostly because of his musical accomplishments, Jackson was held in high regard by most of the people he knew on a professional level in the U.K. Many played his songs, and all of them at least knew his music through and through. Some wrote songs about him in tribute. Sandy Denny wrote "Next Time Around," the first of many musical tributes. Others were compelled to put their feelings down—such was the effect he had on people. Upon hearing that Jackson had left for the States, his friend Roy Harper felt a sudden void left by his compadre, and penned the simple and touchingf (albeit obvious) "My Friend," which appeared on his *Sophisticated Beggar* album. In this very informal recording session, the first fifteen or twenty seconds feature nothing but laughter and comments about a spider walking along the microphone, a humorous and presumably intentional reference to Jackson's habit of talking to and about the microphone in his own performances. Harper was a character of the same fiber as Jackson—brilliant, eccentric and influential. He, like Jackson, held a residency at Les Cousins, a position indicative of someone with a lot of talent and something to say—you had to be able to deliver the goods to have your own night, and Harper certainly did. Being the odd duck/eccentric that Jackson was, it's not a stretch to see him paired with Harper, who was far from typical himself. Harper would later get his own tribute from Led Zeppelin in the form of their tune "Hats Off to Harper."

Many British musicians felt the urge to give songwriting and performing a try, in no small part due to Jackson C. Frank. With Dylan as the God figure, and Jackson as the club level disciple, obviously with his own gifts as a musician and writer, the form began to take shape, although even by late 1965 a 'British Dylan' was hard to come by—most of those who were good at it were musicians first and lyricists and singers second, the bigger names being Jansch, Renbourn, Martin Carthy and a few others. It may sound overly critical to say that most of those musicians mentioned above were less than stellar vocalists, but all things being equal, their true gifts lay in their fingers, not their throats. Donovan was arguably the first, or at least the most notable British disciple of Dylan (the U.S. had already produced its own crop, including Phil Ochs, David Blue and Eric Anderson). Donovan possessed a pleasant voice accompanied by competent guitar skills and a good way with lyrics and melody. Still, it only takes one viewing of the Dylan-Donovan showdown, a lighthearted swordfight, if that is the word, in the seminal D.A. Pennebaker documentary *Don't Look Back* to see how far the British had yet to come to equal Dylan's mastery. Dylan himself was distant and otherworldly and openly tired of the folk music genre. It was his distaste for the sycophantic folkies, performers and fans alike, which kept him apart from the adoring crowds, while Jackson Frank was a far more accessible figure for the aspiring performer to emulate in the clubs and cellars, a position that helped make him the cult figure he is today. It isn't uncommon to read recollections by "folks who were there" who had the chance to hang with Jackson and his peers after a performance, something that you will never hear of with Dylan. (As he continued his "Never-Ending Tour" in 2013, there are some who would say that Dylan seems to have left the building, sometimes as early as the first song. A legend has the right to tarnish his own image, some would say, but it's a sad thing to see for longtime fans.

And there were other Americans- Jackson wasn't alone. The word had gotten across the pond that "swinging England" was the place to be, and the Yanks started coming. There weren't many—it wasn't as if floodgates had burst, but the ones who were there would make quite an impression. Jackson C. Frank was one of them, and as Bert Jansch pointed out in Patrick Humphries' Paul Simon biography *Boy In the Bubble* many years later, his influence on the British folk scene was on par with that of Dylan. That sounds like a wild exaggeration at first since Dylan was and is one of the two or three most influential musicians of the modern era, arguably only behind Louis Armstrong in changing the way music is played and listened to. Upon closer inspection though, it becomes clearer what Jansch was saying.

The comparison with Bob Dylan would seem obvious to an American. Dylan's contemporaries at that time in the United States were performers like Phil Ochs, Eric Andersen, Tom Paxton, Joan Baez, and to a lesser degree, Paul Simon, among a host of others. Anyone who played a steel-stringed acoustic guitar was categorized as a folk singer, whether they liked it or not, in the wake of tremendous commercial success of groups like the Kingston Trio and Peter Paul and Mary.

What passed in America for "pure" folk music was beginning to change from the music that was heard on the field
recordings that John and Alan Lomax, among others, had
collected throughout the rural south, to the dozens of previously released songs that Harry Smith had compiled on
his groundbreaking and still relevant *Anthology of American
Folk Music*. The new perception was, "If it was played on an
acoustic guitar, it was folk music," and that view continues to
this day, where bands like Mumford and Sons and the Avett
Brothers have taken acoustic music to new places. In 2014,
an acoustic guitar anywhere in the mix is often enough to get
the "folk" label on the product, just as a southern twang, no
matter how slight, is likely to earn a song the "country" label,
even if the instrumentation is the same as that of the Jimi
Hendrix Experience—guitar, bass and drums.

Dylan was on a completely different level in a category of
his own, and some would say of his own making. Performers
like Jackson C. Frank, John Renbourn and Bert Jansch were
relegated to playing the small folk clubs, if they were lucky.
Often it was only for food or drink. Still, what they conjured
up on those small and smoky stages would endure, especially
as groups like Led Zeppelin and others began to liberally borrow musical themes and ideas that they picked up from the
folk performers of the mid-sixties. There was even some vicious in-fighting when, as Jackson recalled earlier, Paul Simon
"borrowed" Martin Carthy's arrangement of "Scarborough
Fair" and released it as a duet with Art Garfunkel, even nam-
ing their third album after a phrase from the song, *Parsley,
Sage, Rosemary and Thyme*. It would be over thirty years before Carthy forgave Simon, with the two of them performing
the song together one night in London, in Carthy's original
style.

For the time being, though, Jackson, Renbourn, Jansch,
Davy Graham and others were playing the clubs and colleges
while Dylan played the Albert Hall and the Royal Festival

Hall. It was a musical version of class warfare. John Renbourn relates a story that sums it all up nicely:

Renbourn: "Those places—Albert Hall and Royal Festival Hall—were hallowed bastions of the Empire. British class prejudice was very strong in those days and those were places in which non-conformist types were unwelcome to say the least. The grandiose Albert Hall was the home of the Royal Philharmonic and the tradition of the annual Promenade concerts. Frank Zappa played there around that time and the atmosphere was really tense. When his keyboard player climbed up to the organ loft and played 'Louie Louie' on the hallowed instrument of 'Land of Hope and Glory,' the police came in and arrested him. Apparently when asked 'why?' and 'what for?' all they could come up with was that it was an offense for anyone to touch it without proper qualifications whereupon the keyboard player produced his doctorate from Julliard."

As Renbourn would also relate, when Dylan played the Royal Festival Hall, a lot of people from the folk world went just to see the spectacle of one of their own playing a guitar on that exclusive stage. This was new ground after all. "From what I remember," he says, "the actual performance was kind of secondary and Dylan's accompaniments didn't sound like much his records which were probably mostly [accompanist] Bruce Langhorne. When he got booed at the Albert Hall with the band it wasn't because they were doing something musically revolutionary it was because the sound was terrible. The Albert Hall became notorious for bad amplified sound and that night was probably as bad as it got."

One has to disagree with Renbourn on one thing—the epithets that were shouted at Dylan and his group—call them the Hawks, the Band or the Crackers—were captured nicely on tape at most of his shows on the tour and reveal much audience displeasure with the entire package that Dylan was throwing at them. That wag in Manchester didn't shout out

"Judas!" because the sound was bad—it was because Dylan had plugged in. Hell hath no fury like a purist scorned, indeed.

Put simply though, it would seem that British folk purists didn't equal American folk purists. "Old" in America doesn't mean the same thing in England - there "old" means "really old." There is a village in the Netherlands called Wieuwert, where the steeple and front section of a beautiful church, still operating and in nice condition, were built in the year 1289, over 200 years before Columbus landed in the New World. It is a tough concept for Americans to grasp at first, the concept of age. When I visited the place in 1989 I came away with an entirely different concept of "old." Everything is relative, of course, but when one ventures out into the world and experiences new things it can literally be what many call "life-changing," and in ways you don't expect. But it makes clearer the fact that British folk purists had many, many centuries of songs (the Child Ballads are a good example) to go back to and preserve, which they classified as folk music—literally music of the folk. American history began much later and her music, while derived from European music, especially the Irish and Scottish tunes that came across in the nineteenth century and settled in the rural Appalachian hills and valleys and gained a new life there. It evolved in its own manner into a form that today would be classified as country music. It's an oversimplification but that's another book.

Or maybe Americans were just less concerned. A true purist wouldn't be seen dead at a Bob Dylan concert, and yet at Newport, Forest Hills, and virtually every place Dylan played in 1965 and 1966, there were people, card-carrying members of the "purist's union," with names like Pete Seeger and John Lomax, in attendance, the old guard cautiously, and in Seeger's case at Newport, angrily (if he could have laid his hands on an axe, cables would have been cut, as he said recently) "welcoming" the new guard. While Americans accepted people like Ochs, Paxton, and Dylan as folk singers, the British loosened up enough to accept Cyril Tawney—a seaman turned singer—largely because he still looked like a seaman and, as Renbourn puts it, "his themes in the main were 'acceptably folksy.'"

It seems ridiculous today that such a furor could rage over classification of a style of music, but music wasn't always the commercial venture it is today, and people cared more, and its various proponents can hardly be faulted for wanting to maintain the purity of what they had, rightly or not.

It also helps explain, in a long and circuitous way, what Bert Jansch meant when he once said to Patrick Humphries that Jackson C. Frank was as big an influence as Dylan. In his world Les Cousins was the center of the universe and if you ran into anyone who was around in those days, one of the first names to come up would be Jackson C. Frank.

In Bert Jansch's house, there is a piece of furniture, a handmade bookcase that Bert built himself. It features many of the awards and accolades that Bert has accumulated over the years. One day John Renbourn was visiting and noticed that right in the center of the case, surrounded by Bert's awards, was Jackson's CD, propped up as if it were the center of that microcosm. He related the story for this book, concluding with a note that sometimes there are little things that speak louder than words. A touching little tale, but unfortunately, not exactly the case. According to Loren Jansch, Bert's wife and manager, whose laughter was audible even through her written response to my inquisitive e-mail, on the day that Renbourn visited the Jansch's, they had been listening to Jackson's CD. They happened to set the jewel case where it was when Renbourn took note of it, and through such a common meaningless act, a story was born. Still, it is very clear that Jansch held the man in high esteem. Bert, a shy, reclusive man who rarely granted interviews, did try to express his feelings to Jan Leman for the *Acoustic Routes* film. As he said,

"Jackson was an extraordinary guy. He only produced one album but it has such an effect on singer-songwriters and the way they actually wrote songs. The whole album is actually beautiful—really fine songs..."

I asked Bert to elaborate on that statement.

"All of the folksingers," he explained, "were really impressed by Jackson—quite a few of us, Ralph McTell and others. He certainly had an effect on everyone, the content and everything. You must remember in those days singer-songwriters were few and far between. Singers like myself were just starting out and Jackson had already done this whole album of material, which was all personal, about himself...that in and of itself was quite unusual. It was the early sixties and not too many albums were out in those days. This was either just before Dylan or at the same time but he made more of an impression on me than Dylan did."

(A sad note: Bert Jansch passed away from lung cancer on October 5, 2011.)

At street level, in the basement clubs and folk clubs, the most prominent American singer songwriters were Jackson, Paul Simon and Tom Paxton. Possibly because Paxton was married and came across as somewhat more mature and well balanced, he somehow seemed outside the young contemporary scene. The purists' opinions notwithstanding, he had already written several songs which were in the folk canon and anybody who would lay claim to the title of folk singer had better know how to play "Last Thing On My Mind," "Ramblin' Boy" and "Can't Help But Wonder Where I'm Bound." Paxton is one of the few musicians who can be called the "Woody Guthrie of his generation" and live up to it. When he came to England in 1965 he was already doing full concerts, not in basement clubs but on the bigger stages. He was by far the biggest star from the States to spend any amount of time in England. Paul Simon wasn't a household name yet, but was on his way. Dylan passed through doing his concerts but never stayed longer than his tours required. By booking full tours of the U.K. every year since 1965, Paxton kept his music and image in the public eye. He topped the sixties off in 1969 with a tremendous performance at the Isle of Wight, called back for three encores. He later lived in the U.K. for most of the seventies. His career continues, a shining example of a class act with tremendous talent and humor.

As Al Stewart notes, Jackson and Paxton were both tuned into the same frequency: "I think in some ways Jackson was writing songs that weren't a million miles away from Tom Paxton in style. They both did fingerstyle guitar and very melodic songs. 'Blues Run the Game' is like 'Can't Help But Wonder Where I'm Bound'—eventually half the people on the English folk scene ended up playing it—it just became very popular. That lilting fingerstyle way of playing the guitar coupled with the melodic songs was what was very big in that exact period of time."

It was a style that worked well for Paul Simon, who left England once his ship, literally and figuratively, came in. While Simon was in England, and without his knowledge, CBS producer Tom Wilson had listened to his and Garfunkel's stripped down acoustic version of "Sounds of Silence" from their first album called *Wednesday Morning, 3 AM* and heard possibilities. The Byrds had recently taken Dylan's "Mr. Tambourine Man" and gave it their special brand of 12-string electric guitar treatment. Along with Britain's Animals, who the year before had recorded the old folk blues classic "House of the Rising Sun" with electric guitars, they helped create the folk rock sound. There may always be debate over who did what but both groups took acoustic songs, one traditional and one only a year old but already a classic and electrified them and both can correctly be given credit for the new sound.

Wilson, who had been working with Bob Dylan, borrowed

the rhythm section and some studio players from the Dylan sessions for *Highway 61 Revisited* and overdubbed them onto Simon and Garfunkel's gentle song and a classic was reborn. The re-mixed song was quickly released as a single and went to number one on the charts, almost overnight. When Simon and Garfunkel got word in England they didn't take long packing their bags and headed back to the U.S. to continue their career.

With Simon gone from the scene, only to return sporadically over the next few years, and Paxton for the most part playing the big stages, the vast numbers and main players in the scene were in the clubs and small venues like Les Cousins, and the main man was Jackson C. Frank. His emotional performances coupled with his powerful singing and playing of very serious original songs added a gravitas that was missing from the performances of most other players and really changed the way that folk musicians crafted their work.

And therein lies the answer to what Bert Jansch posited in the Humphries book. Of the three main American performers who made the small stages of London their home during the British folk boom, Jackson, maybe by default, maybe by design, was the one who remained, an exotic figure with a limp and a story, a powerful presence, shy yet commanding onstage, with songs that were both serious and intelligent. He was out there, and people came to see him. They sang his songs, and "Blues Run the Game" became a standard of the day, and other days as well. Musicians tried to copy his style, usually without much success. All he needed now was for something ominous to seal the deal on his legend. Nothing makes a legend more indelible than to have some tragedy befall them. Remember James Dean, Otis Redding, Jimi Hendrix, and others?

On schedule, Jackson C. Frank began to disintegrate. Something had happened at the recording session, or right around that time, that frazzled his synapses. His long slow fade out was about to begin, almost as he was just getting started. Some indefinable turning point had been reached.

Simcha Delft was in the unique position to observe Jackson both before the recording session and later, after it was over. Delft had been away in Manchester while the session was going on, but returned shortly thereafter. According to Delft it had a very powerful effect on Jackson.

"Before the recording, Jackson's performance was warm, intimate, softly accomplished, even though obviously some of the contents of the songs referred to traumatic events. After the recording in the performances I saw he seemed distracted, less present, tense and the stage patter involved a little pantomime about the relationship between him and the large shiny microphone in front of him."

Judith Piepe noticed the difference as well, according to Delft. "Judith described his attitude to performing after the recording as mic-shy." This was something new—there had been a general nervousness in his performances but actually having an irrational fear of the physical microphone wasn't part of that act. It is possible that early symptoms of paranoid schizophrenia were presenting themselves. Certainly it was more than just stage fright, since he had been performing for several years in front of people and all traces of nervousness should have been gone by that time. Ironically, years later, after his re-introduction to the world, as it were, when he would perform at open mic nights in Woodstock, bloated, one-eyed and with fewer, if any teeth, he would perform brilliantly and without a hint of stage-fright.

With the songs on tape and the album already being pressed, Jackson, whether feeling pressure of his own making (likely) or pressure from others (not likely) began to behave differently onstage. It's important to keep the perspective that the stages that Jackson and his peers were playing on were small ones, like Les Cousins, Bunjies, and many other cellar-type clubs as well as colleges and other cozy places. Intimate places where he should have felt most comfortable began to become pressure cookers. Whatever the cause, Delft says, "The change in performance personality over just two or three months was so sharp I personally think he was traumatized by the process of making the recording. I have known others who were never quite the same after making their first album." While Delft knows the music business—she has been a giant in the guitar building and repairing craft for decades—it is unlikely that she ever saw a change as drastic as that which occurred in Jackson C. Frank.

The decline of Jackson's mental health became so noticeable and complete that in early 1966 he entered St. John's Hospital in Lincoln for an evaluation. It appears that none of his colleagues were aware of this, and had been told that he had gone back to the States, but a letter survives from the hospital's consulting psychiatrist, Dr. John Harding Price, to Jackson's mother. Dated July 28, 1966, it relates an ongoing correspondence between Jackson and the Doctor, and reads, in part:

Thank you very much for your long and interesting letter.
Your son's current address is Soho Grill, 49 Greek Street, Soho. This is the last known address at which we contacted him.
I think you should know that his last letter to me was by far the most reasonable and shows considerable improvement.
When I saw him I wanted to admit him to St. John's with a view to full rehabilitation. The difficulty was that the only remunerative employment he has had is as a folk singer and there is not much scope for folk singers in Lincoln. I felt therefore that the proposition he made me that he would be successful as a folksinger should be given a trial. Personally I doubt if, in fact, he will be able to establish himself.
If he cannot establish himself we will be happy to admit him to this hospital and put him through the massive rehabilitation machine in order that he can become a useful member of the

community and support both himself and his wife if he should
decide subsequently to get married.

It's a fascinating document, and a closer examination reveals some details and allows for some assumptions to be made. Just what type of rehabilitation Dr. Price was referring to is not known, and likely will never be. The hospital closed several years later and in 2005 Dr. Price, still in practice, was brought up on charges of inappropriate contact with female patients and his ability to practice medicine in the U.K. was taken away. Though he is still eligible to practice in Ireland, he remains, as of this writing, under intense scrutiny and attempts to contact him have been for naught.

By July of 1966, Jackson had been in the U.K. for a little more than a year. It is known that he blew through his money at an amazing rate, and was likely almost out of funds by the time his album was made. Also, he was now living at the Soho Grill, which was one of the names of the restaurant over Les Cousins, a fact confirmed by Diana Matheou, and the rent there was just a fraction of what it would have been elsewhere. Another hint that he was broke was given by John Boylan, who related that Jackson told him that to get the fare to go back and forth to the U.S. he "flogged" guitars, the British term for hocking, or pawning.

The letter from Dr. Price is also another confirmation that Jackson was in rough shape psychologically and it can be inferred from the Doctor's comments about Jackson's inability to make a living as a folk singer that he needed to make a living—his cash was kaput. He returned to the U.S. with an armful of copies of his album, and headed for Elma, where he returned to his parents' house. He also spent time with Richard Stanley and his wife Kate (Jackson and Kathy had introduced them on a double blind date on April 1, 1964 and they are still together to this day). In 1966 he made another introduction of sorts when an old friend re-appeared, briefly.

The British smoke hashish by rolling it into a cigarette with the tobacco, and Jackson apparently was a practiced hand with it. As Richard Stanley described it, it made him "sick besides stoned" in his own kitchen in East Aurora, New York. Richard Stanley recalls "in the summer of '66 Kathy Henry came back from California with two kilos of excellent weed and about 200 hits of LSD and stayed with us in East Aurora. Jackson was there some of the time as well, but in the summer of '66 the son of the tenant upstairs, who I knew from school, happened through our place. I was perfectly placed to see both their faces as he (Charles Novi) and Katherine first met and knew exactly in the moment what was coming. It was like a little bolt of lightning shot between them. That was the end of her and Jackson, and Katherine and Novi got married within the year."

Elaine

Jackson hadn't exactly been living the bachelor life either. While still in England he had been invited to a party that was attended by a young model who caught his eye. He fell for her hard.

As Jackson told the story to Richard Stanley, another of his cars, the Aston Martin, played a humorous role in the scene where he met his future wife. As related by Stanley:

"He had the car only a short while when he went to a party where he met Elaine. There was lots of hash being consumed and people were blowing smoke into the face of a cat there. Finally, the cat walked up on the arm of a sofa, stood there stock-still for a minute or more, then fell over sideways onto the floor and lay there, feet up, not moving. Everyone thought it was really hilarious (the cat later recovered) and it was the height of the party. Sometime during the evening Jackson was introduced to Elaine and they left together. In the car, a bit befuddled by "substances" Jackson realized he was not totally sure how to start it. The Aston Martin had some kind of a more complicated double switch sequence required to start it and Jackson brought his mind to bear and focus carefully on the process, aware that he must favorably impress his new date. Switch, key, switch, clutch in, out of gear – Contact! Ready for take off. He sat there for a moment reviewing the procedure to be sure he had done everything right, released the emergency brake, depressed the clutch, and put it in gear ready to back out of the parking space when Elaine leaned over and said ever so prettily in her perfect English accent, "Excuse me, but do you customarily drive with the door open?"

§

She was a beautiful blonde. He was a scarred, burnt, limping paranoid schizophrenic genius. A perfect match in some worlds, but not in the one they lived in. Their marriage was short by the standards of the time, about four years. It was turbulent with its share of tragedy, of course, since Jackson C. Frank was involved. Elaine, the blonde, was Elaine Sedgwick, a cousin to Andy Warhol's protégé Edie Sedgwick, and according to Jackson, she had been a body double for Brigitte Bardot. She was smart, beautiful and gifted in the art of creating fashion, and had gone to all the right schools and knew all the right people.

Jackson was smitten. He put the moves on her, charming her in all the right ways, and they were soon a couple. As his star was descending on one horizon, on the other, things were getting a little brighter, and that was where Elaine came in. Well-spoken and well-rounded, she brought a touch of class to his life. Why she was attracted to him at all might be a small mystery, since he was, by the time they met in 1967, broke most of the time, often unkempt and disheveled and prone to odd shifts in behavior that would scare most young ladies of class away. The only logical conclusion to be drawn is that it was true love, if such a thing exists. Jackson would soon be leaving London to return to the States. He had purchased a number of cars, including the Aston-Martin, several Bentleys, Rolls Royces, a Jaguar or two, a Land Rover and a Jeep which he left in London, had paid for their shipment to the States and had to go there to retrieve them.

Elaine soon followed him to the States, where he took her around to see some of his old haunts, and meet his parents and his friends. They decided to get married and did so on February 4, 1967, in Elma, near his parents' house. Jackson's good friend Richard Stanley played the lute at the wedding, which was officiated by the Reverend Edward Gill, and witnessed by John Cunningham and J. Ratvage.

Richard Stanley's take on the wedding: "It was in a church in Elma on Bowen Road. I thought it was an Episcopal church and this would have been a likely fit for Elaine who might have been Anglican. Jackson had no religion, as I remember, being somewhat of a dedicated iconoclast and anti-establishment sort of person. I am amazed at how little I remember of the wedding except that I did the music for it. I played the lute; for the processional, 'Queen Elizabeth's Galliard' by John Dowland; the recessional, 'Kemp's Jig' from the same period. I fancied the 'Queen Elizabeth' especially appropriate; Elaine was truly stunning, almost regal, in an elaborate, beautifully designed white outfit. Jackson, for as much of the time as he spent slouching around in baggy pants, a velour pullover and sockless slippers, could really cut in when he wanted to be well put-together and was every bit a suitable match. I am sure that I would remember if there was a reception. As I remember, Jackson's family was very down on the whole idea and there would have been few, if any, of Elaine's family or friends, perhaps explaining the lack of a reception."

Elaine Frank, who reluctantly spoke on the subject with me in 2008, agreed that Jackson's family was not too keen on the wedding:

"Marilyn was not a particularly welcoming or warm mother-in-law," she says. "There was a lot of tension, and she was right in retrospect. Jackson shouldn't have gotten married. He wasn't ready for responsibility."

The wedding seems to have been cursed from the get-go. Besides having no one from the bride's family in attendance, and a groom's family that was less than keen on the whole deal, other arrangements went awry as well. "There are actually only polaroid photos," says Elaine, "because the actual photographer didn't show up." Still, the whole affair, while a futile exercise in the end, was their best attempt at a classy production, and Elaine had at least one positive memory from that day.

"I remember Richard Stanley played 'Kemp's Jig' at the wedding. It was in winter.... I seem to remember it was a very old church, a small church in Elma, and it was lovely to have the lute played, traditional music."

For a while they lived in the Buffalo area but being around his parents soon proved to be too much for Jackson and especially Elaine, and they decided that the place for them to be was in the Catskills, where Jackson had visited the Boggs family a couple of years earlier with Kathy Henry.

Woodstock was a cool, hip town and a place where a creative couple could find some degree of happiness and maybe even raise a family. The sixties with their attendant peace and love philosophy were in full swing and nowhere was it more evident than in Woodstock. So they made the move, staying for a while with the Boggs's on Boggs Hill, outside of town, until they were able to secure their own apartment, just off Tinker Street, the main street. There they began to mix with the locals and Jackson in particular formed a few ties with the musical community, often playing at the local hot spot, the Café Espresso, which originally was opened by an artist named Franklyn Drake, whose mother Pansy Copeland owned a farm outside of town. It was on her farm that something was brewing that would have a lasting effect on the concept of music festivals and how they were presented. It was also the scene of the crime, so to speak, when the worlds of concept and commerce would collide and where, unfortunately for many, commerce would slink off to the bank, grinning all the way.

The Woodstock Sound Outs

Author's note: The Woodstock Sound Outs were important precursors to the 1969 Bethel event. Every person I spoke with about them told a different story about who, what and when, and the whole thing became a convolution that was almost impossible to sort out to my satisfaction. (The old line that "if you remember the sixties, you weren't there" applies here).

The one thing that everyone agreed upon is that Jackson was indeed a very important part of the early events and has not received the proper credit for his role in developing a tradition that grew to epic proportions at Max Yasgur's farm in 1969.

It was August, and the hippies and peaceniks were gathered in the field. A stage had been set up and the fences were coming down. People were full of the peace vibe, sharing and even feeding each other as three days of peace and music got underway. The sixties were in full bloom and the hills were alive with the sound of music. The list of performers included names like John Sebastian and Tim Hardin. The year was 1967, the Summer of Love. This was the original, the first true "Woodstock Festival." Accept no substitutes. Forget what you've heard and read. This is the (somewhat abbreviated, somewhat convoluted) story:

A forerunner of the more famous Woodstock Festival, which took place a good fifty miles away in the Sullivan County town of Bethel, New York, the Woodstock Sound Out (the name of the first one in 1966), and subsequent Woodstock Sound Festivals (1967, 1968, 1970 and 1971—see, it's getting confusing already!) actually took place in Woodstock and featured several of the performers who would also play, or, in the case of the 1970 and 1971 editions, who had already played at the more famous 1969 Bethel Woodstock Festival.

The roots of the original Woodstock Festival are as follows: From 1957 onward, the Woodstock Festival Committee, a group overseeing publicity for the village and arts colony of the same name, published a booklet each year for the express purpose of giving the place some publicity. The tongue-in-cheek name that they gave the colony of the arts was The Woodstock Festival, and the booklet advertised the local shops and businesses, along with the services they provided. Also included were galleries' schedules, art schools and classes, as well as concerts, plays, poetry readings, dramatic offerings and dances. Pretty much the same type of publication that most cities with any type of cultural leaning have today, but for the time it was fairly unique.

Each year, it was traditional for artists to submit their drawings of a dove (beginning to sound familiar?) and the winning dove, as it were, was selected, with great honor to the artist, for viewing on the cover of the publication. This went on until 1969, and then it stopped for a year, to return in 1970 under the aegis of the Woodstock Chamber of Commerce. The claim can be made, fairly convincingly, that the creators, especially Michael Lang, of the Bethel concert of 1969, took both the name and symbol of their event from the earlier public tradition. There was more that was borrowed, or stolen, (your choice) from the Soundouts/Festivals as well. The entire scene, ambience, setting—was borrowed liberally by the Bethel organizers, who had tried to stage their festival in Woodstock but were denied.

The whole tradition of bohemian Woodstock music concerts under the open skies of August goes all the way back to the Maverick Festivals, which started in 1916 and are still ongoing. In the 1960's, a woman named Pansy (Pan) Copeland and her friends decided to continue that Woodstock tradition of artistic and cultural gatherings—and today, there are, or have been, at various times Byrdcliffe Chamber concerts, as well as the Maverick Festivals, Art Students League picnics, Library Fairs, Pan's Woodstock Sound Festivals, the Playhouse, Full Moon circles at Mead's Mt. Magic Meadow and Sunday Drum circles on the Village Green.

Jackson C. Frank was one of the people helping Pan Copeland get the ball rolling. His connections to the music scene in London were still fairly strong and he was instrumental in securing some memorable acts, including his old friends The Young Tradition as well as a new group called Chrysalis, the Blues Magoos (whose bass player Michael Esposito would become a lifelong friend and neighbor in Woodstock) and the avante garde jazz fusion group called Soft Machine. It was their appearance that shines a light on just how massive disorganization can skirt the edges of disaster and yet still come off fairly successfully.

It was a memorable near-disaster due to a lack of communication between the group, who were based in the U.K., and Jackson, who was in Woodstock. According to Julius Bruggeman, one of the original organizers of the festivals, the group, who had never played in the States to that point, had agreed to perform at the Sound Festival of 1967, but the communication breakdown led to a substantial amount of doubt as to whether the group was actually going to show up and perform. They had been scheduled to play an evening set, but when showtime approached there was no word from the group, so it was assumed they weren't coming. In reality, the group had landed in New York, rented a U-Haul truck for their equipment and were on their way to Woodstock, arriving at roughly the same time that a folkie performer was set to go on as the group's replacement.

The crowd didn't want folk music—they were stoked and toked and wanted something heavier and began to grow restless. The U-Haul arrived, and was driven across the fields of Copeland's farm, only to get stuck in a mud bog that had formed in a depression in the ground. Local hardware store owner Frank Anderson was called in with his tractor to pull the truck free and the band was soon able to unload their gear and get set up on the stage. The stage was a makeshift affair built by Bruggeman after a group of citizens from nearby Saugerties, opposed to the idea of a few hundred hippies having a good time, had stealthily burned the original one the night before the Sound Festival started.

The group set up and began to play, a heavy mix of jazz and rock, "Coltrane-style," according to Bruggeman. The replacement stage, being a quickie job, (this was before it was decided to use flatbed trucks as a more viable alternative) was not suitably solid to withstand the vibrations from heavy drumming and as a result, the drums began to do their own dance across the surface of the wood. Julius Bruggeman, apparently feeling the weight of responsibility, decided to help out by lying on the floor and physically holding the moving parts of the kit in place, with the drummer pounding away furiously, and loudly, above him. Bruggeman is positive that his subsequent high end hearing loss was a direct result of his decision to lay down his body for the cause that night. Afterward, the group, again due to the lack of communication, had no place to stay, so Bruggeman and his girlfriend Christine Anderson gave up their house to the group and slept at a friend's for the night. They returned home the next day to a mess, garbage and dirty dishes all over. The Soft Machine had come, they had played and they had left a mess.

In stark contrast to the Soft Machine, who were stablemates in the management firm representing Jimi Hendrix and who had in fact toured with Hendrix, was another group that Jackson had booked for the Sound Festival—his friends from England, The Young Tradition, featuring Heather Wood, at whose flat in London Jackson had stayed for a time a couple years before, as well as Royston Wood and Peter Bellamy. Their a cappella approach to traditional celtic folk songs was certainly a long way off from the balls-out approach of the Soft Machine and others. Still, they were a welcome addition to the scene and a nice contrast to the bombast of some of the heavier acts.

The Sound Out, the original one in 1966, had been the brainchild of a man named Jocko Moffitt. It was held indoors at the Woodstock Playhouse but set the tone for the future events with a peace and love attitude. Space being a problem, it was decided to move any subsequent events to an outside venue. Pan Copeland, who in her own small way was an American Judith Piepe, taking in all manner of lost souls, owned a farm with substantial acreage on the outskirts of Woodstock, in the area known as Zena–Highwoods, and she volunteered the use of the property for the events.

Here is a description of the arrangements, as well as a not too subtle dig at Michael Lang, from a website article, sadly no longer functioning, about the Sound Festivals:

"Simple sanitary facilities as well as a single food concession were both constructed from re-furbished chicken coops. $15 for the week-end got you the show and the 'scene'. It even included parking, water and firewood. Concert goers were happy campers, generally cooking their own meals and readily sharing with others in an atmosphere of hip comraderie & adventure. It was already being called the Woodstock Festival. In '69 certain would-be music promoters learned of this new recipe the people had created and grabbed it up. Calling themselves Woodstock Ventures, they flashed money, humped up the hype and, calling it the Woodstock Festival, laid claim to everything. That August, a generation recognized their own youth culture was being sold back to them. They promptly tore the fences down (early Friday eve.) and continued the popular non-commercial mystique. Performers however, demanded cash in the office trailer (behind the stage) before going on. Woodstock Ventures and Warner Bros. never shared the proceeds of this 'Woodstock' phenomenon they did not create but claimed for their own. By '69, a generation of Americans instantly recognized the unique authenticity and appeal of Peace and Love rather than war and greed. It made of the name Woodstock a great symbol for the beauty of cheerful sanity in a mad world of alienation and ecocide. Your youthful enthusiasm and 'joie de vivre' became the miracle in the mud. The Woodstock Notion of 'caring & sharing in Peace and Love' belongs to all of us; belongs to history."

The Woodstock, Pan Copeland Farm events themselves were certainly prototypical to the Bethel event. They were three days long, held in mid-August in a pastoral, farm setting, featured some of the same performers, like John Sebastian, Tim Hardin and others, and preached the vibe of peace and love and were accompanied by a great visual called the Pablo Light Show. As Michael Lang and his cohorts moved in and literally stole the show for profitable gain, a bitterness formed in the founders of the Sound Festivals that still exists in high levels today. Only a delay by Pan Copeland in registering the Woodstock Festival name allowed that to be co-opted.

Julius Bruggeman still has the check, made out but unsent

by Copeland. It is a small but powerful reminder of what small details left unattended to can do. To his credit, Michael Lange later admitted that he had taken the idea and run with it. Questioned, humorously, as to whether he had tried to sell water for six dollars at the event, he replied that actually he was shooting for ten bucks.

According to Julius Bruggeman, and corroborated by the Woodstock Week newspaper, on the Sunday evening of the '67 event he looked out and who should be sitting peacefully watching the music but Bob Dylan, who had returned from England the year before as a near casualty of the drug culture he helped foster, only to do himself more harm by crashing his motorcycle on a dewy morning road near his house in the hills of the Byrdcliff section of town. Probably not injured as badly as legend has it (allegedly he broke his neck), still it was likely a wake-up call to slow down and concentrate on the important aspects of life—family and all that comes with it. Dylan had heard about the Sound Festival and had made it known to some that he wanted to be invited to play. After his 1966 tour of England and Australia, where there were as many boos and catcalls and name-calling as there were cheers, to be able to play in front of a friendly, and small crowd would have been a welcome relief for Dylan. The request never got to the right people, and a hurt Dylan showed up a few days after the festival at Anne's Delicatessen on Tinker Street (another Pan Copeland production), where Julius Bruggeman had just opened up at 7:00 AM. Dylan walked in, with the apparent intention of dressing down Julius for not inviting him, which was something that Julius knew nothing about. As Julius describes it, Dylan apparently lost his nerve and ordered a roast beef sandwich instead, unusual for that hour of the morning. As Julius was unwrapping the packaging for the roast beef, he sliced the tip of his finger off. In pain and a nervous wreck, (it was, after all, Bob Dylan's sandwich) he shielded his injury from his Bob-ness, and proceeded to inadvertently bleed all over the sandwich. He quickly wrapped the sandwich and sent the Voice of a Generation on his way. One could say that Dylan got a piece of Julius that morning after all.

Jackson's old friend Richard Stanley was a performer with his group, Time, at the 1967 event and he shares a brief Dylan encounter as well. When one of his group spied Dylan sitting with friends taking in the music, he approached him with a tape the group had made, for Dylan's approval. Dylan, gregarious as ever, replied, "Naw, man, I ain't no critic."

Richard Stanley: "I ran into Jackson on East 9th St. in NYC. I had not seen him since late '64 before he went to England, made the album produced by Paul Simon and did the European tour in support of the album release. I had been doing Renaissance and Medieval music from '63 through early '67, but had recently joined a very avant garde rock band and we were in the midst of relocating from Buffalo to NYC. Jackson told me that, 'some folks in Woodstock thought a summer music festival would be a nice idea' and that 'he was organizing it.' He said he had a couple of acts lined up and what if the band I was in would be the opener. I don't remember if we even submitted a tape, but he put us on the bill and by the time that I found an apartment in New York in May of '67 the event was confirmed with our group Time as the opener that day, The Blues Magoos as headliner, and Tim Hardin, who stiffed me for a $25 job the next year.

"We stayed in an abandoned farm house adjacent to the site from Friday through Sunday. The weather was beautiful all the time we were there. The field in which it was held was lightly sprinkled with slightly weathered cow pies and sloped downhill a bit toward the stage area which was the trailer section of a large flatbed truck. Total attendance each day could not have been more than about 200 persons.

"Jackson and Elaine were living in Woodstock at the time and I spent a little time with them there. The only impression

I retain about their domestic scene was that the place was littered and messy, but mostly I remember Elaine as being tight-lipped and bad tempered as though she was constantly impatient and disconcerted. (The only other time that I saw much of her was at the time of their wedding.)

"In the early fall I again ran into Jackson in NYC. He said, 'Everyone thought the festival was great and that he was going to do it again the next year ('68).' The rest, as they say, is history. That was the last time that I saw Jackson."

§

For his part, Jackson made himself scarce at the concerts, performing a short set at the 1967 Sound Festival, and then demanding to be paid for his role of treasurer (all of the performers were unpaid) on the planning committee for the event. It was the only aspect of the thing that was going to bring any payment to the planners, and according to Bruggeman, Jackson was the first to demand his money, which did cast a bit of a pall over the general feeling of good will that pervaded the event. It is likely that he was broke. At any rate, he received his money, a little over five hundred dollars, and went on his way, leaving a little bit of a bad vibe in the others who had worked a lot harder and were paid less.

He had returned from England a few months earlier, gotten married and had been working at a local leather shop for some extra cash, in between the odd gig or two. His wife was pregnant for the second time, after having suffering a miscarriage months earlier. Fortunately though, this time the baby was expected to make it to full term. For some reason he made a trip back home to Buffalo, where he tried to re-unite with Kathy Henry by showing up unannounced at her door, only to be turned away without a chance to go inside. He visited his parents for a little while and headed back home to Ulster County. He was going to be a father.

The Woodstock Week, February 15, 1968
A Review of Jackson C. Frank at the Café Espresso
(Author Unknown)

It was a typical, bitter cold Woodstock night. Why is it that any night you want to go out the temperature seems to drop 10 degrees? The Café Espresso was nearly full, with the usual assortment of "types," ranging from the "in crowd" with art work on their faces, to the "first timers" in single breasted business suits, trying to look nonchalant. Table candles punctuate the smoke in the room like runaway markers at a London airport. The yellow spotlight came on and the small talk died.

On the "stage" (a platform placed over a circular bar-b-que pit, built entirely without Federal funds from Perdenales Papa) a young man tossed a thick mane of blond hair back from his eyes, cleared his throat a number of times and announced "I'm Jackson Frank."

He apologized for his bad throat, and started to perform his own work. With a guitar style that somehow had a hint of harpsichord, he played and sang "I Want to be Alone." Jackson had originally named it "Dialogue with four voices" until some wag pointed out that a dialogue implies two voices. (It may have been the same friend who rushed over one day to tell Jackson that a pigeon had been seen riding the "tube" (British Subway) from Liverpool to Charing Cross). He went on to perform "You Never Wanted Me," "Milk and Honey" and "Carnival."

Jackson Frank has the unusual facility of saying something to everyone who listens to his songs, and it's seldom the same thing to any two people.

"Just like anything. . .to sing. . .to sing…is a state of mind. Death gives no reason, so why should I? Death has no season, so I know I'll never die. . . If I had a penny, I'd throw it in the sea, to

see if it would float away or grow a penny tree. . ."

Quite a talent, Jackson Frank. Now if he can only be convinced that he should practice more, he will gain confidence and
stop negating his performances by putting himself down.

It's Cold and It's Lonesome. . . .

It was the late winter, early 1968. The buds of the trees had not
yet begun to open, meaning that the ample Catskill mountain woods around the Ashokan Reservoir still carried a dark
gray pallor that was in direct contradiction to the beautiful
waters of the lake, man-made though it was. In a car that was
parked at a small viewing area near one of the pump buildings
that occasionally dot the roads around the reservoir, Jackson
C. Frank, a man possessed by grief, sat with Marianne Welch.
His former band mate in the Grosvenor Singers, she was an
unconditional friend who would, throughout their lives, try
to be there for him when he was going through hard times,
which seemed to be a chronic condition for him, although
nothing as terrible as this had happened before, at least not
since the fire that had maimed him and killed so many of his
friends. The sun went down and the moon rose slowly over
the water.

Several hours before, Jackson's wife Elaine had finally giv-
en birth to a baby boy. She had already miscarried one baby
in the previous year, after moving to Woodstock from the
Buffalo area where they had lived for a short time after their
wedding in Elma. This pregnancy would end just as disas-
trously. The baby, who never had a chance to be named, was
born with a rare and unfortunate condition that caused his
lungs to be on the outside of his body. He only managed to
hold on for ten hours before succumbing to this cruelty of

nature. It was more than Jackson could bear, and he went into a deep, deep funk. Marianne Welch was with him that day as he fell into his grief. After spending some time at the Café Espresso, drinking wine, they took the twenty minute ride through the beautiful back roads of Ulster County, arriving at the Ashokan Reservoir in Boiceville, where they parked and sat quietly as day turned to night.

The death of the baby was quite possibly the last straw on the delicate camel's back of Jackson's frail psyche, and his will snapped. While his behaviors had always been excessive and on the fringe of eccentricity, he had managed to keep his wits about him most of the time, but after his son's death he began to seriously unravel. The pregnancy had been, at least temporarily the saving grace for his short marriage to Elaine, with whom he had been arguing much of the time. With the baby gone, and very little money coming in, he was feeling the strain of family life and needed to do something to change the situation. He had hoped that the baby and having a real family would be his reward for doing all of the right things but that was never in the cards for him. He did make one last attempt at normalcy, though, as he headed through the snow one night to Lorraine Lilja's house, intent on securing a job as an editor at her newspaper, the small, weekly Woodstock Week. The insurance money he had gotten was as much a curse to him as it was a blessing. He had never learned to earn a real living because he knew that money was on its way when he turned twenty one. Instead of having the foresight to use the money to plan for his future, he decided to piss it all away. Even his music career, abbreviated as it was, had only happened because Paul Simon had seen his talents and wanted to capture them before they, or he, disappeared.

And so it was in the early part of 1968, that Jackson, married and needing to support himself and Elaine, returned to newspaper work, hired after walking that snowy route one cold night. Lilja eventually put him to work editing and doing some writing but he started his tenure as an on-air correspondent for the local leading news radio station, WKNY-AM radio in Kingston, New York. Through an arrangement with the station the staff at the Woodstock Week would air short news segments each week and Jackson was one of the on-air readers. Unfortunately, no air checks survive, but after a short stint as the WKNY correspondent he was rewarded with the editorial job he wanted at the paper.

He had gotten the job at the paper by applying the old fashioned way—he went to the general manager's house and asked for the position.

Lorraine Lilja, the manager in question, and now retired to the Adirondack Mountains of upstate New York, remembers that day.

Lilja: "He showed up at my door in Woodstock, coming to my home through the snow in a dramatic black cape with a standing collar. He was back from England, validated, with a beautiful wife. I hired him, and he did a good job. He loved Woodstock with its assortment of characters, just as I have since childhood. He had a ready laugh, and smiled a lot. His fine, flaxen hair was always falling into his face. That may have been intentional, for his face bore the shiny, puckered scars of severe burns. He seemed to enjoy writing about Woodstock, and always met his deadlines, being totally responsible."

Lilja knew Jackson had been through the gauntlet of life, but she never pressed him about what had happened. Being from another generation, she was a busy single mom and wasn't able to take part in the lives of the younger people around, comfortable to provide them with a nice little paper to keep them informed and enlightened. Looking back, years later, through the archives at the Woodstock Library, with its boxes full of more formal publications, one is almost amused to see the Woodstock Week's archives, with their sometimes hand drawn sub-headlines, but the level of writing, by Jackson and others, is generally of the highest order, and reveals an attention to detail missing from most of today's journalism. He did several stories each week, some long, some little more than blurbs for various functions. He also wrote a weekly (for the most part) column called Notes From a Layman, each column focusing on some issue of the day, often with wit and humor. What follows is an example of that humor, a short piece he did for Valentine's Day, 1968. It was his second week working for the paper.

Woodstock Week, *February 15, 1968*
Defensive Valentine's Greetings
by Jackson C. Frank

I was driving through downtown deserted Kingston last week and, as I contemplated a bricks-for-bookshelves foray into the midst of the grim no-mans-land all around me I came upon a group of 300 or so "hippies," I believe they are called, fighting in a vacant lot between a cigar store and an abandoned Sinclair service station. Bells furiously pounded out an incredible anti-rhythm, long hair knotted and whirled, pigeons were de-masting from roof tops for blocks. Frightening, I'll tell you....

Anyway, I decided that, for some insane reason I should service the cause of post-war (what?) journalism to a point exceeding valor and fringing on morbid and insatiable curiosity by ploughing into the melee and finding out what the ruckus was all about. In the center of the beating frenzy, after much elbowing and kicking to reach that storm apex, I found a calm man in a business suit who had assumed the position of meditation most employed by Indian Fakirs. His eyes were small and smoke seemed to dribble continuously through his fat and livery lips. Incredibly a beard and mustache, wiry and faultlessly hairy, began to spout from the man's face as I stood watching. I cursed the luck that brought me here camera-less. As the hair-ification process continued its

Werewolves-like course, his business suit began to fray at the cuffs, to come apart magically at each seam. His blue worsted jacket visibly transmogrified in a short time to a lamb's wool pelt hung like a tent about his shoulders. His oxfords stripped themselves of excess leather and became sandals of tire casements attached by leather thongs, his suit pants to jeans bony white with bleaching. I was about to slip over the edge of God knows what abyss when the newly created whatever he was rose up and joined the crowd in a hypnotic trance which seemed akin to stupor. Someone grabbed me and then many hands, all around me, were pushing me to the center of the circle, to the spot of ground formerly occupied, I was later to learn, by a truant officer. Someone stuck a cigarette in my mouth (it looked like a cigarette) and all withdrew to the former tight circle of frenzy I had, so short a time ago joined.

After the third butt was crushed and nothing had come over me to change my outward appearance, the crowd had become deathly still, hanging on every drag I took, some were fumbling with useless hands at their bead chains. When I lit up the fourth from my Dupont Chinese Laquer lighter, the edges of the inner circle started to fray and blur enmasse.....I shook my head and started at the expanses of crooked teeth buildings in the distance over the crowds heads...It wasn't me, nothing was blurred there. Suddenly the crowd lurched and a great noise burst above them like dry stick and cinders crushing into each other....the crowd became wobbly, faces and bodies flickered and dimmed, and abruptly became...nothing.

The Truant officer sat dazed at what had been the outer edges of the mob, shook his head and got angularly up from the ground, dusting himself off in the process. He looked at me in a very odd way and said, "Happy Valentines Day, I think. Could I have a ride into town with you? I can't seem to find my car."

It's an amazingly cheery piece of writing, one of the last things he would write that bore much humor, given the upcoming tidal wave of sadness that would hit him because of the death of his son, just a couple of weeks away.

As with everything else in Jackson's life, unfortunately, the gig at the Week was temporary, and the urge to return to England began to eat at him. Woodstock was another place where there were bad memories festering, and he needed to get away for a while. The clues were there in his writings for the paper, which often included little snippets of British references and language. It should be noted that Jackson's legend has always contained the statement that he had not written any new musical material because of a massive writer's block. What isn't as clear is whether that block ever really existed at all. He was writing prolifically for the newspaper, often turning in articles in excess of two thousand words, which are very long articles by newspaper standards, and which showed that he was capable of turning a phrase with the best of them. He did have a restlessness about him—the "England thing" was still gnawing at him. It was the only place he had been a success and he felt a strong urge to go back. Finally, he succumbed to his demons and made the decision to return to the place he loved so well. He declared his intentions in a long, elegant article that summer, which laid out his reasons for loving England and what the world traveler would experience should he or she ever want to make the trip over on a cruise ship. The title was a pun on Roger Miller's song called "England Swings" (a song that Jackson hated with a passion, according to Marianne Welch).

England Sings
by Jackson C. Frank

Well, the Pound is de-valued, Parliament runs the Prime Minister and if you hold an Asian British passport you are out of luck... nonetheless I am going to return to jolly old England one of these days. It is really my second home and I have as much love for her as for my own America. That sounds hard to believe, but let me help you understand why I can say it so easily and without any trace of feeling non-patriotic.

Patriotism is largely a matter of where you are born. I was born here in the good old USA, but this matter of being born to a flag and drum beating bears up very badly in peace time, especially if one travels at all and leaves his or her "Ugly America" syndrome behind. The very idea of "Ugly American–ism" and the popularity it enjoyed seems to show in a sado-masochistic fashion the pre-occupation we have in being an insular people. If isolationism recurs in the not too distant future it is only going to be due to the fact that we choose to believe the rest of the world is against us and then we take an abominable and odious stance of defense more rightly paranoia than patriotism. We wish to believe ill in ourselves and that, in the first and last sense of the word, is the worst thing we can do.

When I decided to travel to England I had some fairly idiotic ideas of the whole affair. I had no real anticipation of anything more than a stuffy country filled with books and a lost sense of empire dotted heavily with monuments to a history at least equally stuffy and loss-inspired. The first thing I wanted to do was head for France, to tell the truth. The idea of spending two years anywhere outside the United States had very little reality to me at all then. But two years it was, and I only wish it had been more and I had begun sooner to explore the world.

What is a trip across the ocean except an initial amount of red tape, less than you go through to get Medicare and much more rewarding. We can afford to travel better than any nation in the world today and yet until a very short time ago this travel thing was regarded as the privilege of the very few indeed. It seems Americans have a very leery attitude towards recrossing the Big Ditch having made such a fuss over getting across the first time. I should think that a trip back to the Old Country was the very best indication of what we have accomplished, both to the world and ourselves, nonetheless it would also appear that three-quar-

ters of the population here disagrees violently with me.

Why do I love England then is a job for a raconteur. Since I am not quite the story teller I should like to be I hope you will forgive any rough edges in the following descriptions of my trip and I hope even more fervently that this doesn't appear to be a semi-home films travelogue. I have a purpose in mind and wish you to share it with me.

If you arrive by ship in England it will most likely mean after a short trip from Cherbourg, France, across the coldly green glint of the Channel to Espy, perhaps the most heartlessly industrial waste you have ever known. The port is filled with studies in charcoal and ships spread their bulk like a large machine, devoid of the romantic ocean, in triplicate as far as the eye can see. Towards dusk the lights of heavy cranes and the ships themselves seem to wink almost too tired or busy to appear evil, and yet do, across the grey smudge of the harbor. This is Southampton and the traveler who has envisioned England as a damp and murky land feels the portals of Hell and not just an unpleasant experience await him. It is all to a purpose however, for the bustle of saying goodbye to your deck porters and hauling luggage frantically up and out into the yellow lit railway hall serves as a masterful transition to the true England. In no time at all you have had a friendly word, in the midst of all the exotic bustle, from the customs officials, the accents have become second nature and the hiring, direction and payment, of a porter are all your own affair. The point is the English would rather make you feel competent than coddled. The value of dancing girls meeting you at the end of a runway singing native songs and throwing leis is completely lost upon them. I daresay the result is more beneficial to all concerned.

You may generally expect the Cunard boat train to break down several times along the ninety mile route into Waterloo Station, London. Here too no effort is spared to make you feel actually a part of what is happening rather than a suckling pig in the honored spot. As the English train fares, so do you. All of you. People break out lunches, dinners, what have you and carry on conversation in normal tones of voice about the "bloody" British rails. The antique-but-not-really coaches are clean, comfortable and seem to have lived just long enough to become restful in the embrace of the rickety-rack of rail travel. You start to wonder, if you are a good American and only on a pleasure tour, especially if you are alone, whether or not this is typical public apathy on the part of the English. After all, tempers would be to the point of murder in the States and by now stateside trains would have brought out a new engine to meet the train and "expedite" matters. Strangely, however, the night and the quietude of one's surroundings begin to imbue you with an altered sense of things as you had always supposed them to be, taking the bad as inevitable and the good as a level of critique at best. It is really more important to read a paper and get along with peace of mind than it is to cultivate a larger ulcer within seconds over a machine with perhaps more personality than purpose.

It seems that every new experience in the English frame of life is an adventure for the tourist or the person who had dedicated himself to staying clear of guided tours. Perhaps the quality of self determinant thought which is made such constant usage of in England is what leads little old women to return after fifteen days guided tour yabbering profoundly about the splendor of St. Paul's and Westminster, but totally convinced that the English are a cold fish race. To put a point in for the English, the truth is much more likely that the little old ladies were a bit handicapped for the experience. Again, and not simply American in essence, the point has to be made that tourists lump together and gather very little from their forays. They are singularly determined to leave one foot in the place they have just come from, h-o-m-e.

At Waterloo Station the traveler is all on his lonesome. The only thing to do is carry on with baggage procedure, storing it for future pick-up and tipping the porters once more. Then you are for a moment, just for a moment, the loneliest human being alive. The country is strange, you are cut off from all convenient telephone calls and you have to make your way from that point on entirely dependent upon yourself. After the initial shock it is amazing what wonders that feeling can work.

Down to a cabby, ask for the accommodations you desire and thence over the Thames into the suddenly warm evening of London. Lights, buildings, the well-proportioned streets, a potpourri of colors, sounds and people you will never forget.

After the business of establishing your base, most of your energy seems to return and though you may verge on the thin line of utter exhaustion, there is too much to see and learn to sleep now. I took a cab at 1 AM and directed the driver to the Palace, I had to get it over with. Buckingham slept at the end of the mall in a solid grey mass quite unlike the normal idea of a palace. It had an administrative air to it. On the way back we passed Trafalgar.... the fountain lights had been switched off and everything seemed strangely remote but well-ordered in the gentle evening. Unlike most cities there appears to be only one section which remains alive all night. The Strand and The Mall, Trafalgar and sections of Shaftesbury Avenue seem to be abandoned. Soho is the raging quasar of night light, from it all life radiates and the only spin-off are the hundreds of taxis hustling people home from Cambridge Circus, from the edge of the giant pinwheel.

Soho neither sleeps nor will ever die. It is a strange and harlequin place, a country onto itself, fade-away land....

One of the centers of this bright pattern lies along Greek Street, which runs between Soho Square and its French church, Soho Hospital and RCA recording studios, to Compton Road. Compton is about where the action stops, though Greek Street carries on beyond this intersection for some blocks. This is the border of Soho and is the home of "the Establishment," L'Escargot," "LeKilt" and "Les Cousins." "Sin City" also occupies a prominent position on Greek Street, but around the corner on Compton are the larger strip clubs such as "the Phoenix." Sex is an important commodity in any society but in Soho it is something that people come to look at and for. One mustn't shrink away from the human condition *no matter what their feelings if that condition may be understood rationally. Tourists think it is cute, risqué, or perhaps go home to speak of the evils involved. I know that Soho has produced some of the major hells of living. I know Soho well. Yet, she has given much more than heartbreak. Soho is the center of a moving and cogent world, the young come there for a good time and learn through many teachers how actually small their lives have been previously. Music is on the upswing all over the world. There has been a revival in folk-form and compositions in England which will yet work its wiles on our listening....and it happened in Soho, in clubs like "Les Cousins," the largest folk music club in the world.*

At any rate, the story of old men in the streets who play mandolin and violin with as much expertise as the finest scholarly musician could hope to attain, the corner stands selling roasted chestnuts, meat pies and jellied eels, the "Read Me's" of the newsstands, young people from many lands, the dark recesses of a suddenly wider world as well as its brightness is quite too much for me to write in full here. In fact, I see that I have done little to tell you why it is better to travel than remain in one place. Perhaps this is because such values are personal and each of us forms them separately, personally. Yet, no one can fail to be increased as a person if they can travel with the single thought in mind to become, for a short space of time, a part of the place they visit. I think that is what I learned above all in England and is all the reason I love her so. She taught me the value of remaining open to all things.

§

Jackson left the paper in late 1968. Elaine had miraculously gotten pregnant again, and Jackson, feeling still another bit of level-headedness, and seeing his music as a way to support a family, was getting his act together in preparation for heading back to England for another grasp at the ring. That summer he and Elaine had opened a clothing shop at 8 Mill

Hill Road in town with the help, according to Jackson, of a three thousand dollar loan from Paul Simon. Simon had, as a condition of the loan, required Jackson to sign over the publishing rights to his songs as collateral and had made Jackson sign a promissory note as well. It would be almost thirty years before Jackson got his music publishing returned to him. Simon had been a true friend, though, and was one well that Jackson had visited many times and with his help once again the Franks were able to open the shop. It was called Bell Bows Boutique, and featured fashion designs by "coutourier" Elaine herself. She had many years of experience in the industry, first studying design art at age 15 at the City of London Guild of Arts and Crafts and moving on the jobs at Gucci's, Bond Street, and even gaining accreditation as a Max Factor beauty consultant. She was also an instructor in the toney world of equestrian dressage, an assistant stage manager with a repertory theater and a photographic stylist with Photo Center, one of London's largest studios.

Being married to Jackson was, understandably not satisfying enough and Elaine had to feel somewhat stifled when it came to her own abilities, which were not insubstantial. The boutique would be a good way to express her own creativity, and it might even make a few bucks as well, since Jackson wasn't making much at the paper, prolific though he was. There was a nice centerfold spread in the August 1, 1968 issue of the Woodstock Week that featured several photos of Elaine and some of her creations and was accompanied by text almost certainly written by Jackson, who was no longer officially with the paper, having written his last articles for it several weeks prior.

Ironically the same issue that featured the story of Elaine and the boutique also had a great photo of Jackson on the back page, sitting with his guitar on stone steps next to what looks like a stuffed parrot and an American flag. The caption, rather flowery and unusual, reads, "Jackson Frank, former editor of the Week, will perform at England's Royal Festival Hall in late September, followed by a singing tour. Frank sings songs of his own composition, the lyrics by the voice within, sung in a clear baritone that paints water colors of scenes captured by the mind's eye."

The photo on the back of the newspaper was evidently not a one-shot affair. When the official program for the Royal Festival Hall performance came out, it featured another photo of Jackson, alongside an old car, on Tinker Street in Woodstock, wearing the same clothing, hairstyle, and with the same familiar stuffed parrot perched in the car window....

§

The boutique didn't last long, unfortunately, since even in those days three thousand dollars wasn't enough to make the place as well equipped as was needed to keep up with advertising, rent, fees and all of the other expenses that come with having a small business. As she recalled years later, "At that point in time it wasn't very lucrative. Most people were into doing Indian and Afghani imports as opposed to designer type clothes. I later went on to design costumes for the Woodstock Playhouse. That was much better for me."

With the added pressure of expecting another baby, Elaine needed to curtail her activity somewhat anyway. With Jackson in England she was by herself, and, unable to keep up with running the place alone, she closed up shop and made plans to join her husband in England.

And in England, Jackson was having a mixed bag of a time. His first performance upon his return was as one of a group of performers at a Roy Guest-produced show at the Royal Festival Hall featuring, besides Jackson, a young Joni Mitchell, Al Stewart, the Johnsons, featuring a young Paul Brady and Fairport Convention, with Jackson's old flame Sandy Denny, back on lead vocals. The show, was supposed to be a showcase for Al Stewart, according to Chris Jones, a musician who was in attendance, but according to Jones, Jackson absolutely stole the show. This was confirmed by a review in the *Daily Telegraph* of September 30, 1968.

Imaginative U.S. Folk Singer
By Maurice Rosenbaum

In a twilight era of pop-folk whimsy, where fey singers slide around in a blancmange of pseudo-poetry, it is heartening to be reminded of the clear, hard light of genius.

This was the most rewarding aspect of the "Festival of Contemporary Song" at the Festival Hall on Saturday evening, when the power of true originality was the keynote.

The best of contemporary song consists of largely autobiographical crystallisations of our time, and the quality depends on the creative integrity and resources of the writer and singer through whom the spirit of the time is expressed. It was all the more gratifying therefore to have Jackson C. Frank back with us.

This American song-writer and singer is one of the most profoundly imaginative to have emerged from the folk revival. He is aware of the limitations of his medium—"To sing is a state of mind that can include all states of mind," he says, "and therein lies the danger in communicating through song alone"—and he has the prophetic attributes of humility and vision.

Joni Mitchell, the young Canadian singer who, though she would be the last to claim it, owes little to others, also held the crowd enthralled with the beauty of her voice and the poetry of her songs.

Al Stewart, himself a truly original song-writer and a very good guitarist, was in excellent form both in his new ballad, "Love's Chronicle" (sic) and in Peter Morgan's poem, "My enemies have sweet voices."

The Fairport Convention—amplified guitars, percussion and two singers, Ian Macdonald and Sandy Denny—gave a performance of Richard Farina's "Reno, Nevada" which, I think, Farina himself would have liked, and have great promise. The Johnstons made a lively opening to a remarkable concert.

It was at this show that Al Stewart recalls a new song that Jackson performed, called "Four O' Clock in the Morning" which Al felt had "hit" written all over it, as he told Andrew Means in an interview with Folk Roots many years later. "It was very catchy," Stewart says. "Absolutely right on the ball and just the sort of thing that would have taken off." And, as Means wrote, and which Jackson would verify, he couldn't recall any such song. "I don't even remember a song called 'Four O' Clock In The Morning,' he said. "I was still doing the stuff that I did in '65. I hadn't written anything new." Stewart, among others, recalled what happened in the months after the show: "He proceeded to fall apart before our eyes. His style that everybody loved was melancholy, very tuneful things, and this new one, 'Four O' Clock In The Morning' was in that style. But immediately thereafter he started doing things that were completely impenetrable. They were basically about psychological angst played at full volume with lots of thrashing. I don't remember a single word of them, but it just did not work. There was one review that said he belonged on a psychiatrist's couch. Then shortly after that he high-tailed it back to Woodstock again, because he wasn't getting work." Years later I discovered a recording of a great and catchy song called "Four in the Morning" that sounded almost exactly like Jackson. Same guitar style, same voice, and I thought I had solved the mystery, but the song and recording turned out to be a track from the Jesse Colin Young's eponymous first album. I ran it by Al Stewart but he was adamant that he had never heard Jesse Colin Young and that he only knew the song from Jackson's Festival Hall performance. Another dead end. It is a puzzle to this day. In a phone interview, Al Stewart even sang me a bit of the melody, but by the time we spoke, Jackson was dead, and the song, if there was one, seems to have gone with him.

A short (and not too profitable) unofficial farewell tour of England followed the Festival Hall show, but nothing much new was revealed in Jackson's sets, and witnesses described him as looking very "uncared for" and not physically too well, although, as always, and almost inexplicably, his performances were of the highest quality. As Al Stewart would recall, what new material he had brought along was, while poetic, very psychotic sounding in theme, and the songs failed to make much of an impression on anyone. The problem, besides the lack of good and new material was that the sizes of the venues hadn't changed. He was still playing small clubs and colleges and wasn't making enough money to stay in the U.K.

At some point, someone got the idea to go back into a studio and record something new for the public. And once again Al Stewart would appear on another Jackson Frank recording, playing nameless tambourine on a new song called "Can't Get Away From My Love," which was destined to become a B-side of an alternate version of "Blues Run the Game."

"Yes, that was me on tambourine," says Stewart. "I remember the session. Jackson doubled his guitar part, but that indeed was me on the tambourine."

On the A-side, an almost pointless loose version of "Blues Run The Game," there is quite clearly a second guitar on the track, playing bluesy lead notes. Stewart denies playing the guitar, but in Neville Judd's biography of Al, it says quite clearly, and with documentation to boot, that Al not only played second guitar on the track but also got some nice notice in the local press for it. Whatever the case, the 45-rpm record barely made a sound when released and today is considered one of the rarest finds in the record collecting world.

An October appearance on John Peel's Nightride program didn't help his cause much, although the four surviving songs ("Blues Run the Game" was cut from the only known existing fan recording) he performed on it were well done, including "Just Like Anything," "My Name Is Carnival," "You Never Wanted Me" and a song called "Jimmy Clay," written and recorded that year by Patrick Sky, a Native American/Scottish songwriter who he had briefly met at Heather Wood's flat one evening. The BBC wiped the Peel tape clean as well, and only recently has the fan's recording of it come to light. Substandard though the recordings are, the brilliance of his performances, especially on "Jimmy Clay," cannot be ignored. But, in the end his touring and promoting was all for naught. After a while the amount of work fizzled out and he was forced to make plans to go home yet again.

It was more than just a lack of work that pushed Jackson back to Woodstock. His career path was definitely not going the way he had hoped, even though his return had been, for a short time, semi-successful, at least in terms of the critical acclaim. Elaine had closed the boutique on Mill Hill Road in Woodstock and moved to London to be with Jackson. They moved into her parents' flat on Peckham Park Road and she gave birth to their daughter Angeline on January 27, 1969. The baby girl was healthy and Jackson, who should have been thrilled at having a complete family, instead began to run around exhibiting odd behaviors and chasing after women other than his wife. There was one woman in particular, a married mother-to-be named Caroline that he fancied strongly and to whom he pledged his undying love. She also was the woman mentioned by Al Stewart as being part of the British aristocracy and who was the woman that Jackson had become fixated on for a while.

Elaine found out about Jackson's obsession with Caroline and in a letter to Marilyn Frank wrote of wanting to be rid of

Jackson once and for all. She wrote:

It is apparent that Jack is determined to destroy his own life and that of those around him or it is his intention to re-enact Jack Jones, and I intend to divorce him as soon as I am financially able. In short Jackson was seeing Caroline... behind my back, the week after we arrived. She is married and expecting a child in May but said she would leave her husband for Jack. He told her to go back to her way of life and her husband (they live in Malta). I'm afraid my reaction was to break up. Jack got out of the house rather than cope with my hysteria and it was left to the family doctor to put me on sedatives and sleeping pills. Several days later Jack moved back in. I had calmed down and for two weeks listened to Jack's pros and cons of our marriage. I told him to go after her if he wanted. He insisted it wasn't then I found four love letters to Carol saying he wished he was free and he loved her. I told him to get out (during that time he made no attempt to get us an apartment and was out every night returning to my parents' flat between 3-7 AM. He has made little effort to find a place since. He is now living in a house with four other people. He has had some 700 pounds of bookings. Over the past four weeks he has at least given me support coming to 140 pounds and is making some little show in repaying my mother part of the 200 pounds she paid for our fares over. He has done nothing to repay outstanding debts in America i.e. Bell Tel, rent, credit account, I have been paying storage rent on our household goods, also a doctors bill and part of the credit account. I have most of the money that Jack has given me as I will need it as rent on a flat I have been looking for a place for five weeks solid. It is unbelievably hard to find a flat that will take a baby. I do not want to stay at home as this has been such a strain to my mother who is not in good health.
I have not made set plans except to determine to support myself and the baby and that Jack will not affect my life any more. I hope he runs after his whore friend...they deserve each other. I

will be returning to Woodstock within the next six months. Jack
I feel will be staying here for some time....

Elaine was wrong in only one respect. Jackson wasn't too far
behind her in returning to Woodstock. As Andrew Means
put it in *Dirty Linen*, "the final push, according to Jackson,
came from Her Majesty's Government, which indicated that
a foreigner approaching indigency was no longer welcome.
Jackson lost heart, and headed for home."

Chris Jones, from London, and a musician himself, but at
that time more of a fan of Jackson and his peers, describes another possible scenario that may have been a factor in Jackson
deciding to return to the States.

As he told me in 2013: "The Cambridge was the 'home'
pub to London buskers. I don't think any connections remain
but in 1968 it was a power house of the London Music Street
Mafia. The buskers were okay and many in those days na-
tionally famous. The most famous being Don Partridge who
had hits here with 'Rosie' and 'Blue Eyes.' The other famous
singer was an old lady called Meg or Megan. She was a real
top dog and would often put in an appearance at the Cousins. She'd do a couple of numbers and then pass her famous
'church collecting bag' to hand around the club. She'd make
more money in those two numbers than the guest would see
for a whole night's show! Megan was about 80 with few or no
teeth. A sort of aged warbling soprano but she always went
down a storm.

"The buskers were a union that organized how busking
would be run, such as a cinema queue. The lowest performers
would work the queue first and then one by one you'd get to
Don Partridge, top artists as the last act.

"It was this group that I believe Jack fell foul of and that
was the conversation I came across one night at the bottom
of the stairs of Cousins. It was Jack talking to Andy about the
threats he had received from the buskers. Jack thought they

were going to knife him but maybe his paranoia was getting the better of him...maybe not. I think Jack thought, as I did, that anyone could busk anywhere in London and the only threat was the police who generally would warn and move you on. If you persisted then you could be locked up for a night and fined but that was rare. The buskers were a bunch not to be messed with and you treated them at arm's length, Today London busking is strictly controlled by the authorities."

Whatever the reasons, Jackson soon returned home where, despite his recent income, as related by Elaine, he still spent more than he made. The old habits apparently wouldn't die easily and money, or rather the keeping of it, continued to be a problem and he quickly fell into the same situation he was in before—broke, asking for loans, and a place to crash, from friends.

After floundering from couch to couch for a while, he reunited with Elaine and baby Angeline, sharing a house in the hills south of Woodstock, where their relationship was strained at best, and where Jackson spent as much time out of the house as in it. He wasn't bringing in much money, back to playing the odd gig and doing other jobs, working in the leather shop for a while, where he made a guitar strap and a belt that he presented to Norm Boggs, who had moved to his family's house on Boggs Hill with his wife, Marianne (who had been Marianne Welch from the Grosvenor Singers). Norm Boggs still has the strap and belt to this day and they are a treasured part of his past.

Jackson often spent time with the Boggs family when he wasn't at home with his own family. At one point he had begun to hear voices and, this being a new symptom of his illness, he reacted by doffing his clothes and running around Woodstock (apparently the voices were from spiritual nudists), especially in the heart of the village, near the highly populous Village Green on Tinker Street. Sometimes he wore a long cape and carried his six-foot sword and a ball and chain contraption, fancying himself a character named Lochinvar, from Sir Walter Scott's poem of the same name. Ironically, a few years later when Norm Boggs and Marianne divorced, he kept the ball and chain and she kept the sword, which she hung onto until Jackson stopped by one day to retrieve it. By then Norm had moved away and had taken the ball and chain with him. Jackson was arrested a few times by the local police but by and large his problems and reputation were becoming known by the village officials and they tried to turn a blind eye when possible. Had Jackson's psychological issues manifested themselves twenty years in the future, a treatment plan likely would have been implemented fairly quickly but in the post-sixties, still drug-addled world of Woodstock it was hard to tell what was the cause of odd behavior—a bad trip or a bad brain. As it was he would eventually be institutionalized many times, in what would become a tragic pattern of life for him.

At any rate, his behavior, usually induced by the voices in his head, had gotten so bad and disturbing that Elaine, in defense of young Angeline, had to demand that Jackson leave the house for good.

Her life with Jackson had been living hell, and Elaine, who had the talent and the drive to move on with her life, began to take steps to put Jackson in the past, and toward that end, according to a family friend many years later, she began to tell young Angeline that "daddy is dead." This was an illusion that her daughter believed for many years until one day when, as a teen riding with friends, someone pointed to a disheveled and homeless Jackson hanging around the Green in Woodstock and said to her, "There's your father." Elaine now denies the story, which is understandable, but the friend maintains that it did indeed happen, and who could blame her anyway?

For Elaine herself, "bittersweet" might be too gentle a word to describe her feelings about her ex-husband. She must have seen something in him that brought out her nurturing side, but a few cutting words from Jackson and the nurturing feelings were a thing of the past.

"He was incredibly talented," she says, "and it is a great sadness that when one is very young one thinks that you can change people or give them motivation or inspiration but apparently he was much, much more intent on being destructive. Maybe that was part of the creativity, but he was a very difficult and tormented person. He behaved extremely cruel. It was on purpose, and it was one of the reasons I don't have fond memories. Jackson had immense talent and it's very, very sad that he was so destructive. He couldn't seem to find something to give his life meaning."

If she had reckoned that marrying Jackson and helping to make his life productive and normal was going to be a simple task, Elaine had made a gross miscalculation in judgment. She wasn't blind to his problems, though, and it is admirable that she took on the task at all.

"He certainly could be charming. He certainly was very intelligent and was very interesting and very stimulating to be around but the price that you paid for that wasn't worth it. He was obviously mentally disturbed and I think it was a combination of several things. The fire obviously had been a great influence but it went even beyond that. I think there were things before the fire ever happened that made him very troubled and tormented but he was equally capable of torturing the people who were closest to him who tried to help."

Elaine finally gave up, of course, since trying to help a stubborn, mentally confused Jackson Frank was akin to fighting the tide with a spoon. At one point in 1971 or 1972, Lorraine Lilja, his old boss at the newspaper ran into Elaine on the street and was told, after inquiring about Jackson, that they were no longer together because he had, in Elaine's words, been "a bad boy," a reference to either his disrobing habit or, more likely, his philandering. Either way, the marriage was kaput, and Jackson began his bouncing from couch-to-couch journey.

In one of the more touching stories to come from Jackson's acquaintances of the time, he ended up living for a part of a year with a writer named Tom (Stuart) Nusbaumer, who related the following story on a website years later. Nusbaumer is a Vietnam veteran who had come back severely damaged by that senseless conflict, and Jackson was staying with him. His story:

"In the early 1970s, I was living in Woodstock. I had rented a house, and Jackson lived in the house with me and another person. Before I rented the house, I shared a room with Jackson in a boarding house, also on Tinker Street. We used to stay up all right listening to music and write, it was a great time. When I rented the house, Jackson rented a room in the house. But soon he ran out of money, and then slept in the living room. Finally, I told him to leave. Soon, I remember this like it was yesterday, I saw him on the street during a snowstorm, his beard covered in snow and ice, he was standing up against a building trying to protect himself from the cold wind. It was so sad. I of course allowed him to return to the house and live there for free for the rest of the winter. Then I moved from Woodstock to New York City and never saw him again. But I have often wondered what happened to Jackson. Jackson was a tormented man, as, at the time, I was. I had come back from Vietnam disabled, and was bitter. Jackson and I had something in common, we had both survived a horror, but the legacy continued to give us great pain. He was a good man and I am sad to hear he is gone."

Today, Nusbaumer is an acclaimed writer and reporter who has moved on with his life, and who specializes in covering war related issues for various publications. He still has fond memories of Jackson. Such was the dichotomy of Jackson C. Frank. His personality and talent were so tremendous that forgiving him his trespasses was an easy thing to do, and thus was done by almost everyone he met, famous or just plain folks.

It was in 1971 that Jackson had an opportunity to make a small comeback of sorts. Art Garfunkel, whom, according to Marianne Welch, Jackson had never really liked, had shown up in Woodstock one day looking for Jackson. He had just broken up his partnership with Paul Simon, following the huge, multi-Grammy winning success of *Bridge Over Troubled Water*, and was looking for new material. He wanted to know what Jackson had written that was new, so that he might record the songs on a solo album. Jackson told him he had a song or two, including one called "Juliette," which he was willing to let Garfunkel have, and which would have been a major source of income if it became a hit since Garfunkel was still riding the big wave of success after *Bridge* won all its awards. The two of them made an appointment to meet a bit later at a café just off Rock City Road to go over the song. Jackson, in typical fashion, began to unravel and by the time he was to meet Garfunkel, was a nervous wreck. He arrived late, accompanied by a clique of Woodstock's great unwashed (read: hippie types), who began to harass Garfunkel, teasing him about his college boy looks and making him feel very uncomfortable. Frightened, or annoyed, or both, he pleaded with Jackson to get rid of the thugs, and when no relief was given, got in his car and drove away, not to return. It was another blown opportunity for Jackson, and it would be the last time that anyone of stature would make an effort to help him in any big way.

With Garfunkel out of the picture, Jackson decided to at least try to get his songs recorded for his own use and on June 5, 1972 he was booked for a session at Andy Robinson's Shotwell Music Recording in Woodstock where he laid down three songs, with Woodstock resident and well-known performer Tim Moore (who ironically was the composer of

"Second Avenue," a featured tune on an Art Garfunkel LP, on second guitar. They recorded "Juliette," "Madonna of Swans" and "China Blue." Two years later, on May 9, 1974, Jackson returned to Andy Robinson, this time in Robinson's Rude Sound Studio in Woodstock, and with an uncredited bass player, and Artie Traum on second guitar, added another four songs to the tape—"Spanish Moss," "Cover Me With Roses," "Box Canyon" and "Stitch in Time." The tape completed, Jackson left it with Andy Robinson, who would keep it in his possession for the next 38 years. Jackson never returned for it. It was also around this time that Al Stewart made a trip to Woodstock to see Jackson, but the reception that he received was not what he expected. And neither was his friend. As he recalled, "The first time I realized there was something distinctly wrong was when I went to Woodstock in 1970—he had real long hair and was living with Elaine at that point. He was hostile and paranoid and Elaine was sort of not digging it at all. I think he was sort of chasing her around the furniture and being rather odd. I got that impression.'

Stewart returned yet again to the States in 1974 as part of a tour with Fairport Convention, who had recently re-installed Sandy Denny as lead vocalist. Stewart:

"The next time I saw him was 1974. I was doing a short tour with Fairport Convention which Jackson couldn't resist because he gets two for the price of one and he turned up—I think by 1974 he was absolutely broke and he wanted to borrow money off both me and Sandy. We probably gave him some. I don't know...he said he needed money to buy a guitar. I think Sandy probably gave him some. By 1974 he'd basically lost his possessions and was pretty broke."

It is clear that Jackson was hanging on by a thread to his old life, but his sickness was too powerful to let him live the normal life he craved.

Another friend who ran into Jackson in Woodstock, almost, was John Renbourn. Invited to town by Happy Traum,

Artie's brother and a master guitarist himself, Renbourn had earlier received a letter out of the blue from Jackson. In it he recounted the old days, and talked a bit about his music. Renbourn called it "a lonely sort of letter."

When he got to Woodstock, and Happy Traum's place in the hills, he called the number that had been given in the letter, and as he recalls, "The voice that answered was hesitant and nervous sounding. I think it was Jackson all right but he sounded frightened. We arranged to meet but nobody showed up."

Happy Traum had never met Jackson at that point and when Renbourn described him to him, he said that he reminded him of a character who was always wandering around in town looking lost, which, as Renbourn said, "had to have taken some doing in the druggy Woodstock of those days." Happy must have seen Jackson standing around on the sidewalks, as he was prone to spending some of his days just wandering around Tinker Street. Once you wandered off Tinker there wasn't much going on.

Renbourn also recounts hearing about Jackson from afar, in the years immediately preceding his trip to the US: "Later when most of us were touring and losing touch I heard a few stories about him and none of them were nice. Karl Dallas told me he had seen him playing again and he was like 'the straw man' meaning 'not there.'" Dallas, by the way, has no recollection of using that term, but no matter, it was apparent that something was terribly wrong with Jackson by the early part of the seventies. Around this time Sandy Denny received a strange piece of mail. An envelope, addressed to her, obviously by Jackson, who had apparently misplaced or had never written the letter that he intended to send to her, appeared in her post. Inside was nothing, but written on the flap of the envelope were the words, "the May wind...."

John Boylan also tried to pay a visit to Jackson at one point during the time after he had returned from England. "I remember when I went to see him, and he would not let me in the house. He met me at the door and wouldn't let me in. He said 'We have cats.' I think we went to the Espresso and had coffee or something and had a little chat and that was it and I got the feeling that this guy doesn't want anybody from his past in his life right now."

By the mid-70's Jackson had spent quite a bit of time in and out of the Hudson River State Hospital, as well as the psychiatric ward of the Benedictine Hospital in Kingston. At Hudson River the diagnosis of paranoid schizophrenia was firmly established and a proper course of treatment was implemented, including Thorazine, which helped alleviate the symptoms and quiet the voices in his head a bit. He then went home to Buffalo and spent almost two years living with his parents, who made sure that he kept up with his meds and got healthy again. Sending him home for the extended time period was an experimental trip that the facility had decided was worth the risk. As prickly as Jackson's relationship was with his mother, trips home always seemed to rejuvenate him and the difference was notable immediately afterward. A similar though much shorter trip home in 1994 would yield positive results as well. The trips seemed to recharge his psychic batteries, as well as get him cleaned up and restored to some semblance of normality. At any rate, free of the voices for a while, he resumed writing and playing music, coming up with enough good material, including the tracks he had left with Andy Robinson, for his prospective second album. He left Buffalo and returned to Woodstock, where he began playing gigs on Saturday nights at Manny Katz's Deli on Tinker Street. It was only for food and whatever the hat would pick up while being passed around but it gave him a chance to work out his musical kinks and get a little recognition. On November 21, 1975 he appeared on a local TV broadcast from the deli. In letters to his mother he was thrilled at the prospect and was grateful for some new clothes she had sent him especially for the gig. Nothing more is known about the program, which apparently was not recorded but was probably a live broadcast. The letters are the only clue that there even was a show.

In a letter home in early 1975 he related to his mother that he was involved with a program where he was the entertainment director. While the letter does not get specific he related that there was a puppet show, a drama show and entertainers to be dealt with. Having lived in the area myself and knowing a bit about what goes on that features things like puppet shows and so on, it wouldn't be a stretch to think that it was probably the annual Woodstock Library Fair (where the head librarian was D. J. Boggs Stern, his old friend from Buffalo) that he was involved with. In between the duties that he had taken on, he also had a muse nagging him, and she was a demanding one at that.

In another letter to his mother that year, he described one particularly productive period.

He wrote: "It wasn't until late last night, after spending two days on my own work, three thousand words including five-six songs, one poem-short story and nearly the first chapter of my first book (intended) called *Society Doll* and getting to bed last night after 8 A.M., I suddenly realized I was running out of energy rather badly."

What is more specific is a lovely bit of writing describing his songwriting process:

I have to take the time to arrange and compose some song melodies. The words and form are already written. It is like a marathon with me now. I do many differing forms at the same time, songs and poems and stories, and that is different than the way I wrote when I was younger. Then I had all the material in a little pocket that just had to be opened up and there it was, whatever it was, now I start on several skeletons and flesh them out afterwards, meantime the ideas simply keep pouring around me till

I am dazed and unable to keep up with them and exhaustion of a sort sets in. I prefer the old way although it is not so prolific and indeed provides little proof or substantiation that I am in any way gifted or in the right work to begin with. Anybody can sit there and type endless bits of poesy or word thoughts, quality and formation is what counts. I have gotten a lot of praise from a lot of people here lately on what I have done. But that is part of this type of community and can as easily pass as a warm and common handshake as a mark of distinction worth the bearing. It can also be plain crap from people who would like to write but cannot or haven't tried.

Elsewhere in the letter Jackson mentions that a tape he is making is going to cost fifty dollars, and that he would be in need of financial help from home since the entertainment job he has been doing for the library fair was an unpaid one. Given the date of the letter, early February of 1975, and the recording date of the session (in May of that same year) for what was intended to be his second album, the tape mentioned in the letter was in all likelihood from the very same session.

In May 1975, he went into a small studio in Lake Hill, just outside of Woodstock, owned by a man named Peter Mekeel, and recorded the songs, doing several takes of each song. (Three of the songs he did that day were repeats of songs that he had recorded a few years earlier with Andy Robinson: "Spanish Moss," "Cover Me With Roses" and "Madonna of Swans.") This was in stark contrast to the New Bond Street session that produced his first album. The mic shyness seemed to be gone and the performances were terrifically confident. The recordings finished, he departed the studio and left the recordings there for safekeeping. Typical of his modus operandi he would never go back for them. It would not be until 1994 that Peter Mekeel would re-discover the tapes and would make an attempt to give them to Jackson. Ironically, it was only after he accidently recorded over one of the songs on the reel that he realized what he had and stopped. He transferred the songs from one side of the reel onto cassette and brought it to Jackson, who was now living in Lake Hill, just down the road from the studio. The five songs he transferred that day, "Marlene," "Marcy's Song," "The Visit," "Madonna of Swans" and "Relations" would eventually be released as bonus tracks by Mooncrest as part of the first CD re-issue of his 1965 album. It was only several years later when the original reel to reel tape was sent to a major studio for remastering that four additional tracks, "Cover Me With Roses," "Spanish Moss," "Cryin' Like a Baby," and the track Mekeel almost completely recorded over, "Have You Seen the Unicorn?" were discovered. As it was, "…Unicorn" was chopped off at a particular spot where the snippet that was left was a perfect 39-second two-line gem.

The absolute highlight of the Lake Hill recordings, and arguably one of the greatest songs he ever recorded, however, is "Marlene," his tribute/apology to Marlene Dupont, his girlfriend from 1954, who was burned so badly in the fire that only a swatch of fabric was left to identify her. It is also one of the most pain-filled songs ever written by anyone, anywhere. Almost as sad is the story of the little girl to whom it was written and sung.

Marlene

The ghost of her hair floats over there
And her smile, her smile it seems so lonely.
She gave me her hand as they struck up the band
And she seemed to say, seemed to say "You're the only."
And we danced like two snowflakes in the falling wind,
In the wind.
Well, do me a favor, God...
Won't you let Marlene come in?
The gymnasium floor, the brassbound door,
The jungle bird, the jungle bird that she showed me
Her love was so clean, to tell the truth Marlene,
The sound of your tambourine still haunts me.
We were so young then now that I'm old,
I know, oh, I know
I loved you right then, but I made Marlene let go.
My friends in the bars, hell, they only see the scars
And they do not give a damn,
They do not give a damn that I loved you.
I don't know why but once you've seen the sky
You think you know all birds are lovely
But there's snow on the ground in Woodstock tonight
It's twenty two years dear since I saw the light
The world did explode in such a high powered glow,
To run to run to run was all they left me.
Up here there's breeze, high in the clouds we're free to fly
To fly away was the lesson,
Though the fire it burned her life out
It left me little more,
I am a crippled singer and it evens up the score,
The ghost of her hair floats over there
And her smile her smile, it seems so lonely
She gave me her hand as they struck up the band,

And she seemed to sigh she seemed to say
"You're the only."
And we danced like two snowflakes in the falling wind,
In the wind.
Well, do me a favor, God...
Won't you let Marlene come in?
Do me a favor, God...
Won't you let Marlene come in?

"Marlene," by Jackson C. Frank © 1975

Of all the children who died in the Cleveland Hill School fire, there was one who would never leave the memory of Jackson C. Frank. That she would still be on his mind over twenty years later is important, since, as he told T. J. McGrath, he fully intended to name his never-released second album after her.

Marlene Dupont was Jackson's first love. In more jaded times it is easy to say that such a thing is passé, a remnant of a bygone era. For eleven-year-olds, that spark that comes to us all is never passé, never corny. From the vantage point of later years, the young love between eleven-year-old Jackson and his little lady was a sad and beautiful thing

Marlene Dupont was the daughter of Joseph Dupont and his wife, whose name is not known. She was a beautiful but perpetually sad girl who wore her troubles on her sleeve, but she also bore that special trait of vulnerability that made others take notice, and for inexplicable reasons those who knew her would never forget her as the years passed.

For instance: Francis X. Maier, now Chancellor of the Catholic Diocese of Denver. As a child, he lived in the house next door to the William Axford family. In a letter he wrote in response to an online article about the Cleveland Hill School fire, with accompanying photos of the victims, he said: "I was

149

in kindergarten in 1954, a student at Cleveland Hill School in Cheektowaga, New York. I happened to be home with the flu on the day of the fire. One of my close friends was Marlene Dupont, a sixth grader who died in the fire; she was a foster child who lived with the family next door. I've never forgotten Marlene. Not for a day. In fact, I've prayed for her on and off, pretty regularly, for more than 50 years. I was surprised and moved to see her face again in the photo on your page, looking out over the decades."

Marlene was an unhappy, quiet girl, most likely because of the loss of her mother, either to death or divorce. She was an adolescent girl living in a motherless home with her father and his brother, two men who by all accounts were not prepared to raise a young girl. As far as can be determined, it was not a case of untoward activities in the home, just two men trying their best but ultimately unequipped and unable to cope with the situation. The result was that Marlene was forced or at least enrolled against her will into the foster care system by a father who undoubtedly loved her but had no clue about raising her. As it turned out she was placed with the family of William and Ceil Axford, who lived next door to Francis X. Maier, just a few hundred feet from the Cleveland Hill School.

Her foster sister, Kathleen Axford Nealy, recalls that on the day of the fire, there had been an argument over a clothing accessory: "Mama made clothes for us and we had the same plaid dresses...I think Marlene's was green and mine was blue because that was my favorite color. We fought all the way to school because I had to wear those old snow leggings and she didn't have to, and it was kind of sad to remember that we fought all the way."

It would be a single, unburned swatch of material from those outfits that provided identification and a tiny bit of comfort to the family, allowing them to know for certain which one of the tiny victims was their foster daughter.

Marlene's funeral was held a few days later, and she was buried in a cemetery a few blocks from the school. A memorial tree was planted for her, as were trees planted for all of the children who died. A Funeral Mass was held and in one of life's little ironies, first grade soloist Marianne Welch, who would later be a member of the Grosvenor Singers with Jackson, soloed on the "Mass of the Angels" for Marlene. Twenty-two years later, still carrying the hurt and scars from that day, and from the loss of the first love of his life, Jackson C. Frank would sing his heart and soul out for her.

In the meantime, Jackson, in good form once again, clear headed and creating music, made a crucial mistake. In what would be another vicious cycle of his life, he declared himself "cured" by his medications and being better, did not need to bother taking them any longer. So he stopped. The speed of his decline was startling, and in short order he was back on the streets running around naked and waving his theatrical sword, "Jackson-as-Lochinvar" once again. Old friends who once welcomed his presence now would discreetly duck into storefronts to avoid him when they saw him hobbling their way. He often ended up sleeping on the ground or on park benches or on the occasional couch of a friend. His disregard for basic hygiene at times made his presence highly noticeable, and not particularly desirable. Like many cases of addiction, his relapse into mental illness made things progressively worse each time it happened. Once again he ended up in Hudson River, trying to get his mind right with the help of the staff and continuous support from home, although his mother was beginning to tire from her exertions on his behalf. Although the idea that he would spend a good portion of his life in institutions is a sad one, the fact is that at least they were available to him when there was no place else to go. He probably slept on more strange couches than anyone he knew, with a lot of friends, including the tireless Mark Anderson eventually growing weary of having to deal with him or no longer able, for personal reasons, to continue giving him room and sometimes board. Even Marianne Welch (now Collins), who for a time near the end of the decade was running the Creative Music Studio in Hurley, New York, a short drive from Woodstock, gave him free room and meals at the facility for several months. Just about every time he would find any kind of stability, even for a few weeks, it would be circumvented by his own behavior, whether psychologically or chemically induced. Jackson had been a bit of a drinker earlier in his life and once he discovered the marijuana world it was "Katie bar the door." He smoked quite a lot of weed and at times it became a priority. As Mark Anderson remembered of a particular incident, Jackson wouldn't dream of helping him put a roof on a shed, but was content to sit on the sidelines smoking pot and offering unsolicited commentary. It has been theorized by several of his friends and former employers that his drug use was fairly excessive, including all kinds of substances, but the alcohol and marijuana are the only ones that anyone seems to have eye witnessed, so anything else is speculation. What is sure is that, given his psychological problems, the chemical additives could not have been much help. Letters to his mother and father from this time, though, show a clearheaded writer, a vivid imagination and even include at least one nearly complete song lyric, a good example of what he referred to above as a song skeleton, called "St. Madeleine."

St. Madeleine

St. Madeleine framed by the church gate
Arts of work and love
I live on the street grate
Our heavens up above

She goes to the quiet hour
I go to the fray
St. Madeleine by the church gate
I live in France today
Save what you can of the old lace
The weather will be new
Each day you spend in the old place
The secret grew and grew
Little cars come humming
Each to each they sigh
Man is our believer, we are just his pictures
Singing you must try
Madeleine lived in Cherbourg
She goes to hallows now
Her books she left in Cherbourg
Good linen cools her brow
Our little passion saves us
As we sail upon our breath
Forming words is serious
Betting thoughts of death
She knows of our reasoning
The bluebirds fill her ring
She is married to the love of us
Our vows are to this king
Peaches I have offered her
She takes my cheese and wine
Times can change they rearrange
But Madeleine is mine
The news appears in marble
The famous sculptures dance
No widows are in church today
A man must take his chance
But I have been with Madeleine
By the pool of Lourdes
I have seen the angels heal

I am stricken, she assures
A bracelet of fishes
Holding mouth to tail
Was offered to the serpent god
And these believed we'd fail
The nets of mind wrought ivory
Still let the breezes pass
Madeleine of the convent
Has held me in the grass
St. Madeleine lived in Cherbourg
She goes to hallows now
Her books she left in Cherbourg
Good linen cools her brow.

"St. Madeleine," by Jackson C. Frank © 1975

Unfortunately, as with almost every other example of Jackson's unrecorded songs, the melody was kept in his head and is thus gone forever, barring any unforeseen appearance of previously unknown tapes. The one exception to the "no melody rule" is a composition that he wrote for the Young Tradition in 1966 or 1967, and which might be called "Joshua." Written out in his own hand, it features three verses and a chorus, with a basic melody written on a hand-drawn staff, with no chords. Since it was written for the Young Tradition, who performed mostly a cappella numbers, it probably was not intended to have accompaniment. The group, however, never recorded it and Heather Wood only recently discovered the sheets he had written it on in her belongings.

Joshua

Joshua bends the boughs to the ground
Gathers the fruit and hands it all round
Martha is waiting down by the road
Joshua comes to carry her load

Chorus: Song, song, a cymbal, a song
Some of them dead but all of them gone

Who is the child that stands by the door?
Takes what is offered and wants nothing more?
He brings a song to brighten your day
Call out the dogs to chase him away.

Chorus

Under the bridge where the water runs deep
There on the bank lies Simon, asleep
Out of the rain and out of the sun
Out of the sight of everyone

Chorus

The eye of the moon looks silently down
Calling the souls from out of the town
Calling the lovers, the fools and the blind
Leave all the chains of daylight behind

Chorus

Several other songs known to exist but with no known recordings or even lyrics are "Frank's Blues," registered with BMI in 1970, "She's Just Gone Again" from 1966 and "You Don't Know My Mind" from 1967. It's possible the last two were songs recorded for but not released on the original LP, although all parties involved who contributed to this book remember nothing about those titles. Jackson's creative activities seemed to ebb and flow with his psychological difficulties, and as a result his song output was very sporadic, although what songs he did write were never less than interesting and poetic.

In 1978, it appeared that there might be a re-appearance of the man himself, when a re-issue of his Columbia-EMI album appeared on the shelves of record stores in England. The master tapes for his first album had been licensed by a company called B&C for re-issue, but the images that were on the original release were not, apparently, and an awful drawing of Jackson as he looked in 1978 or so, long hair, jewelry on his wrist, appeared instead. Also, Paul Simon's name as producer was removed, apparently at his own request, according to Jackson, who added, "I think Paul was too big for his britches."

The album was re-issued in 1978 as *Jackson Again* and for many years was viewed as a quasi-bootleg, probably due to its tacky, amateurish looking appearance, although it was indeed an official release. There was little fanfare and it came and went almost as fast as the original, but there were several things about it that made it different than the Columbia-EMI version. Gone were the liner notes by Jackson. In their stead was something different: a letter that Jackson had earlier sent to Karl Dallas, which managed to find its way onto the B&C re-issue.

Hi Karl——As a native of Woodstock these last more or less twelve years I have produced a noticeable affect on the matter of work, I only do, in most part, what I wish to. I was born in 1943 in Buffalo New York and headed with my family to a wartime world in Elyria, Ohio... big house, chickens in the backyard and country and western on the radio 24 hours a day. I began singing somewhere in that time. There is a Dukedom in my background and several relatives in Ireland, France, Canada... who knows? Africa? I began seriously to consider music as a passion after being nearly burned to death in a school fire during music class. 50% of the class did not make it out of the venue. This resulted in being crippled for life with a rare though traceable malfunction and a record player and Burl Ives records while recuperating in 1954. It had me from then on, in a folk sense. In 1957 or so the family was collecting Elvis records and we wound up on a trip down south at his home. I got a private meeting with Elvis and was zonked. White blues. music anticipating little follow-along writers like Mailer -- 'The White Negro'... well. Receiving a set amount after being put out of whack permanently I bought guitars, many guitars, and tickets to places like London. 1965 was the year I first came to England and I had just begun writing songs consistently at that point. I still remember someone saying 'Well, you are a singer-songwriter, Why didn't you stay in America? Look at Dylan.' And I replied 'The reason I didn't stay was that I looked at Dylan.' Somehow then, at that time, It made sense. I have been interested in writing all my life. Perhaps it is a more enduring desire than singing and jobs have ranged in the word game for me from copy boy to editor on various papers and I have been publicist, ad man, reporter, dictation clerk, short-story, novel and poetry writer. I really would not like to leave all this without a solid crack at a full-length work, I guess it is a moral retentive. In 1968 I returned from London in the middle of cutting a record, which didn't survive the departure, and after discovering and aiding in obtaining their first record for two fellows named Andrew Lloyd Weber and Tim Rice (Jesus Christ!) I lay back to see what the tide brought in. I worked in leather. I played my guitar. I was lonely (as in divorced). Then I got sick.

*Now I am better. I have been at the start of several unanimous-
ly acclaimed (later) events, as most of you who are reading this
have, and really can't get them all un-jumbled enough to start
and stop and fill up in between sensibly. I have had tremendous
respect for writers I have known in England and have followed
their careers to the exclusion of proper sensibilities as regards my
own. Maybe I could make that the reason I got sick. No. Nobody
would believe it, 'sides, it isn't true you see, strictly speaking. Anyway, life in the mountains here is serene and I have produced
some works I wouldn't swap for a ride on the Old Queen E. In
fact I have had some second thoughts, eventually over-ridden as
to whether I should not just hoard them all up and be discovered
somewhere after the grave, even maybe not then. That is the cor-
nerstone, which is a poor but noble object, to dig erosion. The
moments change, the world recedes, concedes, and all the time I
can remember where I have been. A friend has just produced a
book here in which he symbolizes 'it all' by saying that 'the secret is that there is nothing to be gained...' and 'Memory cannot
change a thing' and he makes me proud to know that we are in
the midst thereby of the tail end of the learning process... that
sublime moment when we start to unravel the web which is in
fact our only garment. The seventies served as a prelude-radar
range to the steak we had just claimed at the check-out of 1969.
Now everybody can be a master of Eastern religion AND work
in Bethlehem Steel. What happened? Is it time for me to come out
again? Are my words, my songs, 'relevant'? Is 'discriminate' once
again a word and not a hot concept? Is Julian Jaynes freeing the
masses from their metaphysical drunk? Nonetheless, the moments
change and I see in my passing eye that memory prelude to these
words. Soho Square, the little Tolkien-booth and a statue once
new and arabesque curled, a king I think, whose features even
then, back in my memory, were nearly gone from time, but whose
considered opinion must have been that it was worth it, even
looking like a calcined ice cream cone melting into his original
place. A king, a king of England, preferably when he was young.*

I am emerging from the years of quiet in a backwards-forwards rocking motion, always the best for leaving a cocoon, and hope to see the effort of its only deserved end of presentation. Once the world was burning and now the world is old, once the singing meant me but the story must be told. So, at this presentation of old days which etched and always drew one in finer and finer line to appreciate the hand which held the moment, and in memory of those who have some small interest in the passing scintillion urge to final history, thank you for allowing me to burn in ways I had joy and hope and control over, my youth with you and once young king.

Jackson C. Frank

The letter was a revelation. It reads more like poetry than prose and reveals more about its author than he probably intended. Intelligent and creative, he makes references to myriad people, places and events and touches on his own history with all its pitfalls and missteps. And a bit of mystery. He mentions two names, now well known on Broadway, and his efforts in "discovering and aiding in obtaining their first record for two fellows named Andrew Lloyd Webber and Tim Rice (Jesus Christ!)" Attempts to contact Webber and Rice were met with silence until after many months had passed, when a one-line email arrived from a spokesman for Webber. It said simply, "Andrew has no recollection of anyone named Jackson C. Frank."

In fairness, it appears that this was an attempt by Jackson, who may have also had some delusions of grandeur as part of his affliction, to associate himself with names from the past. He had been involved with Norrie Paramor and had come too late to the party as far as Webber and Rice were concerned, since they already had secured their own deal. It would appear that Jackson was trying to use Karl Dallas as part of a brilliant, albeit unorthodox, means of reintroducing himself to the world. The letter meanders all over the map, often into the ozone at times. There are many vagaries and some exaggerations, but it can be assumed that one of the acclaimed events he was in at the start of was the Woodstock Sound Out, although, to be honest, who can be sure?

Sadly, once the re-release faded from memory after a year on the market, there would be no more re-issues for almost twenty years to remind the listening public of what a brilliant album they were missing, although those who already owned it were happy to spread the word whenever they could. In the United Kingdom, "Blues Run The Game," which had appeared on a Brit-folk multi-LP set called *The Electric Muse*, was still a staple for the floor singers, albeit more of a pleasant remnant of days gone by, and its creator was less and less remembered by the public as time passed.

Above: Jackson age four, 1947.
Bottom Left: Jackson as a toddler in Elyria, OH.
Bottom Right: Studio portrait with Jackson's aunt, grandmother Rochefort, and mother Marilyn.

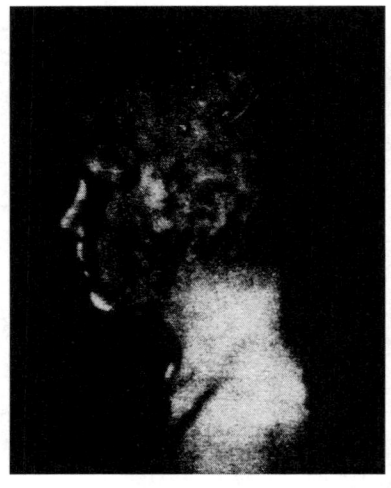

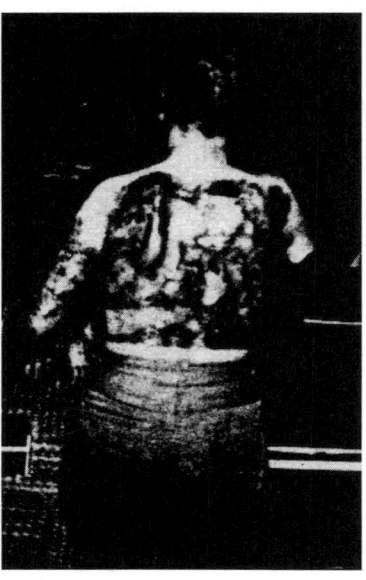

Above: Photocopies of the burns on Jackson's head and back after the Cleveland Hill School Fire. He is 11 years old.

Below: Jackson with Elvis at Graceland, 1957.

Left: Publicity photo for Columbia / EMI.

Right: The only known performance photo of Jackson, taken at the Railway Club by Claire Winstone.

Above: Jackson with girlfriend Linda Ffoulkes.

Left: Jackson with friend and first Silvertone electric guitar.

Right: Jackson with girlfriend Katherine Henry at Stonehenge.

Above: The Grosvenor trio, left to right: Jackson, Ev Neinhouse and Norm Boggs, 1963.

Left: Jackson with Richard Stanley, 1964.

Right: Jackson with teddy bear in 1964, photo courtesy of Richard Stanley.

Below: Jackson with Elmer and three other relatives, date unknown.

Left: Jackson at Timberlyn Heights, Great Barrington, MA, 1998. Photo by Linda Fite.

Below: With Tom Paxton, at a benefit in Saugerties, NY, 1995.

Top: With John Renbourn at SUNY New Paltz, NY, 1995.

Right: Woodstock Manor, 1994.

Bottom: With John Renbourn and Robin Williamson at Suny New Paltz.

The Long Slow Decline

Jackson, in the T. J. McGrath interview in 1994: "About 1973, after the divorce, my wife wouldn't let me see the one child who had lived. I had an emotional breakdown—I was just sitting in my house. I had taken off my clothes and I was gonna go to bed and I was just sitting in my house and the neighbors came down and wanted to know what I was doing and then, because they couldn't explain it—I wouldn't come out, so they went and got a local group, FAMILY of Woodstock, and FAMILY went and got the mental wagon, the ambulance, with a straitjacket and so forth and they put me in Hudson River Hospital for seven months saying that I was mentally ill—I wasn't—it was emotional, it was an emotional breakdown. Afterwards I lived on some pills they gave me which made my mind blur and my speech slur and I couldn't think very well. It was called Mellaril [an anti-psychotic drug of low-potency used in the treatment of disorganized and psychotic thinking -ed.]. It's one of these psychiatric drugs they give you—I lived with my mother for two years because I couldn't recover hard enough. I didn't realize it was the pills that were screwing me up—I had a very good idea it was the pills—I didn't live in Woodstock after they took me away—I lost my rental—my rental was gone—when they put me in Hudson River Hospital."

Jackson was referring to an evening from many years earlier, and which, if it hadn't happened, might have changed his life again. Art Garfunkel, whose feelings for Jackson were kind ones even if Jackson didn't always feel the same, showed up one night in mid-May, (the night after Jackson had been taken away) at the door of Jackson's next-door neighbors, Lee and Helen Mycszkowski. A kindly couple, they were very fond of Jackson, and often checked in on him to make sure he was all right. A couple of days earlier Jackson had an episode where he disrobed and then tried to take a walk down Tinker Street to the Green. Lee and Helen had managed to keep him inside, and stayed by his side but he only got worse through the night, imagining voices and forces beyond his control trying to influence him. The Mycszkowski's called a doctor friend to help, and Jackson was taken for observation by FAMILY of Woodstock, a local charity who had helped him often in the past. They took him to Benedictine and then to the Hudson River State Hospital in Poughkeepsie, under the care of a Dr. Armine.

Now Art Garfunkel was standing at their doorway asking about Jackson, and had to be told he was in the hospital. Art explained that he had brought a brand new Martin guitar for Jackson as a gift. The Mycszkowski's offered to hold it for Jackson, for when he returned home, which they did, and Garfunkel left, again never making the connection with Jackson.

Jackson, to T. J. McGrath: "I came back to Woodstock after two years in 1975. I was doing all right and I was on welfare. I didn't have any money and suddenly I was thrown off of welfare, it was about 1983 or 84. [He never mentions that 'suddenly' was almost nine years after he came back to Woodstock!]—And I went out to California to see if I could get another government check out there and to visit some friends in Berkeley, Chris Zaloom, his name was, and he had a guitar store in Woodstock. I got back from California under rough conditions. I didn't quite make it with the check I got, or I thought I'd get and I thought 'What the hell? Why don't I go down and see Paul Simon for some money?'"

§

The seventies were a pot luck/hard luck decade for Jackson. They started out with his return from England in 1970, quickly followed by his writing of "Juliette," one of his most poetically ambitious songs, which Art Garfunkel had wanted to record but never got the chance. He also suffered through the final dissolution of his marriage to Elaine in 1973, and the first of his many hospitalizations in Hudson River State Hospital, where he was a reluctant part of a program called "Gateway" that he felt was for more severely handicapped patients, a category in which he felt he did not belong. Following an extended two year, and by his mother's reckoning, very successful furlough home to Elma, he returned to the hospital, was re-evaluated based on the results of his two years in Elma and released to find his own way once again.

We will never know what Marilyn Frank's idea of a successful furlough home was, but neighbor Marlene Cook took notice of Jackson when he was home, and her description of his behavior is revealing.

Marlene Cook: "To be honest I (and rest of the neighborhood kids) were kind of scared of him and we stayed away from him. I was nine when I moved to Elma and probably thirteen or fourteen when Jack moved in with his parents for a long stretch in the early 80s. Mental illness had taken a strong hold of him by then and he had some strange habits. I remember him walking away from home on the street - people rarely did that as it is a 55-mph country road. He would also sit in the ditch at the edge of the road for hours. He'd just sit there and pick grass.

"Despite his strangeness, the whole neighborhood cut him a lot of slack. I don't ever remember people speaking negatively about him or telling kids to stay away from him. The adults would say something along the lines of 'He was in the

Cleveland Hill fire you know - in the music room!' and they all knew what that meant and that was enough to explain everything about him."

§

Once back in Woodstock, it wasn't long before he was once again living couch to couch in Woodstock for weeks at a time, and that was all before the decade was half over. He had lost his rental and finding a new one wasn't easy for someone with the problems that Jackson was dealing with. He finally managed to get on the Ulster County Department of Social Services welfare program, which took care of the rent on an apartment he secured on Simmons Court. What is sad to consider is that he was getting by on almost nothing per month. His royalties were non-existent at that point because his album had only sold less than 5000 copies, and at that time, pre-internet, there was no mass market to get his music out to the public. With the problems he was undergoing he was certainly eligible for a disability program under the auspices of the federal government's Social Security Administration, which would have provided him with quite a bit more money per month than the meager welfare check. Later, after being brought back to Woodstock in the 90's, he would be put on that program and would live fairly comfortably when he was sticking to his medications. Unfortunately, in the late seventies and early eighties, he found himself thrown off welfare for reasons not clear, since he certainly was eligible for that program. It is likely that the county found out that he was harboring people in his apartment, which is against the rules and which often brings a termination of benefits, after many mailings giving opportunities to appeal any official decisions. For a time he was allowing a woman named Diane Hartwell (now deceased) to live under his roof. Diane was a girl from poor circumstances who, despite a rough outward appearance and a long record of prostitution, had a kind heart and an affection for dolls, which she collected and displayed at local street fairs and events. Jackson also participated in some of these shows, displaying hand-painted ladybugs made from walnut shells.

It is quite possible that the county found out that Diane was living with Jackson and sent him cease and desist letters, which he probably didn't open. Jackson's apathetic attitude toward his mail may have been a contributing factor. He would let unopened mail accumulate and then throw it out when the pile got too bulky, and after deciding that the envelopes did not contain any checks. At any rate, once he was again secure in an apartment on Simmons Court, he began to write again, and things began to look up.

In 1975, as mentioned above, he managed to write and record his second album, only to inexplicably leave the tapes with Peter Mekeel and Andy Robinson for decades, forgotten. He also spent a lot of time just walking the streets of Woodstock, lost to the voices in his head. Despite good friends like Lee and Helen Myczkowski looking after him and despite the authorities in town working with him with what could have been serious charges of repeatedly walking around town naked, waving a six foot sword, and despite having gained quite a bit of recognition for his musical abilities through his regular gigs at Manny Katz's Deli and the Joyous Lake, a club just down the street, Jackson wore out his welcome.

A benefit concert was planned to help him financially but it never came off, and Jackson was forced to make a move, one that would almost cost him his life. No longer welcome at most of the couches in town by the early summer of 1983, after being thrown off welfare, he got a wild hair and decided to head west. His mother told him not to go, but he heard somewhere that if he went to California he could get some type of government money for his disability. With that in mind he caught a bus west. Back in Woodstock, at just the same time that he was on that bus, this writer was perusing the racks of The Collector record store on Tinker Street, and upon finding evidence of Jackson's recent visit to the shop, and inquiring about where he could be found, was told, "He just left for California." I was literally a day late.

Jackson stated (see above) that he went west to see a friend and Woodstock guitarist and music store owner named Chris Zaloom, but Zaloom, asked years later about what Jackson was doing with him in Berkeley, denied ever living in California. He did acknowledge knowing Jackson a bit in Woodstock, but said that he had never been to Berkeley. Whatever Jackson went to California for, it did not work out, as a letter from his mother pointed out later as she was once again reminding him about all of the details of his life in an effort to shame him into adulthood and responsibility. She said, "You…went to California against my advice. You came home from there, sick and broke, to us, and lived here until I got sick and went to the hospital."

Jackson described it a bit differently in an interview years later, saying only that he came back from California "under rough conditions." He had hitchhiked back across the country, taking his chances with the creeps on the road as well as the various snakes and other little surprises that pop up on a three thousand mile journey across this big land. That he made it back alive is no small miracle, given his basic defenselessness. It also is evidence of the survivor that he was.

While it is the job of a biographer, who also happened to be a friend to the subject at hand, to detail the goodness of someone, it would not be honest to exclude the bad deeds of that person as well, and when Jackson went to New York, he did a very bad thing.

As Marilyn Frank said, Jackson returned to the East Coast and wound up back home in Elma, with her and Elmer, arriving a few months before Marilyn became ill and would need to be hospitalized. There it was determined that she had a defective heart valve and would have to undergo open heart surgery. She made it through the operation, which involved the implanting of an artificial heart valve, and was still in the hospital recuperating when Jackson pulled his most devastating disappearing act of all. While his mother was in the hospital, Jackson, who probably had stopped his medications while she was away, left the house, telling no one and leaving no indication as to where he was going, nor showing any curiosity about his mother's condition. He was gone when Elmer brought her home. He didn't write and didn't call. After a year passed with no word they assumed the worst.

Marlene Cook: "I remember him disappearing after Mrs. Frank's pacemaker surgery. At some point she assumed he was dead. I felt so bad for her. She was such a nice lady and really had it rough dealing with Jack's illness and disappearances. Mr. Frank wouldn't let her have a dog, so she spoiled mine. She'd bring the dog 'leftovers' which I think she cooked specially for her!"

There had been no signs of life—no bank activity or any other activity for that matter. Months passed and then, out of the blue, strange messages began coming through the mail from New York City. Then, they stopped. For four long years they heard nothing more from him and once again assumed the worst, until one day, mysterious letters of a desperate and rambling nature began to land in the Franks' mailbox, with a return address at Creedmoor State Hospital in New York City. Four straight years of homelessness had ended and he was, at least for a while, in Creedmoor, where Woody Guthrie had spent the last days of his tortured life some seventeen years earlier.

At Creedmoor his condition improved. Being off the streets after four straight years of hand-to-mouth living certainly made day to day existence manageable. A pair of photos taken by workers show him walking the grounds, feeding some goats that apparently were residents as well. There is also a photo of him on a park bench with a guitar, looking at least 20 years older than his 38 or 39 years. The streets of New York had indeed taken a toll, and they weren't done yet.

The Spectre

Where the street becomes a wall, the spectre fell against it
Without a cry or wail
Here in the darkness his blackened rainbow ran
There's no more lack of conscience that isn't to a plan
Oh the spectre
The spectre had no food, the spectre was in guilt
Yet no light yet no light his shadow overspilt
Across the rugged ranges of curbs and broken lights
The spectre wasn't finished, the spectre was the night
Oh the spectre
Behold the shining silver of a coin held in your hand
The spectre wasn't greedy, he recalls he is a man
While all through the midnight the rushing lonely cries
See oh see the spectre call for a compromise
Oh the spectre
Where the street becomes a wall, the spectre fell against it
Without a cry or wail

"The Spectre," by Jackson C. Frank and Jim Abbott, © *1995*

The homeless man, once a singer, hadn't sung a clean note in years. When he tried, a croak would burst forth from a throat ravaged by nicotine and the harsh conditions in which he traveled. Where the street becomes a wall indeed. He was a spectre, unseen by the moneyed throngs who sped past him every day on their way to work in the World Trade Center towers. Oh, occasionally there were some who could see him.

They were the ones who dutifully put their money in his cup. Sometimes they would buy the typewriters he had salvaged from dumpsters and repaired. Once someone bought a typewriter and discarded it a few hundred yards away, around a corner—a sympathy purchase. He picked it up and sold it again a few hours later. He was a ghost but he was a smart ghost, and he was very good with his hands, scarred as they were. He also pieced together bicycle parts to make a complete machine. He remembered a time when those hands could amaze crowds of college kids in London, a place that had never seemed as far away as it seemed now. He had played with the very best, and they were the ones to come away better for it. How many ghosts, how many homeless, lost spectres had played Royal Festival Hall, for Chrissake?

§

Jackson had been in and out of the asylums for years. Although he was picked up many times and placed in institutions like Creedmoor, the system only allows the facilities to hold patients who have not been committed by a court or doctor against their will for a determinate amount of time, usually a matter of days. In New York, where Jackson was situated, a judge can order a mentally ill person, or someone suspected of mental illness, to be hospitalized for 24 hours to undergo an assessment. If a doctor determines that outpatient treatment is necessary, the judge can order the person to comply with treatment, and if the person refuses, the court can involuntarily commit the person for up to 72 hours. During that period, experts would determine whether long-term involuntary hospitalization is needed. The wily street people of New York, a large group that now included Jackson C. Frank, knew the rules. After that period of time was up they had to be released or there could be legal ramifications for violations of their constitutional rights. After all, they were not criminals, a fact that too many people forget. The years on the streets had not been kind to Jackson. They had cost him his teeth, as well as his frame of reference. Later in life, he would still exhibit behaviors that were typical of someone who is living rough. He would hide his belongings under his pillow, lay down on the sidewalk to rest, even though a bench might be available nearby. He would also pocket various foods, for later consumption.

Simple acts like going to the bathroom are different for the homeless. They often have to make the best of the situation and when they are often banned from using restrooms for their appearance or hygiene, they are forced to improvise. He remembered how he got there, and it wasn't pretty. It was new to him. As he recalled to T. J. McGrath:

"I went down to New York and almost immediately was picked up as being indigent almost as soon as I walked off the bus. I was down by City Hall in New York and there's a park there which has become kind of infested with people who live off the streets and so on."

Being from a rural background in Elma, where homeless-ness was not a prevalent condition, Jackson got a wakeup call from the real world.

"I had never heard of them—the homeless—I had never heard about these people in my life and had never seen them. I was taking a couple of days off before I called Paul to see if I could get a hold of him and they picked me up with a van that has a group of people who pass out sandwiches. They have a psychiatrist and a cop in the van—the mayor's name was Koch. It was Mayor Koch's idea of what to do with the homeless."

Jackson had that part right. One of the more controver-sial plans that Mayor Edward Koch had implemented was his plan to rid the streets of the so called "obviously mentally ill" because it didn't reflect kindly on the city to have her wackos on the loose. It all became a huge public controversy when a woman who went by the name of Billie Boggs, but whose real name was Joyce Brown, was picked up for defecating on the street. At first she seemed to be out of it but shortly after being picked up her mind cleared up due to her medications being properly administered, and she began screaming at the press for an attorney to protect her rights. The whole thing became quite a mess and the program was discontinued. Jackson, again to T.J. McGrath, years later:

"They kept picking me up and putting me in mental hospitals, because when they asked me if I had been in a mental hospital before, I had to say 'yes.' Finally when they started bouncing me on the street with medicine—different medicine every time—and I was getting very sick...I managed to spend four years on the street living a hand-to-mouth existence—nobody knew where I was and I couldn't think of where Paul would be and I tried all kinds of different numbers and I never thought of Charing Cross Music (Paul's Music Publishing Company) which is where he was."

In actuality, Simon was in the Brill Building, located at 1619 Broadway in Manhattan, where his fifth floor offices, no longer called Charing Cross Music, but now operating as Paul Simon Music, were situated. In all likelihood Jackson walked past the building many times as he panhandled and did what he had to, to survive. His appearance, based on the Creedmoor photo, had changed so radically that it is unlikely that Simon would have recognized him if he had run into him.

It's also likely that Jackson had stopped taking his meds, causing his thoughts and memory to become jumbled and confused: "I didn't realize it until I was put in a different place and I decided to clean up my act and do it myself because I was believing I was crazy—they almost had me believing I was mentally ill and I know damn well I wasn't."

The mentally ill label was still anathema to him, as it would be until the end of his life:

"They kept calling me paranoid schizophrenic and these are things that people know about. You talk somebody down out of these situations when they get into a problem. That's the way you do it—you don't do it the way these guys do it. There are a lot of people in there who don't deserve to be in. For a period of about 10 years I was locked away, and became more crippled because you can't lock me up. I need to have different surfaces to walk on than a hospital corridor. In the hospital they say you either walk in the corridor or you sit and you watch TV and that's all you can do. They don't let you out all day long. Finally after all the various homes that they put me in, I wound up in Creedmoor of all places, which is a really crazy place. What I didn't know was that for a long time someone had been looking for me."

Jackson would stay at Creedmoor on and off for several years. He eventually made it out of the big institution into a smaller, less regulated halfway house branch of the facility called the Leben Home for Adults, in Elmhurst, Queens. It was then that the person looking for him managed to ask the right question to the right person and a tiny speck of daylight could be seen in the tunnel.

Searching for Jackson

I first became aware of Jackson C. Frank in 1983, but aware of him was all I was for several years. It wasn't until the mid-1980's that I first heard any of his music, and then only a not terribly well-recorded cover version at that. It was enough, however, to get me started on an adventure that I will never forget, and one that taught me that one person can be a saint, a sinner, generous to a fault as well as an infuriating pain in the ass, all at once.

It was sometime in the summer of 1983 that I drove the thirty miles from my home in Kerhonkson, New York, to Woodstock, the renowned artist's colony nestled in the Catskill Mountains in Ulster County. Woodstock had once been, and for many was still home to Lee Marvin, Van Morrison, John Sebastian, and scores of other famous musicians and artists—most notable among them Bob Dylan, who had first visited the area in 1963. By 1965 he was living there full-time, returning to New York City in the early seventies when he was driven out of Woodstock by fans and the curious trespassing on his property and inside his house (and as he related in his memoir, *Chronicles*, he once came home to find two "hippies" having sex on his bed). They, in many cases were also looking for the site of the famous 1969 festival, which was actually held in the Sullivan County town of Bethel, 50 miles to the south, and a million miles away philosophically, but that's another story.

By the 1980's though, Woodstock had lost the magic that it once had and was no longer a quiet haven for the creative, becoming instead more of a sanctuary for the entrepreneurial capitalists who opened the seemingly ten thousand shops and galleries lining Tinker Street, the town's main drag. The shops, or shoppes, as it were, were in stark contrast to the aging hippies who remained and could be seen strumming guitars, surreptitiously puffing some weed or just hanging out eating pizza on the benches in the Village Green in the center of town, living advertisements for an era that was a generation in the past.

Personally, I liked to go to Woodstock for the records. Aside from Bruce Talbott's Truck Stop Records, a legendary shop in Kingston, the coolest and best-stocked record store in the area was The Collector, owned by Lester Nafzger. In the days when vinyl was making its last hurrah, those were the stores to hit if you wanted something fine, something sublime; or as happened to me, something odd.

It was on a summer's day in 1983. I made the 40-minute trek from my home in Kerhonkson, in southern Ulster County to The Collector to check out the used record bins. The used bins there and at Truck Stop were favorite spots to find the best stuff (hell, my first Richard Thompson album, *Live! (More or Less)* came from the used bin at Truck Stop for a buck!)

At the front of the row of albums was a familiar old one, Al Stewart's 1976 classic *Year of the Cat*, warped and looking like it had been dropped in a bathtub. Since the records in The Collector usually were rejected if they looked that way, I picked it up and gave it a look. It was then that I saw the handwritten dedication that would change my life, and (I guess) save another one, for a while at least.

> *Regards To Jackson.*
> *The Blues Run the Game.*
> *Al*

Looking closer I could see that the record inside, although the cover was a mess, was not only in pristine condition, but that it was on the British RCA orange label, which was not the same label as the US release, which was on Janus Records. I marched up to Lester Nafzger, who looked like a thinner, mustachioed Elliot Gould, and asked about the record. "Who is 'Jackson?' What does 'the Blues Run the Game mean?'" "Why would Al Stewart sign an album (and the British release at that) to this guy?" And why would the album end up in the used record bin at The Collector in Woodstock, New York on a hot summer day in 1983? I was a fount of questions.

That last question was the only one that Lester could answer authoritatively. "He sold the record to get money for food," he told me. Lester then began to tell me a tale about this man, Jackson, who was known as a street dweller from Woodstock and who, according to local legend, had been badly injured when a car battery exploded in his face. Lester gathered momentum as he spoke. Clearly I had touched a nerve, and he proceeded on to a diatribe about Paul Simon, Al Stewart, and Jackson. He said that he had heard that Jackson, before his accident, was a songwriter and musician who would write songs for other people (like Paul Simon and Al Stewart) and would sell the songs to them for money for food, rent and other necessities. He even claimed that Jackson used to come in with checks from Paul Simon and would want to cash them. He then went on to slam Paul Simon specifically as a phony and a rotten guy who stole "Bridge Over Troubled Water" from Lester's own girlfriend, who sadly had recently passed away from cancer. It was quite a tale and really got the "inquiring minds want to know" part of my personality engaged.

Though I didn't realize it at the time, almost none of what Lester Nafzger told me that day was completely accurate, but there were grains of truth in almost all of it. The real story was much sadder, much more interesting, and would take more than ten years to discover.

§

When I left The Collector on that summer day, all I knew about Jackson was that he was a street guy with very visible facial scars. I actually walked around town for a couple of hours and looked carefully at anyone who looked disheveled or who might be described as a "street guy." Lester hadn't seen him for a few days and when I made the rounds of the characters who haunt the Green, no one knew where he was. Most denied knowing who he was. Finally I ran into a man named Michael Esposito, once bass player for the Blues Magoos and now Woodstock denizen and Old Catholic priest, who told me that I had just missed him. Jackson, he said, had departed for California a few days earlier. It was a setback and

I began to wonder if I would ever solve the riddle of "Who was Jackson?" A little disappointed, I headed for home, but I could never quite get the mystery out of my mind. Over the next few years I would search any libraries and music reference books I came across, but I never found any mention of this enigmatic burned-up Woodstock street guy. Over the course of those years I would revisit Woodstock many times in search of Jackson. But all my efforts were in vain. The man was a ghost.

Then, out of the blue, came a lead in the form of a John Renbourn LP, serendipitously sitting in the used record bin at Truck Stop Records in Kingston. Released in 1973, *So Clear* wasn't a notable piece of work and the recordings on it sound less than stellar. At the time, I had never heard of Renbourn but the cover looked interesting so I picked it up. It didn't stand out right away but at some point I noticed the track listing included a song called "Blues Run the Game." On the label, in small print, were the songwriting credits and next to this song were the magic words: "Jackson C. Frank." Progress at last. Jackson had a surname.

For years I had searched all over for any reference to Jackson C. Frank and when I found the song on the Renbourn album it was like discovering a satchel with a million bucks on my porch. I listened to the song a number of times, liking it but not loving it. My reservations were mostly due to poor sound quality; either this was a poor pressing or my cheap record player wasn't up to the job, or likely a combination of the two. Still, I could appreciate the composition. A great song is a great song and the melody and words were memorable, as was the guitar pattern. It was a start but that is all it was.

Another few years passed and I did finally back off from my Jackson obsession a bit, until one day in a bookstore I happened to see a biography of Paul Simon by a British writer named Patrick Humphries. Casual page turning led me to a chapter called "England Swings" and my pulse began to race when my eye caught sight of the name Jackson C. Frank. The chapter went on to tell the story of how Paul Simon, displeased with the way his musical career was going in the United States, decided to try his fortunes in London. While there, he stayed at a flat owned by a woman named Judith Piepe, who as we now know was a mother-hen type with a soft spot for young people and other, down-on-their luck addicts and waifs. Among the many who passed through her doors were Simon, Al Stewart, Sandy Denny and Jackson C. Frank.

The chapter went on to recount how, as a child, Jackson was badly burned in a school fire, slowly recuperated in the hospital and eventually received insurance money for his injuries when he turned twenty-one years of age. Humphries' book told the story of how Jackson moved to London, immersed himself in the folk scene and recorded an album with Paul Simon on production duties. Ultimately, according to book, the LP sold less than a thousand copies and sank without a trace, as did its creator. The chapter ends abruptly. So there was an album....

And yet, as a serious collector of records at the time, I knew most of what was out there, old and new, and I had never heard of this one. I checked various music publications like Goldmine and old almanacs but nary a mention of good old Jackson C.

Then, in 1992, I went to college, ten years past my prime. When the manufacturer I was working for closed, I enrolled at our local community college in a liberal arts and teaching program with Communications as a minor. One day during a radio class I mentioned to the teacher, a bright and tremendously capable guy named Mark Anderson, that I was a folk music fan. He acknowledged that he was as well, so I asked him if he had ever heard of Jackson C. Frank. His reply stopped me dead. "Why, yes," he said. "In fact, I just got a letter from him."

As it turned out, Mark had been college buddies with Jackson and had loaned him the use of his couch back in the seventies when such a thing was do-able. Now, however, married and with a family and a respectable job and a very busy schedule, he simply didn't have the time for Jackson anymore. So Mark posed a question that would change two lives.

He asked me: "Do you feel like helping a down-on-his-luck folk singer?"

I said: "Why not?"

Jackson Found: Last Chance

Mark Anderson gave me his letter from Jackson the following day. I could barely read any of the writing but managed to pick out the phone number from the script. It was a very strange letter inasmuch as while it was practically hieroglyphic in appearance, you could see that the author was incredibly intelligent. I don't remember anything else from that day, but at some point I did go home and make the call to the Leben Home for Adults, in Queens, New York, and was actually able to get Jackson on the phone in short order. My only recollection of the call is that I told him I would try to help him but that I was just one little guy against the system, and that he shouldn't expect a lot from me. I gave him my number and address and told him to hang in there, and that I would get to work trying to determine what options were available. Mark Anderson had told me a bit about Jackson and his lifestyle as he last knew it to be, and I began to hesitate. The whole situation was almost too much for me to digest—it was all new to me and a big change in the way my days were spent. I was close to putting it on the back burner, and began thinking of graceful ways to back out. Then a letter arrived in the mail.

Dear Jim, it began,
I write in handscript as no other method is available....
I, as I grow older in this chilling kind of world, lose a lot of perspective on the important matters. I am also late this week with my laundry and need a shave. I guess you could say I have had the shit kicked out of me. Pardon that rough usage. I guess it's the dream of everyone who goes down and out that at a certain time someone out there takes an interest and helps them....

I've lost over half my life to the death of my son when I was 26 or 25 and I can say I know I'll never get better in here....

Jackson was still, after all that had happened to him, feeling the deep pain and helplessness that resulted from the death of his son over twenty-five years later. He continued:

I'd planned on going to Mark and Eleanor's [the Andersons] and thence to an apartment if it was all right with them. The day I was to leave I was told by the owner of this place that I could not leave without an address [unintelligible] given them. I did not and collapsed into a blue funk.
As for my illness, it is a series of things that have happened to me that make/made me get sick. Foremost was being put in the street with nothing. I'd go through episodes where young children I'd see were dying or abused I fancied or thought.
I thought nothing of or from by myself—it was autohypnotic. After a while I'd talk to myself and get along with food from begging or from the garbage, I sank pretty low.
I don't know that it is over—I just got myself organized not to be sick when I was put in hospital or here. It doesn't take long before a life of hard knocks does you in. That it took nine to ten years to get it together to call Paul Simon, a very good friend, shows you how low I was. There is a psychiatrist and a cop who pick up street people and put them in mental hospitals by offering them

lunch and a place to stay or get clean. I grew to fear them a great deal as they continued to pick me up and throw me in 9 months at a time. The cops arrested me 5 times I believe for having a cap gun I purchased in Chinatown, for the fireworks there are legally sold—I lived in Chinatown like a bum but not a drunkard and by the World Trade Center for months at a time, collecting antiques and business machinery that was thrown out, bicycles too, to sell for a dollar or two in Chinatown's antique district.

That was the bulk of the letter that he sent me. As he said elsewhere in it, it was a rough estimate of his life since he left Woodstock in 1983. I was touched in a way that I had never been touched before. I called the number he had included at the bottom, and after a few minutes he was suddenly there on the phone. I remember it distinctly—a lot of huffing and puffing and a rough voice saying, "Hello?" I was suddenly hit by that realization that there was no turning back. Someone in bad shape was now depending on me for help, and I needed to at least make the effort to do what I could. We talked for a few minutes and made arrangements for a meeting the following Saturday. I had a lot to think about.

I don't remember much about the two hour drive that Saturday, but I managed to arrive on the Queens, New York street where the Leben Home was located, fifteen minutes late. Because it was a Saturday the streets were fairly clear of cars and I was able to find a parking spot quickly. My next problem was knowing who I was looking for. The only picture I had seen was the album cover photo, which Mark Anderson assured me was a very flattering shot. It was also taken almost thirty years earlier, so I really had no idea who I was going to look for. I lined up to parallel park and before I could back the car in, I saw an older, heavyset man hobbling down the sidewalk, shuffling really, and in a flash I knew it was him. "Jackson?!," I half yelled.

"Jim?!," he half yelled back.

I parked and quickly caught up with him. As we shook hands I noticed right away the terrible scarring on his hands and face, where his longish hair was only partially covering some pretty bad ones. He reminded me I was late, only joking a little. As I would soon come to learn, if you told him you were going to be somewhere at a certain time for him, you had better be there on time. For some reason, the reverse wasn't true—his dedication to punctuality was truly abysmal. I saw that he was headed away from the Leben Home and asked him where he was going. He said, "I figured you weren't coming and decided to go have some lunch. Come on, let's go get a hamburger. My treat."

We walked down the sidewalk for about a block, when all of a sudden he stopped and dropped to the ground without a word. I stood above him as he proceeded to lay on his side, right there on the decidedly dirty New York concrete with his right arm propping his head up, almost as if on a couch watching TV. "What happened?" I asked him, mildly alarmed. "Are you all right?"

"I just have to rest," he said. "My leg is killing me."

"There is a bench right over there," I observed, to no avail.

"This is more comfortable. Just give me a few minutes."

So there I stood, about two minutes into my first encounter with the elusive Jackson C. Frank and he is prostrate on the sidewalks of New York, choosing the "comfort" of a sidewalk over a perfectly good, and clean, park bench ten feet away, while people passed by and had to maneuver around him. I fought the urge, the very strong urge, I might add, to head for the car and the sanity of the mountains. Thankfully for both of us I did not.

He lay there for several minutes, as if it were the most natural thing in the world (turns out it was, for him) and finally asked me to help him up. I grabbed his hand and gave a pull, which brought forth the most painful cry, startling me so much that I almost let go and let him fall back to the sidewalk. I held on though, and in a minute we were hamburg-er-bound once again.

There are some memories in life that burn themselves into your brain forever, and that day with Jackson was one of those for me. We sat at a corner diner, a nice place really, with good burgers, and he recounted the story of how he had been living in Woodstock, had gone to California for a while "just to see the place" and had come back to Buffalo for a while. He then headed to New York and was picked up as mentally ill and thrown into the mental health system, and which he now felt was keeping him prisoner against his will. As he told the story, he had come to New York to find his old friend Paul Simon, to borrow some money to live on. His arrival in New York had coincided with a local furor over then-Mayor Ed Koch and his plan to rid the streets of the mentally ill by scooping up anyone who looked crazy, basically, and institutionalizing them. Jackson on a good day looked pretty rough, and fit the bill, so to speak. After traveling a long distance to get to New York he must have been a sight. He was summari-ly lured into a van that the city workers drove around in, and as was their plan, he was offered sandwiches, which he accept-ed, then was restrained and brought to Creedmoor. So began his nearly ten year, distinctly New York odyssey, in and out of psychiatric institutions, back and forth from the streets to the "crazy house" as he liked to call it. A section of the law only allowed the mentally ill to be confined without cause for a de-terminate period of time. After their time was up they had to be released. With nowhere to go, and pumped full of various medicines, a confused and sick Jackson C. Frank began his life on the streets, occasionally being re-institutionalized and re-released—a savage cycle.

"I used to sit outside the World Trade Center with my cup," he recalled in 1994. "The bankers had gotten to know me and were quite generous—there were days I made over a hundred dollars without having to move from my spot."

He also supplemented his panhandling by recovering discarded business machines from trash bins and restoring them to workability. "I couldn't make head nor tail of anything," he told British writer Andrew Means in 1995. "I was living out of garbage pails and living on the street with a blanket." At times he would find old motorcycle parts to sell, or he would refurbish discarded bicycle frames and sell them for a buck or two.

"I would go through construction sites, dumpsters and various other things," he told Means. "I once got a violin that was marked '1827 Mozart.' I picked that up. They'd give me a dollar in the morning for that sort of stuff. I got some coffee and a roll, and I'd hang around for the rest of the day and maybe bum some money off the people in the street, or people that I knew would give me five bucks for a pack of cigarettes and something to eat."

Another haunt was on the lower east side of Manhattan, near the Hell's Angels clubhouse. There he found discarded bike parts, antiques and other treasures and was able to clean them up and sell them on Canal Street, a popular flea market area where just about anything can be had for a price. He slept at night in the many city parks and on benches and the sidewalks near subway grates when it was cold. He was picked up several times by the police who would then send him back to Creedmoor or Bellevue. There he would be put back on his medications, get better for a long enough period of time, and be released to wander the streets again, where he didn't have his medications and went right back to hearing the voices and exhibiting the odd behavior that the homeless often display. Thus he had ended up at the Leben Home for Adults in Queens. A subsidiary of Creedmoor, it was a type of halfway house, it was meant to be a place where the mentally ill in possession of their faculties could stay as long as they followed the rules and took their medications. Each resident was assigned to a caseworker, and Jackson was placed in the hands of a woman named Janice Duncan. Whatever it was I was trying to do for Jackson would have to be approved by Miss Duncan before it could come to fruition.

I guess this is as good a place as any to address the subject of his mental illness. Jackson was never as passionate about anything as he was about what he called "the lies" about his condition. As a layman I can only spout pop culture diagnoses, but based on my research, and after reading his medical reports, I can say pretty decisively that Jackson C. Frank was indeed a paranoid schizophrenic. His was a classic case of denial, blaming the fire, blaming his body chemistry, blaming the medications, blaming God Himself, but not wanting to suffer the stigma of being declared mentally ill. He would blame his rapid weight gain on the parathyroid gland problems, which had nothing to do with weight gain. He said the medications muddled up his mind but when he was on them he was as clearheaded and creative as ever. His symptoms were there and were classic. Later, he would tell me that voices were talking to him, even as he and I were having our own conversation. His medications were the appropriate ones for the diagnosis and when he took them he would improve dramatically, as would his creative output. Once he achieved what is euphemistically today called "wellness" he would declare himself healed and would immediately cease his medications. And the circle goes round and round.

The Leben Home, aka "Hell on Earth"

After Jackson finished telling me his story we left the diner and headed back to the Leben Home for Adults. Entering through the front door we encountered a plexi-glassed reception/security room. We walked straight past it into what might have been a lobby in a hotel—if it had a floor. The entire floor, excepting the edges around the walls, was missing, a huge open sand-filled area littered will all manner of filth and garbage. We skirted the pit and made it to a hallway where his room was located. The day was a very hot one and the humidity was stifling. Flies were all over the walls and there was a faint smell of decay everywhere.

Entering the room I noticed that it was almost empty. He had a bed, a chair, and a dresser, which held a small radio, a desktop fan with exposed metal blades, and a pair of glasses. I began to cry as I realized that this 50-year-old man had everything he owned right there in a tiny sweltering room in a place that he hated enough to ask a complete stranger to get him out of it.

He motioned for me to take the chair, which I did, as he went to a closet and pulled out a cheap battered guitar that Miss Duncan had found for him. He said, "I guess I better play something for you."

"You don't have to do anything," I replied.

"No, I want to," he said.

He proceeded to sing the first few verses of "Blues Run the Game," his most famous song, but the heat, his out of tune guitar and his shot voice all forced him to cut it short. As much as anything else it was his cutting short the song that firmed up my commitment to help him. As a musician myself who had been through some difficult years there were times I only had my music and guitar, and to not be able to play when that is what you are born to do can be devastating to the psyche. And Jackson's psyche was damaged enough. I left him soon after that, with no promises left other than that I would try to do something of meaning for him.

The following Monday I looked up and called the number for the Ulster County Department of Mental Health, told them who I was and what I wanted to do. I gave them the contact information for Janice Duncan. They told me they would give her a call and that I should look around for an appropriate place for Jackson to go in the event that what I was trying to do came to pass. The kind folks at Ulster County Mental Health gave me a list of suitable places for Jackson to possibly land, given his needs, which, although I didn't know it at the time, were many and great. I began to search in earnest. One name on the list stood out immediately. It was a place called Woodstock Manor and it was located in Lake Hill, just a few miles outside of Woodstock. Run by a man named Henry Howard and his wife, it was a boarding house setup with monitored medication distribution. Basically, as long as someone lived there and followed the rules, and took their medication as they were told to, they had a home for as long as they wanted or needed. They were free to come and go as they pleased and the setting was the Catskill Mountains, which are beautiful indeed. I figured that Jackson would fit right in. I called Janice Duncan and the county, and the powers that be did their jobs and just a few days later I got a call from Ms. Duncan informing me that she would be coming up from New York to visit Woodstock Manor later that week. I was invited to tag along since I had been the catalyst for the possible move for Jackson. Jackson was not coming along.

It was a sunny day when Ms. Duncan arrived and the meeting and tour went smoothly. Mr. and Mrs. Howard were professional in their presentation and a nice lunch was prepared while they talked about Jackson. I mostly listened. The Howards were taken aback a bit by my last name—Abbott. In a rather famous incident, their daughter, Susan, had been married to a man named Richard Adan, who was an aspiring actor and playwright working as a waiter at a café owned by the Howards in New York City. A convicted murderer named Jack Henry Abbott had written a book in prison called *In the Belly of the Beast* and it was so well received that luminaries like Norman Mailer championed his cause for early release. With other celebrities like Susan Sarandon pushing for his parole, he was released in June of 1981. Six weeks later, this new toast of the literary world walked into the café and tried to use the restroom, a rare commodity in Manhattan. Adan told him that the restroom was for staff only. The short-tempered Abbott then stabbed Adan in the chest, killing him. Abbott went back to prison and eventually hanged himself in 2002.

This information made me uneasy even though there was no connection between myself and Jack Henry. The Howards were kind though and decided to give Jackson a chance. The necessary paperwork was drawn up and a date for his move was set for two weeks later.

I can't and won't cast blame as to whose fault it was but on the day that Jackson was to move to Woodstock Manor, the dark cloud moved in and the trip was delayed. Used to such disappointment, Jackson went about his day, smoking and hanging around the streets near Leben Home. Late that afternoon, when he should have been checking out his new room in Lake Hill, he was instead sitting on a bench near Leben Home. Suddenly, as a group of teenagers were running through the area, Jackson felt a sharp pain in his left eye, which immediately went dark. As he later recalled, "I was just sitting there when I heard a kid say, 'let's get the homeless guy,' and the next thing I knew I was shot in the eye." One of the teens apparently figured that shooting a pellet gun at the homeless or mentally impaired was good fun. The pellet pierced Jackson's left eye and became lodged in his skull.

He recalled, "I got up with blood pouring down my face, and walked into Leben Home. I told the security desk that I had been shot and they told me to not get blood on the counter and that they would call an ambulance." An ambulance arrived and he was taken to Bellevue Hospital, where doctors were able to save the eye proper but not his sight. The pellet would stay in his skull for the rest of his life.

A few years later, the Leben Home made national headlines when it was discovered that the owners had been making many thousands of dollars through some shady dealings with some local ophthalmologists and urologists. In these dealings they basically were using their mostly mentally ill residents as surgical fodder, sending them out on buses for un-necessary eye and prostate surgeries. The surgeons would perform the procedures, and because the patients were wards of the state or city, would bill the government for their fees, which was in turn split with the owners of the Leben Home.

Fortunately, it was a fate that Jackson escaped.

By the Time I got to Woodstock...

It was several weeks later when he was finally able to make the move. I drove to Woodstock Manor to await his arrival. He came a few minutes after I got there and with a laugh declared, "I'm home!" I was amazed to find that other than a casual mention of having depth perception problems, he was very stoic about what had happened. Having survived everything he had been through, it was clear, and sad, that something as life affecting as getting blinded in one eye didn't really bother him, at least outwardly.

Within weeks he was settled in. The country air suited him well and his very appearance seemed to improve. I visited almost every evening after work (I was working as a dog warden for the Town of Rochester, where I lived, as well as delivering newspapers at night in the mountains around Woodstock) and we talked about music and life in general. Sometimes we would sit out on the porch in rocking chairs and just watch the cars go by. He began to trust me more and more and one day asked me if I wanted to be his manager when his musical career resumed. I told him I was flattered but that I knew nothing about the business. He asked me to do him a favor and look up the phone number for BMI, which is Broadcast Music Incorporated, a royalty distribution service, where he had registered his songs so many years before. He was certain he had royalties due him from his music being broadcast on the radio over the years. I told him I would try to find the information but that I seriously doubted that he would have any airplay royalties for his songs. An avid radio listener, I had never heard any of his music even once on the radio, so the idea that any royalties that might be backlogged would amount to anything was a stretch for me. I located BMI's number and gave them a call, told them Jackson's story, and after a moment they informed me that he did indeed have almost a thousand dollars waiting for him. They had been unable to locate him for ten years so the payments simply accrued in an account somewhere. I gave them his new address and other information.

The check arrived and he was ecstatic. He immediately called his mother and gave her the good news, and then told me that he had to have a guitar. He had been playing my Martin and said it reminded him of one that he used to have in England. His check wasn't nearly enough for a new Martin, especially after he spent a good portion of it on food and cigarettes. (Although meals were provided at Woodstock Manor, it soon became evident that it wasn't enough for Jackson.)

I drove him into Kingston where the best place for a musician to get a guitar was Allegro Music, owned and operated by Ed Surowitz. He had heard Jackson's sad story and would take good care of his guitar needs. An hour later we were on our way back to Woodstock Manor with a new Washburn acoustic, which Jackson described as a "poor man's Martin" and which had a great sound. It was coming on spring in 1994. He was armed and ready for an attempt at a comeback. I didn't know if he would be able to pull it off, given his general appearance and condition, which included a voice ravaged by years of living rough and constant smoking.

At this point I was still visiting Jackson every other day or so when I could make it. My wife was getting upset with me and my Jackson "obsession" and I must say I was a bit over the top trying to help him. Even though I had spoken by phone to his mother in Buffalo, she had informed me that due to her defective artificial heart valve that she had received a decade earlier, and which the doctors were loathe to replace due to her age, she was unable to travel. I felt as though I was the only person who could help him outside of the system—most of his old friends from Woodstock had died or moved away, and he barely knew anyone when we would go to Tinker Street to hang out.

A minor miracle happened one day while we were sitting on the porch. A middle-aged guy, obviously from Jackson's era came up the steps of Woodstock Manor and introduced himself to me. Jackson knew him right away. His name was Peter Mekeel, and he had been a friend in the old days. As described earlier, he had heard about Jackson being back in town and had brought a cassette tape of the 1975 sessions with him. Ironically, Mekeel had only dubbed five songs from the reel to reel onto the cassette, apparently not realizing at the time that there were four additional songs on the flip side of the original tape. It wouldn't be discovered until 2002 that there were other songs when the engineers at Hollywood Records, at the behest of Geoffrey Weiss, A&R man for the company, and a tremendous fan of Jackson's music, went over the tape to remaster it. When they sent me the results on a CD, I was shocked to hear three-and a fraction songs that I had never heard before.

It was at this time, late 1993, that a modest letter-writing barrage was helpful in getting Jackson's 1965 album re-issued on CD. Mooncrest Records, a small company in London, managed to secure the license to re-issue the album and when we were notified of their decision we sent them the five tracks from the cassette that Peter Mekeel had brought to us. Mekeel had misplaced the reel to reel after dubbing the songs to cassette so we had to use what we had, which led to the five songs from 1975 being transferred to CD at a slightly higher speed than they should have been. No one noticed, but when the reel to reel was finally located (after Mekeel had almost completely recorded over one entire song) the difference was notable. A subsequent re-issue on Castle a couple of years later was speed corrected, as was a two disc anthology in 2003. But that was all in the future, and for the time being Jackson needed to get his creativity back, and Woodstock was certainly the right place for that.

As a musician myself it was really exciting playing and singing with him on the porch at Woodstock Manor, and I even wrote a few songs, or the beginnings of songs, and showed them to him. Before he had written anything new he took a couple of mine, changed them around, added lines and verses, and came out with his own far superior works. Apparently this inadvertently kick-started something in him because a couple of weeks later when I showed up one Saturday he had a whole fistful of songs that he had typed up on an old typewriter that I had found for him at the Salvation Army.

One evening I noticed that Tom Paxton was playing a small benefit show at a school in Saugerties. Jackson had mentioned that he had known Paxton in England so I thought it would be nice to bring him to see his old friend. We arrived early, in time for the sound check and just walked in and sat down in the front row. Paxton came out to test the levels etc. and noticed Jackson sitting in front of him. He stopped playing the song he was playing and began singing, "Catch a boat to England, baby..." and it almost made me cry. When the sound check was over he hopped down from the stage and ushered us backstage. He and Jackson had a great visit, with Paxton talking about how Jackson was his host while he was in the U.K. and how Jackson took him all around the continent and

England. I shot a few photos, and we went back out and took our seats for the show. Jackson had a great time and it seemed to stimulate his creative juices a bit.

§

I showed up one day a week or so later to be greeted by a Jackson who was very happy to tell me about his own adventures of the previous evening. He had slung his guitar over his shoulder and hit the highway into town, Woody Guthrie-style, he called it, hitching a ride to the Tinker Street Café, formerly Bernard Paturel's Café Espresso. The Tinker Street club was famous for having Bob Dylan as a resident in the apartment over the bar, and was where he wrote many of his best-known songs. The Café hosted an open mic night every Tuesday and Jackson had gotten wind of it. As he told me later, after his short set he was approached by a tall bald Englishman who introduced himself as Julian Dawson. Dawson remembered Jackson from his own teen years in the U.K. and was kind enough to tell Jackson how he had been an influence early on in his life and how much he had enjoyed the set. At roughly this same time, T.J. McGrath, a writer for Dirty Linen, an American-based world music monthly publication specializing in Celtic music, was looking for the heretofore-elusive Jackson C. Frank. He had gotten the word out that he was searching for the lost singer, and Julian Dawson had seen the plea. Dawson, a veteran singer-songwriter himself, got in touch with McGrath and let him know that he had just happened to catch Jackson performing in Woodstock. Somehow I had become Jackson's de facto representative, I guess, because I soon got a call from T. J. McGrath requesting an interview with Jackson. I gave him Jackson's number in Lake Hill and they had a conversation shortly after that, on June 25, 1994.

Late in that summer of 1994, Jackson decided he wanted

to record the new songs he had written. Re-enter Mark Anderson, who was still functioning as an adjunct professor at Ulster County Community College (now called SUNY Ulster), and was in fact running the radio and recording facilities there. He offered up the recording studio to us so Jackson could get his songs on tape. So, one sunny September day Jackson and I walked through throngs of teenagers and young people, all of them pretty much self-absorbed on their way to class and not noticing the man with the limp, carrying a gig bag and a sheaf of papers. With Mark engineering, Jackson recorded 6 songs that day. They were "Goodbye to My Lovin' You," "Mystery," "I Don't Want to Love You No More," "October," "Halloween" and "Young Child."

At this point his guitar playing had, amazingly, returned to something approximating what it had been in the London days. He was a little slower but still clean and steady. His fingers had grown (more) stubby so he would often use semi-barre chords to make regular chords, as in using two fingers for a D chord instead of the usual three. It was a concession he had to make but the effect was the same, and sometimes allowed him to voice certain chords differently, giving them a slightly unusual ring. He showed me how he played most of his 1965 songs and was proudest of the fact that Bert Jansch, one of the finest guitar players to come out of Britain (or anywhere), was unable to copy his accompaniment to "My Name Is Carnival." He showed me how he played it and as with a lot of his playing, as well as that of Jansch, it sounds fairly simple to play, until you try it. I am a fairly accomplished player myself, with over 40 years on the instrument, but some of his stuff is very tricky. When one considers that he came up with the songs, both lyrics and the accompaniment, in just a few months, after playing basic arrangements of old folk and country tunes for his entire career before England, it becomes clear just what a tremendous talent he was.

As with the 1965 sessions, Jackson ran through the six songs in a run of first takes. His physical condition—obese, and with what certainly seemed to be the beginnings of emphysema, allowed him very little room for error, and his breathing difficulties can be heard on some of the quieter moments on the recordings. Unlike the earlier sessions he was not at all shy and seemed to be as comfortable as was possible in his condition. He had actually written a couple of other songs to be recorded that day, but got tired and wanted to leave before he could get them on tape, figuring he could just come another day and tape them. He never did, and while I have the lyrics on paper, the melodies remained in his head. Later, after his death, a notebook containing several more complete song lyrics was presented to me, all with no known melodies. The lyrics are included elsewhere in this book and anyone wishing to have a go at them and add a melody is welcome to do so.

The session went well and the tapes were mastered and copied for mailing to various record companies for their perusal. Our first thought was to send a copy to Columbia-EMI but they were no longer a company per se, and besides, SONY had taken over and had no idea about Jackson. We sent SONY a copy of the tapes with a gentle reminder about who Jackson was and what his history with Columbia had been, but all we received was a polite letter declining any interest in the songs, saying that they "do not fit our current needs." Letters from other companies, including B&C were all just as curt, and our enthusiasm waned quickly.

Then the *Dirty Linen* article came out, T. J. McGrath's words and some photos that I had sent him. Called "Lost Singer Found," it was a fine primer on the life and music of Jackson C. Frank and it started the ball rolling for his re-emergence into the real world.

Soon after the *Dirty Linen* piece came out, Andrew Means of *Folk Roots*, the world music magazine from England, was on the phone for an interview and in short order had his own article in print, complete with one of the photos of Jackson and Tom Paxton from the evening in Saugerties. Things were happening. Another night sometime later that summer Wizz Jones, the ultimate British hippie musician, was playing a set in Massachusetts. Charles "Chip" Reynolds, a folk music devotee, came down from Vermont and collected Jackson to take him to the show. A longtime fan, Reynolds ran a website that was devoted almost entirely to the world of English music, and a big part of his inventory was folk music. He actually purchased a copy of Jackson's 45-rpm single of an alternate version of "Blues Run the Game" backed with "Can't Get Away From My Love," which he then transferred to digital. It was his digital copy that was ultimately used a few years later in the CD anthology of all of Jackson's known recorded works, and a belated thanks is in order here.

What Goes Up. . .

Of course, as a man with a dark cloud following him, it was time for Jackson's parade to get some rain. Seeding the cloud on this occasion was the man himself. Unable to just maintain the status quo, Jackson, who had been taking his medications and had been generally very amiable to the Howards and the other residents of Woodstock Manor, decided to pull off his own mini-rebellion. His room was situated about 20 feet from a door which led to a nice wrap-around porch about 25 feet off the ground, and which overlooked the Lake Hill countryside around Woodstock Manor. The porch was about 75 feet from Route 212, the main road, which ran past the Manor, and which Jackson decided was just the perfect place to take care of his bladder issues as they might arise. He apparently did this many times, instead of making the 20-foot walk to his room with its own toilet. Eventually he was seen, and Henry Howard gave him warnings to cease and desist, which he did not. In short order Henry Howard was on the phone letting me know that Jackson was history there and that he had been removed from the facility, and placed in a different location in the city of Kingston, New York, about 15 miles away. At this point I was no longer acting as anything approaching official in Jackson's life, just his friend, so the call to me was just a courtesy.

The place in Kingston was a dump, and was located in the middle of a difficult to reach residential area filled with shady characters and lots of hills, which meant that Jackson, with his bad legs, wasn't going to be able to walk too far, not that there was much to walk to. He was a good 10 miles or more from Woodstock now, and he complained about it ad nauseum. For the first time I began to see what a tough task this was going to be.

Then, another minor miracle came to pass. Jackson's parents, still alive and fairly well in Buffalo, were on the phone with a plan. They were going to have him come home for a two week stay leading up to Thanksgiving in late November, at which time I would fly to Buffalo, and drive Jackson and myself back to Woodstock in a rental truck full of furniture. My job, if I was willing, was to secure him an apartment in Woodstock as close to the food stores and the center of town as possible. His mother would take care of his rent and expenses from any royalties he received. As his backlogged checks began to flow finally, all money was sent to his mother and was duly dispensed by her as the need arose. He was terrible with money, even money he actually deserved to have. I guess the survivor's guilt aspect of his personality, when it came to having money, never left.

And so, on a cool November morning I drove Jackson to the bus depot in Kingston for the seven-hour bus ride "home" to Elma. It was to be his first time back to the Buffalo area since 1984, and would turn out to be the last time he ever saw his family. While he was there, I got to work on an apartment search for him. I managed to locate a ground floor, easily accessible studio-type flat on Tinker Street, located just a few thousand feet from the Village Green, and easily within walking distance of necessary food stores and even the Tinker Street Café, formerly Café Espresso, where he would appear at several open mic nights over the next couple of years. I spoke to the landlord, explained the deal with Jackson, and necessary paperwork was filled out and submitted to Social Services and the place was his. I later found out that Jackson had lived in or stayed on a couch at some point in almost every house for a two-mile stretch of Tinker Street during the late sixties and throughout the seventies.

When the time came after the Thanksgiving holiday, I was sent a plane ticket from Albany, New York to Buffalo and I flew there the following day. Elmer Frank was waiting for me with Jackson in the car, and I was amazed what a couple of weeks at home had done for him. His mother and father had gotten him a haircut and new clothing, but the most amazing thing were a new set of dentures and a neat mustache and a new man appeared, looking a lot like an older version of the album cover from 1965. It was truly an amazing transformation and a photo from that day is included elsewhere in this book. It was a twenty-minute trip from the airport to the house, where, sure enough, the Ryder truck sat waiting, loaded and gassed up for the long ride to Ulster County.

My stay at the Franks' house was brief—barely an hour, and then it was time to leave—Woodstock was waiting. The truck was already packed and ready when I got there. Neighbors had pitched in and helped with the heavy lifting since the Franks were both in their seventies and Mrs. Frank especially was a bit on the frail side, due to her defective heart valve. A round of photos was taken, food was bagged up for the long ride to Ulster County and we were on our way. It would be the last time Jackson would ever see his parents, although there was no way that anyone could have convinced me of that on that day. It was a perfect day in many respects—Jackson was the best I had ever seen him, he was clean, smelled good, looked great with his new dentures, was full of good home cooking, caught up on his medications and in great spirits. The eight-hour ride to Woodstock was a true pleasure and it flew by. Unfortunately so did the daylight and it was dark by the time we got there.

In hindsight I had probably envisioned an easy unload of the truck, Jackson and myself working well together bringing in the dressers, chairs, a small couch and other large items. Not so, as Jackson absolutely refused to lift anything heavier than a suitcase which, coincidently was about the only item he unloaded. Mark Anderson had related a story to me about a time when he briefly saw Jackson again in 1970 after all of the years apart. Mark was now married and living in Ulster Park, New York, just outside of Kingston, and he had inherited a house there that needed some work. He brought Jackson to see the place and thought that maybe if they worked on something together it would help them reconnect a bit. The project he chose was a simple one—put a new set of shingles on the small roof of a shed on the property. Jackson would have none of it. His preferred activity at that point was to sit off to the side and smoke as much marijuana as he could and try to convince Mark and his wife Eleanor to try it too. As Mark said, "That didn't work for us," and he gradually lost touch with Jackson again.

Jackson liked the apartment I had found, and recalled living in each of the houses on either side back in the 70's. Several hours later I was finished, tired but no worse for the wear, and he was all set for his first night in his new apartment. For Jackson it was the culmination of years of dreaming about just such a night. I was, and still am proud to have been able to help make it come to fruition.

He still needed to make a living. Although I had been able

to track down back royalties from BMI, they didn't amount to much in the grand scheme of things, since his album had been out of print for so many years and his songs only occasionally were played on British radio. I began to look into who had the rights to his songs, and the answer came quickly from Jackson himself. Paul Simon had the rights to the songs. I had heard all of the stories about Paul and his legendary cheapness and his being compared to a mynah bird and could only imagine how he had finagled the songs from Jackson. Amazingly, after all of the years and hardships that Jackson had endured, he still knew Paul's mailing address at the famed Brill Building on Broadway in New York City from memory, and I typed a letter to the man. I explained who I was and what I was trying to do, and Jackson added some sentences for verification and we sent it off. I never expected much— after all, Simon was the guy who had brazenly taken Martin Carthy's signature song from under England's collective noses and copyrighted it as his own, and Carthy was someone who was able to fight back, but chose not to. Amazingly, a week later a package came in the mail from Paul's office, with a series of copyright registrations, a letter and a small official promissory note, made out years ago by Jackson. He had borrowed fifteen hundred dollars from Paul with the songs as collateral on the note. Now Paul was returning them, with the letter listing the songs that were in his control, and which were now being returned, and a note saying that the debt was canceled and the songs were once again Jackson's. Why a multimillionaire like Paul Simon would force an obviously destitute friend to not only go the promissory note route, but to take his songs, which were his only real collateral, is a question that defies reason, but that is what happened. Whatever Paul had been in the past, however, he did the right thing by Jackson this time. Now Jackson was able to use his songs as he wanted, but what to do with them? The album had been out of print for decades.

§

Jackson was a creature of excess by the time I knew him. It may have been a result of his medications, it could have been a residual effect of his years on the streets or it might have been something else entirely. The fact is that when he wanted something, he wanted it in large amounts or the world would feel his wrath. On Saturdays it became almost routine for us to go into Kingston and visit the "all you can eat buffet" at Kentucky Fried Chicken. Not that I minded, of course—good chicken is good chicken, and I piled my plate high. Jackson, however, was like the obsessed Richard Dreyfuss character in *Close Encounters of the Third Kind*. He would stack one plate with a mound of mashed potatoes exactly like the models of Devil's Tower in Wyoming. He would then make a volcano-like cone on top and fill it with gravy-lava and would sprinkle corn all around it. The other plate he would stack with chicken—lots of chicken. Our KFC experience culminated in disaster one night as Jackson was returning to our table with his potato mountain plate. Always walking with a limp, his gait was very uneven and that was bad enough but on this particular evening his hips were quite bad and when he sat down he missed the chair almost completely and ended up on his back, potatoes, gravy and corn all over him, me and the people at the next table. Employees rushed to help clean up, and amazingly he insisted on getting a duplicate plate of potatoes, gravy and corn. We made it through the dinner but it was the last time we went to KFC. For various reasons they discontinued the all-you-can-eat policy the very next week and that was that.

Other food foibles: He would send me to the local Grand Union Supermarket. In the United States, Grand Union was one of the big chains in the northeast, and the one in Woodstock was especially fun to shop at because you never knew who might be there buying what. I saw purple-haired Todd Rundgren in the vegetable section one day with a small dog, also purple, in his cart. The members of The Band and NRBQ also used to shop there, as did whoever might be recording at Bearsville Studios down the road. Jackson almost never shopped there himself but he knew what they sold and it was my job to buy it for him. He would often send me in search of "cooked on a rotisserie" chickens, buying them two at a time, and he would then eat them two at a time. The same went for large cooked hams, which he would eat not all at once like the chickens, but over the course of the week. Also many, many boxes of cereal, cookies, soda, and a host of very fattening, non-nutritious crap.

And cigarettes. By the carton, he would buy and smoke the demon things. I began to see fairly quickly what his mother was always railing about with the smoking. I tried to convince him to slow down and wean himself off of them but it was no use. While I spent vast hours with him I wasn't his keeper and he was free to do as he pleased. Part of his being able to have his own place—he was still under the auspices of the mental health department which was paid in part through a government program called Supplemental Security Income, or SSI—was that he had to agree to have a home health aide come a couple of times a week to help him clean up and bathe, etc. He went through a number of young ladies, at whom he would berate and scream for no other reason than he didn't want them there. In part his body may have been the reason he didn't want a woman coming and helping him bathe. His chicken and soda diet had put a huge amount of weight on him and the scale wasn't lying when it recorded him at almost 300 pounds one day. Not a tall man, his normal weight was in the 160 pound range, so he was close to double what his normal size should be, dangerously obese. Naked, his appearance was very grotesque, in part because of the fat. He also looked almost translucent in an odd way.

His skin, especially on his back and limbs, was so severely scarred from the fire that it wouldn't grow in the way normal skin would to accommodate weight gain. Instead it stretched, getting thinner and showing his veins and the subcutaneous layers of fat, yellow and rippled. It was a while before I got used to seeing him that way, and it still disturbs me a bit to this day.

One lingering injury that I can't shake the memory of was a gaping hole in his left elbow. Jackson couldn't remember when it appeared there but he had it as long as I knew him, possibly a remnant of life on the streets—an inch wide hole in the scar tissue near the point of his elbow that drained constantly, a stinking yellow ooze that was probably pus. It got on his clothing and everything else he touched. When he stayed at my house we had to throw out his linens afterward because of the yellow and green stains on them. When he went to a doctor as a requirement of the SSI office, a doctor saw the hole and immediately scheduled a date to fix it. A short operation later and the hole was closed, never to return. His mother had maintained, and so had Jackson, that his weight gain was the result of the medications that he was taking, but having seen him graze at the trough, I knew he was responsible for most of it himself. I tried to help him, but in that respect I failed miserably, and I remember a moment of clarity one day when it occurred to me that his life was never going to get any better, so let him enjoy himself. In a way he deserved it. He had survived so much to get here—who was I to tell him to lose weight or stop smoking? When Mark Anderson first told me about the letter he was amazed that Jackson was still alive. "He is a truly helpless individual—he can't defend himself from anything" were the words he used that day. Now Jackson was safe, and he didn't have anyone to worry about except himself. He was doing great.

One day I stopped by and he was obviously high. I morphed for a moment into his mother, scolding him for smoking weed, and then caught myself. Then it occurred to me that the son of a gun had actually gotten his hands on some marijuana, and I was just hoping that he wasn't spending money I had given him (at this point he really had no money except for what his mother and I would give him. She gave him about 50 dollars a week, I gave him maybe half of that) on it, as I am pretty anti-drug, and wouldn't want my money going to buy that nonsense. Then I remembered my moment of clarity, to let him enjoy his life, and I lightened up. I asked him where he had gotten the stuff and he told me about a girlfriend named Roxy Dawn that had stopped by. I was shocked to hear about a girlfriend, but he only meant a female friend. He suggested that we go to her place and hang out after a stop at the bank, so we headed out, and finally ended up at her apartment. She turned out to be a Janis Joplin lookalike with yellow skin. She was quite nice and we sat around while Jackson and she smoked a joint. She produced a cassette of Jackson playing new music from the 70's that she had held on to all those years. I begged her for a copy and she said to come back the next day and she would let me have the tape to take home and dub a copy. I went back the next day as she told me to, and found her absolutely beside herself, upset—she had accidently recorded a radio program over the music Jackson was playing. A one of a kind recording—gone. To make a bad day worse, he got robbed that evening. It had been his SSI check day—his rent was automatically paid and he got a few hundred dollars extra each month for food and other expenses, including his lights, phone and cable TV bills. After we went to the bank and he cashed the check, we headed to Roxy's place, and then back to his. He took his wallet and set it on the table near his front door. I told him as I was leaving to put his wallet away in a drawer so no one would be tempted. (His door and windows were next to a fairly busy sidewalk). I said goodnight and left. The next morning early I woke to the phone ringing.

"I got robbed" was all he said.

When? "Last night. I was sleeping and I heard a sound. There were two men in my apartment. I made a noise and they ran out the door. Took all the money out of my wallet."

What was there to say? I gave him all the money I had except for a few dollars that I needed for gas to get to work. I didn't want to tell his mother because it would just get her agitated that he wasn't more careful. He was, after all, about 53 years old.

Surprisingly, the loss of the Roxy Dawn tape spurred one last creative gasp in Jackson. He had been keen to listen to it over and over to re-learn the songs on it and when she erased it that went out the window and so, I figured, did his enthusiasm for making music. But he had a surprise in store: the very next week when I arrived he smiled and pushed a button on his cheap, mono cassette recorder, the kind that has a condenser microphone built into the body of the machine. From the tinny speaker came his guitar and vocals, with new songs, including one that I had started myself and that he had finished to something terrific, that he had written over the course of a couple days and which he wanted to get on tape as soon as possible. The recordings were primitive and rough but listenable. They eventually ended up being called "the Kitchen Table Demos" and were released on a posthumous double CD set in 2003.

It was around this time that something wonderful almost happened. Through my constant letter writing and digging, I had gotten in touch with someone who knew Jackson's daughter, Angeline. Out of the blue one day I arrived home to find a message on my machine from her. A very lovely and dignified voice, with a modest British accent, was asking permission for a letter to be forwarded by me to Jackson. I called the number back and got her answering machine, and left a positive response. The next day I got another answering machine message while I was out that a letter had been sent. I called back and got... the machine. Several more attempts were all met with an electronic answer, so I gave up. The letter, actually a card, came in a few days, and I gave it to Jackson. Inside was a photo of a beautiful young blonde woman, mid-twenties, and very pleasing to the eye. "Dear Jackson," the letter began. She went on to explain that she didn't know him and it would take a while before she would feel comfortable calling him "Dad," if ever. She just wanted to take the first step, and she went on to tell him about herself and her life. She was pleased to tell him that she was living with a musician and they traveled a lot to gigs and at the moment were on a break from his band's tour. She also left him her address and asked him to please write to her. In all, a touching letter and I thought it might be really good for him to heal this wound. He had, after all, been thrown out of the house when she was an infant and had little or no contact for all those years.

The next day I arrived to visit and he proudly showed me a letter to her that he had written. I read it quickly and immediately knew that if he sent it that it was over, and that there would be no reconciliation. In it, he happily took on the role of father and criticized almost every aspect of her card, including her grammar, and gave his opinion that she should not be living with anybody until she was married, as if he had the right to say a word to this poor girl. He was a good person, a well-meaning guy with a big heart but this was one time I got very angry with him. I told him not to mail that letter and that he should be thankful that she had even bothered to make the attempt. I also told him that he should write another letter and be very nice to her. The next day, I called him to say hi, and the first thing out of his mouth was, "I mailed the first letter."

It should be noted that he never received another letter, card or phone call from Angeline, not even an attempt at one. She did, however, establish a relationship with her extended family several years later. In 2005, a year before Marilyn Frank died, she called me asking for a favor. She wanted me to track down Angeline so she could talk to her. I wasn't aware that they had never met, or even spoken. I managed to get in touch with someone who had Angeline's number in London and passed the info on to Marilyn. Happily, they maintained a relationship until Marilyn died in January 2006.

The ebb and flow of Jackson's successful rehabilitation began to be more ebb than flow, as slight changes in his behavior and demeanor manifested themselves. While he had been fairly fastidious about how his place looked, everything in its place, he began to leave things on the floor and the place became a mess, only cleaned up by Roy, his aide, and when Roy was reassigned, another aide named Pete. Eventually Pete was taken off the case when supervisors became aware somehow of Jackson's overly abusive and uncooperative nature. As Pete and Roy came from a private agency, they had no obligation to continue care, so a county employee was scheduled to work with him several times a week. He had become negligent with his meds and missed many doses. As with a lot of paranoid schizophrenics, when he took his meds he was great, as was the case in 1994 when he went home to Buffalo. He reached a plateau of "normalcy" and declared himself cured. And out went the medications, with the usual excuses that they made him drowsy and caused him to gain weight. The end of his independence was near.

Great Barrington: Game Over

The final straw came one evening in the fall of that year, 1996. It was a cool night and he was heating his apartment with a kerosene space heater that we had picked up somewhere.

It has all kinds of safety features built in so it's almost impossible to have a mishap, but Jackson found a way. He had gotten even more obese and had a hard time getting in and out of bed. One particular night he wet the bed while asleep. Instead of getting up and either changing the sheets (which would have been hard for him to do anyway) or moving to the couch to sleep, he flung his wet comforter over the heater to dry. You would think that someone so damaged by fire and its effects would be careful, but not Jackson. When his new, county-employed (this means a "by the book" official) aide showed up early the next morning she discovered that the comforter had melted and was dripping hot goo all over the floor (fortunately it was flame retardant and as such had not immediately burst into flame) and probably would have eventually gotten so hot that a fire would have broken out. With the stroke of a pen on paper Jackson was declared to be a danger to himself and others (he could have burned the house down, and there were tenants upstairs) and unable to care for himself. He was removed from the apartment, never to return, and taken to the psychiatric ward of Benedictine Hospital in Kingston. Part of a Catholic hospital, the Benedictine psych ward was the target of a lot of local ridicule and was known as a dumping ground for petty criminals who would be sent there if the courts didn't send them to jail, and as a result, at various times there was not a lot of actual care for the mentally ill, just maintenance until a place could be found for them. In later years though, conditions improved and the hospital's reputation improved to a great degree.

Jackson hadn't committed any crime, and being released to the streets wasn't an option—this wasn't Leben Home, after all, or New York City either for that matter, so Jackson languished there for months, with no plan in sight. I visited him as often as I could, and he was miserable. When brilliant minds, warped as they may be, are surrounded by craziness, what possible good can that do? He was really having it bad there and I wondered what could possibly be next for the poor guy. I was powerless to do anything other than visit. Then I got a call from Marilyn Frank. She had received a letter from the hospital informing her that they were going to need the bed space and Jackson could no longer stay there. He had already been there almost 6 months and for the hospital, that was too long and he had to be placed somewhere. The hospital requested that she find him a place to live where he could be supervised and suggested he be sent home to Buffalo. An eighty-year-old woman with a defective heart valve who was unable to travel, she could not have Jackson and his myriad problems come home to roost, so she had to decline. It was then that the hospital informed her that they were planning on making a legal move and would be filing a request with the local courts to be declared Jackson's legal guardian. By doing so, and if the courts approved their request, they could decide his fate. Shortly thereafter I got a call from the Franks. They were embarrassed and humbled but wanted to know if I would consider becoming Jackson's legal guardian, to prevent the hospital from doing something unpleasant to their son. What could I say? Of course I would do it.

The whole process took only a couple of weeks. The Franks had hired an attorney from Buffalo who oversaw things to make sure the process was done properly. Jackson was evaluated by a court ordered psychiatrist to verify his incapacity. The doctor met with him for five minutes, and even though Jackson was in fine form and as clearheaded and lucid as I had ever seen him, declared him to be classically paranoid schizophrenic. I had to make an appearance in court to take an oath and sign papers. The judge was a very kind man who asked me if I was aware of the importance of this action and the responsibilities I was taking on. I told him I was aware and accepted the job, as it were. With the motion granted, the next task was to locate a suitable place for Jackson. Because he was only in his mid- fifties, none of the nursing homes and senior care facilities in the area were willing to take him on, especially in light of his reputation for being difficult. The hospital, despite being beaten to the punch by the Franks and myself, then became quite helpful. It's not that they were bad, or evil—they just needed to get him out of there to make room for someone more needy. They compiled a list of facilities that might be willing to give Jackson a chance. Unfortunately they were all out of the state, but one, in Massachusetts, seemed ideal, both in location and in the services they provided. I let the hospital make the proper arrangements as far as the paperwork went. After all, they were the professionals.

And thus it came to pass that Jackson was moved to his final home, a lovely place called Timberlyn Heights, nestled in the beautiful Berkshire mountains in Great Barrington, Massachusetts. It was a nursing home, but an open-minded one, and they were willing to take on Jackson and his difficulties. He was moved there almost immediately, and was in his new room almost before I realized that it was a long ride for me and I would likely not be visiting as much as I was used to doing. Whereas Woodstock was only a 25-mile ride for me, this was more like 100 miles, and took two hours because of the winding route to get there. I resolved to do my best, but gradually had to cut down the number of visits to a couple times a month, and sometimes only once a month. Not that Jackson sat around waiting for me. The facility was good and they were always taking their clients out on trips to local malls for shopping and to just be out and about.

He had few visitors, but every once in a while a surprise would pop up. Not long after he arrived, CBS and Paul Simon and Art Garfunkel decided to release Old Friends, a terrific boxed set of Simon and Garfunkel songs with alternate takes and unreleased material. To Jackson's, and my delight, a cover of "Blues Run the Game" from 1965, never released, was included. The company sent me a couple of copies and I brought one to Jackson, who didn't have a CD player. We took a ride in my car, listening to it over and over. He was thrilled with it, and kept saying, over and over, "They did a nice job, didn't they?"

The recording would bring him a check for over six-thousand dollars, which, as usual, was sent to his mother in Buffalo, where she would dispense it as needed. She was the best banker he ever had. It would keep him in candy and cigarettes for a long time.

A couple of writers called me and made appointments to stop by for interviews. One was Pamela Murray Winters, who made a drive up from Virginia and who was doing research for a biography of Sandy Denny. The other was Linda Fite, a features writer and editor for the Times Herald Record, a newspaper based in Middletown, New York. Fite, a longtime friend, had heard the story of my search for and finding of Jackson and thought that an article was a good proposition. Her interview turned into a nice four-page cover story/article in the Sunday Magazine section, complete with a picture of the Jaguar that Jackson had lusted after, drawn by her husband, Marvel Comics artist Herb Trimpe, and a great photo on the cover of the magazine of Jackson and his guitar. She also took several more photos that capture him, as he was, cigarette smoking and looking like he'd lived through the hell that he had.

It was possibly the last highlight of his life. It was only a few months afterwards that I began to notice that he was really letting himself go. His weight ballooned skyward and he got very bloated and had a look of perpetual pain, which, of course he had, but never as bad as it was at this juncture.

I knew his time was running out. I saw an advertisement for a concert at the State University of New York at New Paltz. The show was a pairing of two of Jackson's old friends, Robin Williamson, of the Incredible String Band and John Renbourn. I called him up and told him I was coming to pick him up for something special, and he seemed eager to go. I made the hour and a half drive to Great Barrington to pick him up. He was wearing a white shirt, blue trousers and, as was his custom due to not being able to bend, no socks. And he had an amusing little accessory—a stretched out wire hanger that he had fashioned into a scratcher of sorts, to get to the places his tightened skin and obesity wouldn't allow his arms to reach. I told him he could leave the hanger and I would scratch him if he really needed it but he insisted on bringing it along.

We made the two-hour trip to New Paltz, and I was thankful it went by quickly. We parked and walked in, very early, and happily he didn't see the small poster for the show, so he had no idea who we were going to see. We managed to just walk in—colleges are not like commercial venues with security and ten people to get past before you can sit down. As with the Paxton show, we just walked in and he sat down. I told him to wait a moment and I would be right back. I ventured backstage looking for the dressing rooms and happened to catch a glimpse of John Renbourn sitting with a newspaper. I noticed Robin Williamson sitting at a nearby table in a corner. I boldly walked up to them and introduced myself. When I mentioned that an old friend was in the auditorium, they were curious, and when I told them it was Jackson, their reaction was almost comical. "Robin, Jackson Frank is outside! What are we waiting for??" exclaimed Renbourn as they rushed for the door.

They approached Jackson and sat down on seats nearby, happy and amazed at the same time. I was watching their faces for signs of shock at his condition, which was very bad at that point, but they were true professionals and registered nothing but delight. The conversation was light and pleasant and then it was time to get ready to do the show. I took several pictures of them with Jackson and off they went. Jackson and I had great seats for the show. The first half was brilliant as the two old masters played beautifully. Separately and together, they were great. At intermission, Jackson told me he wanted to leave. I tried to convince him to stay—after all, we'd come a long way. He was insistent though, so begrudgingly I brought him outside to the car. As we were making our way back to Great Barrington, it was mostly quiet in the car, and then he asked me a simple question that blew my mind: "Who was that we just saw?"

I thought, "His mind is gone—he had a whole conversation and didn't know who he was talking to???" He had an idea who it was but was embarrassed to ask, he told me later, but I wondered if he was just trying to downplay the whole thing. He explained, and I had not thought of this, that the last time he saw Renbourn, he was thin, had a head full of hair and only a small tuft of beard. Now he was bald, much heavier and possessed a full beard. The time had slipped away and it had been thirty years since he had seen John, and Williamson was much the same—older, heavier and with a full beard, after having no beard at all in the sixties. Looking at photos of both Renbourn and Williamson in the different decades, it was easy to see where there could be some doubt in both cases.

A funny thing happened backstage before they came out to see Jackson. Just before we hit the door, Renbourn stopped me and said, "Before we go out there you must tell me, because he never would. What does the 'C' in his middle name stand for?" When I told him, "Carey" he seemed disappointed, just as he related to me later.

We drove back to Great Barrington and I dropped him off and went home, arriving at my own home at 2:30 AM, to the chagrin of my wife. She had been angry with me for spending so much time with him and giving him money that we really needed for ourselves, and she was right. Our marriage was about over and in fact ended within a couple of months, when she showed me to the door. A lot of our problems weren't related to Jackson, but then again, a lot of them were.

I found a new place to live in Accord, New York and went about my business, trying to re-establish myself and get back on my feet. I visited Jackson every couple of weeks and we talked about him getting well again and getting another apartment when he was well, but I knew it wouldn't happen. He was getting more and more obese and walking was harder than ever for him. He was supposed to be on a regulated diet but when I would visit he always had bags of chips, candy and other junk in his room. I figured, live and let live, let him enjoy himself, and that was that.

I saw him for the last time on his birthday, March 2, 1999. I picked up some snacks for him and brought my guitar along, but he was not feeling well, had no desire to play, and had nothing much to say. I left after a short time and headed home. I went to work the next day (I was teaching school at the time, along with being the town's Dog Control Officer, a position I held for seven years) and the day was uneventful, until I got home that evening and the phone rang. It was Penny McCoy, the head nurse at Timberlyn Heights.

"Mr. Abbott, I just wanted to let you know that Jackson passed away last night."

"From what?"

"I'm not sure, but he just didn't wake up this morning. I'm sorry for your loss. I know he meant a great deal to you."

It turned out to be a combination of pneumonia and cardiac arrest that did him in. The fire, the years on the streets, the cold winters on sidewalks and being shot in the eye by punks couldn't kill him but bacteria did. I called his mother as soon as I hung up from talking to Ms. McCoy, to give her the news but she had already been called that morning. Mrs. Frank was devastated. She had obviously been crying all day. She told me that she had been expecting this and felt like she had already lost her son many times in the past—after the fire, when he started taking up with Kathy Henry, when he went to England, when he took off from the house while she was having her heart surgery, when he went to New York City...but this time she knew it was final.

And so it was. In the end, it was his old nemesis, fire, that ensured that he would not rise again for another song. He was cremated on March 9, 1999 by the Finnerty and Stevens Funeral Home in Great Barrington, and his ashes were placed in an urn and sent to his mother and father in Buffalo, where they were placed among other urns containing the ashes of family members. There was no service, or even mention in any of the music press about his passing. That may have been my fault—as guardian I was probably supposed to notify those folks, but all I knew to do was write up an obituary for the Kingston Daily Freeman in Ulster County.

He is gone, but his music is still part of my life, and always will be.

Postscript

So what to make of Jackson C. Frank? His legacy is a small treasure trove of fine music, and his story is movie-worthy to be sure, and at least two screenplays have been written for consideration. His influence is still heard in the music of Bert Jansch, John Renbourn and other survivors of that time who are around and performing today. It isn't a stretch that Jackson's influence carried into the rock world as well. It has been well publicized that Neil Young himself has called Bert Jansch one of his guitar idols, the acoustic equivalent of Jimi Hendrix. Led Zeppelin was also tremendously influenced by Bert Jansch, as well as others from the scene. Sandy Denny even sang on Zeppelin's *ZoSo* (the untitled 4th album) on the track "Battle of Evermore," her haunting voice singing lines alongside the controlled caterwaul of Robert Plant. Counting Crows, Eddi Reader and others have recorded versions of "Blues Run the Game" and countless, less professional but no less captivating versions of his songs can be found on MySpace and YouTube. On MySpace, in fact, possibly the finest cover of "My Name is Carnival" is performed by Erland and the Carnival, a group led by a young man named Erland Cooper.

In the Jackson v. Paul Simon debate, speculation as to who influenced whom can be laid to rest. Jackson had never heard Paul Simon before he went to England, and Simon had not written his best work yet, but Jackson's influence, with themes of loneliness and solitude can be heard in many of the songs on the Simon and Garfunkel albums that came later, and a jaunty song like "Feelin' Groovy" almost certainly has its roots in "Just Like Anything." The fact that Paul Simon felt compelled to record Jackson is telling, since it is something he has done only a couple of times in his career since, including producing *Seductive Reasoning*, an album by Maggie and Terre, two of the Roche sisters whose albums were full of quirky songs and seamless harmonies.

Not everyone who crossed Jackson's path thought highly of him, but these exceptions were few and far between. Certainly friends of Sandy, including Linda Peters, later Thompson, disliked the way he treated her, and they have said so in various publications. Joe Boyd, legendary producer of Fairport Convention, among others, in what can only be called a blip on his judgment, didn't get Jackson's talent at all. In an email response for this book, Boyd recalled, "I only met Jackson once, I believe, maybe twice. I certainly knew his story, but it would have been pretty condescending not to dislike a jerk because of his injuries. He never appealed to me as a person or a musician. I used to run out of folk clubs when a floor singer would start in on 'Blues Run the Game!' It takes a Dylan or Nick Drake or Sandy [Denny] to get me interested, as the form itself I find pretty boring. Jackson was fine as an example of the early Anglo-American singer/songwriter form, but that did very little for me. I file him somewhere in the back of my mind with Eric Andersen as a good example of the worst American singer-songwriter cliche mongers. White guys talking about 'the road' and 'leaving her behind' and stuff like that. 'Blues Run the Game?' I'd rather listen to Sleepy John Estes."

While the things that Boyd says about the singer-songwriter gang are arguably generally true, if one wants to be cynical, in Jackson's case the road he traveled was much harder and rougher than those roads traveled by many of Boyd's beloved blues singers. The fact that Boyd dated Sandy Denny later cannot be discounted for his dislike of Jackson. In his brilliant memoir *White Bicycles*, Boyd included the following phrase:

"...I went to hear Sandy Denny at Les Cousins in Soho. I still wasn't convinced: she insisted on performing songs by her American ex-boyfriend Jackson C. Frank and other undistinguished singer-songwriters."

It certainly seems like Boyd's general disdain for singer-songwriters clouded his vision and judgment about some truly talented people, Jackson included. While it is certainly true that there were, and are, no small number of hacks in the business, Jackson Frank was certainly not one of them. It isn't without precedent that one suitor would harbor jealousy toward a previous rival, is it?

Nonetheless, one of Boyd's favorite performers, (not to mention Sandy Denny, who makes two) the doomed Nick Drake, was heavily influenced by Jackson, performing no less than four of his songs, "Blues Run the Game," "Milk and Honey," "Kimbie" and the vastly under-rated "Here Come the Blues." Recordings of those songs eventually saw the light of day officially when they were released in 2007 as part of the Family Tree CD. A generation of singers and performers, some obvious, some not, were thence influenced by Drake. Once again that piece of accidental art featured in Bert Jansch's home would seem to be prophetic and true—Jackson's music lay at the center of that particular musical universe. For Boyd to dismiss Jackson Frank so out of hand, then lionize those who (literally, in Sandy's case) learned at his feet, makes no sense and suggests that there are deeper issues involved.

One true thing is that Jackson C. Frank was an extremely talented musician, with seemingly unlimited potential. His abbreviated catalogue contains a very high ratio of great songs, and of his more polished works, mainly the 1965 LP and the second album, which would have been called *Marlene*, contain no duds at all. Even the rough demos cut in his kitchen are strong lyrically, and the best of them, like "The Spectre," "Goodbye to My Lovin' You," and "Tumble in the Wind" are near-perfect songs. The genius contained in all of seven, recently discovered early- to mid-70's recordings with Artie Traum and Tim Moore put a fine point on the issue of the high quality of the man's work. There is no doubt that given a fair shot at life, free of pitfalls, his name might be mentioned as a true peer of Paul Simon, instead of just an interesting footnote in a bigger story.

This book may be an overstatement. It might be a remembrance of a minor figure in the entertainment world that no one recalls. It is, however, a tale that needed to be told. The story of Jackson C. Frank was not destined to have a happy ending, no matter what I would like to think. That I was able to give him some help at a time when he needed it was a blessing for both of us, and I would do it again, despite the high aggravation that came along with the job. His lack of care for himself and his own well-being as well as his unwavering stubbornness when it came to being right or wrong were major factors in his long demise. I talked to the wall when we spoke of these matters, but he was his own person and made his own decisions, and he lived the way he wanted. Even after becoming his legal guardian, I allowed him to have his way most of the time. I never felt that his destiny was in my hands, and I only agreed to become guardian to prevent the hospital in Kingston from doing something drastic. I succeeded in that regard, and while I don't think they had anything less than his best interests in mind, it isn't a myth that in the U.S. healthcare system, money talks. He was taking up valuable bed space, and thus had to go.

What I am still amazed by is the way that he survived, day in and day out, in chronic pain. To live a life where every waking hour is filled with intense discomfort is inconceivable to me. That he managed to be so stoic and even cheerful once in a while is even more inconceivable, and I can only admire him even more for it. I can only hope that in his final hours he was free of it. But he is gone and I'll never know.

His music lives on, though, and there is no reason to doubt that "Blues Run the Game" will be with us always. The internet has been tremendously helpful in getting his music out to the masses but the fact remains that although he was American, Jackson C. Frank is unknown in his own land. The fact that his album has never been released in this country has aided in keeping him a footnote in the big book. A U.S. release would probably make a significant difference in public recognition of his work, as would a movie about his life. The two screenplays completed about his life, if one or both make it through the process, would do miracles for getting his story a larger audience. A legacy isn't much if no one knows that you existed.

So there you have it. A tragedy, in many acts. The tragedies of the fire, the mental illness, the loss of children, literally and figuratively, the tragedy of homelessness and the tragedy of dying alone, surrounded by many. So many tragedies, and only one life to fit them all into.

Jackson C. Frank. May his story be told and his songs be sung.

*. . .I have traveled long enough, traveled long enough
upon your shoulders. . .*

from "Madonna of Swans," copyright 1975 by Jackson C. Frank

Appendix 1

In this, one of the earliest pieces Jackson wrote for the *Wood-stock Week*, his description of an art gallery exhibition party goes far beyond the norm, including vivid recounting of his own accident and injuring his hand.

Love Thy Labor
by Jackson C. Frank
Woodstock Week, *February 15, 1968*

On Saturday, February 10 the Woodstock Artists Association Gallery opened its doors to the public and let us, in the midst of the wintery gloom, be touched by the many facets of love in a visual diffusion brought more to life by the opening party on that date than the exhibition itself. Nonetheless, separating the happy people and good conversation from the essential structure of the show one found much more than first impressions warranted on the matter. The only real fault of the showing began to be a lack of proper space in which to perform traditional adjustment from one piece to the next. In short there really wasn't enough room. It was as if the paintings were quite attendant and incidental, standing against the walls like guards or waiters. Your reporter may be forgiven a touch of the critique as he had fallen on his face while photographing the WAA billboard outside the gallery and mashed his hand up rather seriously. Not the mood in which to see a show dedicated to Universal Love. One doesn't perform to the nines with muddy clothes and bleeding paw, in fact there is little love lost in the whole affair.

All of us but yours truly seemed in such a festive way and identification phrases pouring so easily forth that in a short time all trace of nursing sorrow vanished, the first stage of alienation was over with. The party carried on.

Clarence Schmidt was in rare form and no one could of course miss the gentle but bright-eyes patriarch as he gadded about, in search of no one in particular. We deemed it wiser to go in search with Robbie, the tape-eating robot with "the big ear"…Grace Swank said hello.

"I worked out a heart theme on three paintings, and, well, …I didn't like it, you know? It went against the grain. So I went back and painted out the heart theme ones and took three small paintings already complete, cut out paper hearts and arrows and pasted them onto the frame. In the old days if you gave a box of candy, a gift, something in silks and so forth, all you had to have was a heart. That's all I had to have, a heart."

Grace also said that the idea of a winter show was a very good one for both the town and the WAA. "We sometimes get lost along about now, there is little contact and nothing to do in the winter…"

Weaving about the tight groups of fluid people, trying at one and the same time to get an impression of the works on exhibit and not to brush good coats with a gory fist. Robbie served as scribe for such titles as "And Then we Slept, Arno, …Gottshuck, The Heart of Wisdom…" and vague and rambling descriptions thereof. Something was lacking. I sat down for a cigarette and a little rethink.

Gladys Plate came by in a floppy hat and I made her look at a portrait of monkeys while I photographed the scene holding my breath. The flash was busted on the camera and the Polaroid light meter was taking seconds to do its work. The film came out blurred. More cigarette.

I decided on additional stroll material and came upon Arnold Blanch's "Portrait of a Nude with My Future." A little further on I met Arnold Himself perusing the photographic exhibit.

"I think the show will bring spring a little closer this year. I also think the paper should mention Mr. And Mrs, Heckeroth came to the opening. Businessmen and tradespeople are the ones we'd like to see come to the show."

Arnold has felt this way twice in the two times I have talked with him and, it seems to me, his ideas have a very pertinent ring to them. The show will be running for some time, on into the 25th of February, from 3-6 p.m. every day. I have a special reason for returning, but that is yet to come...

Talking with various members of the gallery attendance I found reaction pretty much to one viewpoint...that the show was not terribly cohesive but that outstanding pieces could be found, and that the while concept of a mid-winter show was very imaginative. From my past visits to the WAA coffee hour on Thursday of each week, I began to form a picture in my mind of the basic friendship of the WAA for this town and for all visitors. Would it be petty to say my hand was not hurting half so much as before and that I really didn't notice it at the time?

I hadn't heard much n the subject of Valentine's Day, which the show is to run concurrent with, using the occasion, in fact, to inspire the exhibition theme. Suddenly Ken Downer's "Universal Valentine" occupied my full attention. It became a totem to the showing itself. This is not flippancy on my part, as the work is quite massive, but as I stopped looking for something else. I can't even remember what it was. The entire assemblage of people and lights, coffee and art works fit itself together. For a moment it even seemed we were all in a cast, characters and words come alive within the crisp clean white folded walls of a Valentine greeting. Then I succumb, perhaps like a nit, to a painting...I fell in love with an untitled work. All of this begins a bit stickily, *but it is as it happened. I was packing up to leave when my eye caught Ann Roberts' "Untitled" and lost my heart completely to the flowers in her (see the work) hat, the shadow man, the chalk mist woman…Fabulous, but this IS a personal opinion. Nonetheless, if anyone buys her before I get the scratch, my heart will shatter….Happy Valentine's week.*

Appendix 2

Here is an article of a type that, in typical local newspapers, is usually bone dry in its prose. Because Jackson and fire were so well acquainted, he had a deeper feel for the subject and what follows is not the typical public service piece about the hazards of fire, but true poetry. Note the title, as well.

Fire, The Enemy
by Jackson C. Frank
Woodstock Week, *May, 1968*

A somewhat-record of fires reported in the area for this time of year has the Woodstock Fire Company speculating and constantly busy. In the month beginning April 23, almost a dozen fires have been in the local area. Most of these were caused by open burning. There is a ban on open burning and no permits are being issued for this purpose. Nonetheless people carry on it as if they had no idea of what the ban is for.

Let us say what the ban is for…since 1964 drought, plain drought has continually been the word not used but implied in the conditions that come to the local countryside during the summer months. Acres of timber of invaluable beauty and worth have gone the way of tinder in the heat and bone-dryness and usually with the help of man. A match, a cigarette, a campfire left alone...and open rubbish burning. If a tree falls in the forest...the question is not so much of who is there to hear it fall, but of who or what caused it to fall. If a tree burns, the forest burns and who is there to start it? That is what a ban is for, to keep your own ideas of what you can and cannot do about fire free and clear of responsibility for the tree in the forest. The law doesn't think you are stupid, they think we all have to work to keep Woodstock and the surrounding areas as beautiful as possible for as long as possible.

Fire record for any one day:

Saturday:

12 Noon...Brush fire on Delision Lane, Woodstock. Fire spread to a shed owned by William Allen, Woodstock Company No. 1 responded.

12:10...Lake Hill, a house fire in the residence of Norman Wilbur caused extensive damages and was answered by the Lake Hill Fire District and Woodstock assisted.

Appendix 3

An accounting of St Patrick's Day in Woodstock, vaguely about a gentleman who made an appearance at the Café Espresso on Tinker Street, but about much more than that. The piece shows a great deal of humor, something not often seen in his writing, and a welcome relief from the darker material he often wrote.

At the Espresso
by Jackson C. Frank

As crowds from all points and activities in Town flowed in, the Café Espresso prepared itself for the appearance of one Ralph Santinelli. New York has its Parade, Ireland floods the airwaves and somewhere, we are sure, a ghostly figure shakes his misty staff at a fleeing mass of spectre reptiles, sits down on an oversize Shamrock and drinks a well-earned cup o' the Grog with his Leprechaun friends at the end of the day. Woodstock? Woodstock had Ralph Santinelli.

It just goes to show you how really Irish most of us are at heart. Ralph was a bang-up success. Why? Well, for one thing he is a good performer, drinks his whiskey clear and is a nice guy. For another...half of us had forgotten entirely that this was the

Reverend Mr. Patrick's Day weekend at all, the sudden recall to reality was a thunderous boom-clap of fun for everyone. Ralph banjos most of the way, and the technique and earth of material combined amazing (sic) well. The Irish repertoire he set out upon was well-received and, need we say, very appropriate, all things taken into account.

It seems a shame the old-time celebration of St. Pat's has gone the way of the Precinct's Mounted Police...out to pasture. A donnybrook and socking it to the Joycean way of life are very much out of step with Our Thinking Times. Then again, the Irish live in agreement with England at great advantage to us. When something bugs the nationalist and true patriot, they get together and blow something else up...most of the time they just prepare to... it's all the same. Of course that seems unfair to put in print, but then we mean Ireland's Irish...and that is the point. In America St. Patrick's Day is a celebration parade. Usually it rains on that parade and Macy's has a big sale. Big deal...Listening to songs of the Ould Sod one can never really depart from a begrudging admiration for the Irish way of thought...maybe next St. Patrick's Day we can all get together and plan some way to blow up Macy's and paint the whole damn city green.....

Appendix 4

Another piece from Richard Stanley. This contribution shows how righteously indignant Jackson could become when confronted by something he perceived as wrong, much like his anger concerning civil wrongs in "Don't Look Back."

The Burning Land
by Richard Stanley

One Sunday in September, the four of us, Jackson, Katherine, Kate, and I, decided to take a drive to the south of where we all lived, rolling hills flanked lovely flatland. I knew that it support-ed intensive truck farming and that this was where our seasonal produce came from, but I never gave a thought to how the pro-duce got from the fields to my mother's table.

We stopped first in this farming country. It wasn't hard to imagine why someone had thought to name it the Eden Valley. It was a warm day; summer was refusing to give way to the advance of fall. The air was still and a haze hung like smoke, through which the mid-afternoon sun glowed.

On these drives, we were always looking for out-of-the-way, secret-seeming places and would drive off the main road to follow a dirt track wherever it led. On this particular day, we nosed along a narrowing path through woods that ended in a truck farmer's picked-over field, surrounded on all sides by woods. This was just the sort of place we loved; it seemed isolated from all the world around. We left the car and walked around the field until something along the edge of the woodland caught our eye. Getting closer, we found a row of joined concrete cubes about fifty feet long of the rudest sort of construction. A window and a door had been cut into the front of each, but there was no evidence of any actual windows or doors. The floors were bare earth. They looked ruined, but the presence of some debris suggested recent habitation.

We all stood in silence, contemplating this blot on the landscape, framed by the wonderful woods. I noticed that Jackson was starting to act somewhat agitated, moving nervously, his mouth working in tight, twisting expressions. I could not imagine why. Some rage seemed to be building within him and he started to speak in taut, angry tones. "Do you—do you—do you realize?" he said, haltingly, at a loss to express his feelings. "Do you realize what this is?" he said again, almost uncontrollably, as if he were going to speak in tongues or channel the voice of some spirit. I have to admit that I stood there dumbly not realizing anything. "This—this is what they gave them to live in when they were working here! The migrant workers were made to live here. It's not fit for a pig! Jeezus!" He trailed off into incoherent ranting, slowly becoming silent. I felt truly stupid. Of course, it was, but how could anyone live there? There was nothing within those bleak walls. Patterns of black mold were the only decoration. None of us had ever been so directly confronted with the evidence of the near-slave-labor conditions in which the migrant workers lived. The sun was beginning to redden as it lowered in the sky, and the beautiful afternoon suddenly seemed to become threatening. I remember Jackson saying, "Let's get the hell out of here. I can't stand the thought of this!"

We got back to the car and, finding our way back to the main road, continued on our way south into the Alleghany National

Forest and another unexpected experience.

As we slowly descended toward the Alleghany River, the enveloping forest and the fading, early evening light, now thickened with actual smoke, intensified the haze that had persisted through the day. Suddenly we came out of the forest into a scene of devastation. Everywhere we looked, the trees had been cut down and the land bulldozed. We saw that not only trees but also demolished buildings had been pushed into huge piles, and all these heaps of rubble were burning—some vigorously, others with only occasional tongues of flame darting out. It looked like a war zone.

Kate and Katherine walked away from the car. Jackson stood with his back pressed against it and when I turned to look at him from several feet away, he was staring straight ahead, his face set in determination. The fire! I saw the firelight glinting off the scar tissue that covered a lot of his face, constantly changing his expression, although he moved not a muscle. A sudden flare-up reflected so strongly that his face looked ghostly, the way it appears sometimes in pictures taken with a flash, so that parts appear overexposed, white and totally featureless. Jackson remained stoic—he was obviously struggling, but he held his ground.

We were standing on Seneca land that in two years would be under the Kinzua Dam, but that was now burning with the fury of hell. Jackson said, "Buffy [St. Marie] sang about this—the treaty's been broken by Kinzua Dam." (The song is "Now That the Buffalo's Gone.") I imagined that we could hear Buffy's tremulous, wraithlike voice from within the smoke-filled air. The hair on the back of my neck stood up and I was transfixed by the scene and by Jackson's appearance as he faced the fire, standing firm and saying very little. Across his face passed every imaginable human expression, etched by fire. He said only, "They are here, they are here—do you hear them?' The voices of a thousand souls, some who died in fire, some in battle, seemed to mingle with the sound of Buffy's voice in my head. I thought I was about to faint, but Jackson stood there solidly. I think that in those moments he was facing down great horrors of his own.

We stood watching the devastating spectacle until perspiration was running down our faces. On our way home, no one spoke for miles.

Afterward, the pedant in me had to find the Seneca treaty that Jackson had recalled from Buffy's song. Written in 1794, it stated, "This is a new and important security against your being cheated; and shows the faithful care which the United States now means to take for the protection of your lands." Perhaps our young nation was idealistically motivated to such "faithful care" at the time, but in little more that 100 years, plans were under way to abrogate this oldest active treaty with any American Indian group, and by 1965, the faithfully cared for Seneca land would be under five hundred thousand yards of concrete, 3 million cubic yards of landfill, and 1.5 billion cubic yards of water, covering an area of more than 21,000 acres.

Appendix 6

Richard Stanley again, in a hilarious story about a close call at a staid college in upstate New York.

Jackson, Tarred and Feathered in Houghton –
Saved by the Unitarians
by Richard Stanley

Sometime in early 1964 Jackson started talking to me about get-ting down tracks for a possible album. At the time I worked part time for a little recording company, Audio Industries, that main-ly recorded school and church groups and produced LP copies for them. I did primary engineering and tape editing (these were the days of the razor blade and editing block) at which I became quite proficient. We also did a couple of commercial projects. I had access to all of the AI gear and to the MIT acoustic engineer designed auditorium at Houghton College in Houghton, New York, through work that we had done there. I told Jackson that I would do the engineering and tape editing if he would just pay for the tape and suggested the site as having the best acoustics of any available space to which I had access and thought that I could get the school to let us use, based on my connection there recording some of their music programs. I set it up with the school over the phone and we went down (about a one hour trip) packed into my dad's '54 Chevy station wagon on a very hot day in mid-summer.

To appreciate what ensued you must know that the school was run by Fundamentalist Baptists and was more a divinity school than anything else, although they had full liberal arts program. We arrived mid-day and set up with Jackson on the stage, miked to take advantage of the acoustics of the well-designed hall (we had no effects, including delay or echo) and I set up in a room off-stage isolated from the live sound and we proceeded to do practice takes, intending to start in earnest the next day. Jackson ran through some his current repertoire and during this time a few students drifted in and out through the back doors of the auditorium. Late in the afternoon we left, got dinner and spent the night in a motel nearby.

When I got up in the morning there was a message marked "urgent" for me at the front desk to call the office of the president of the school. Being familiar with the nature of the school I had some idea of what this might be about, but nothing could have prepared me for what awaited in the office of the president. I was shown into the office where I faced an inquisitorial quartet consisting of the president and other officials who glowered at me with looks to kill. It was clear they were mighty upset about something, especially the president who was already red in the face. I don't remember the opening salvo, but they attacked in unison, all of them becoming highly colored, shaking with God-ly Christian rage and shouting as sweat ran on their faces. We had besmirched their sacred institution and brought sin to roost among their dear innocent students. Some of the students who had heard us the previous day had reported to the administration and the president said, his overwrought voice cracking and his face growing to ever darker shades of red, that he had been told that we were doing "devil music with a sinful beat and blasphe-mous words" in their institution blessed by God and consecrated in the name of Jesus Christ! Not only that, but somehow they had become aware that Jackson and Katherine were living in sin, having taken a room together at the motel. Did they have spies? Wow! I was scared and could almost see them heating up the torture tongs and boiling oil or tar and feathers for all three of us. We packed up and got out of there in a flash before the wrath of God could strike out down, first sweating, but then, safely out of town, laughing about the whole experience all the way back home.

There remained the problem of a suitable recording site as this near death experience had done nothing but screw our purpose to the sticking point as it were. Later in the week I contacted a friend, Herman Trotter, who was a musician and active in the W. Ferry Street Unitarian Church. They graciously offered the use of the sanctuary for five days at no charge and in this decidedly more amicable environment we recorded 12 tracks of Jackson's material using two mics, a Berlant four-channel mixer and a Premier Electronics Lab Ampex-quality tape deck in mono, full track on ¼" tape. I handed off the only fully edited copy to Jackson when I finished it, not having made a safe-keeping copy nor did I keep the out-takes. The resultant edited master tapes would be the first album length professional quality recordings made of Jackson and, although they were done without even a simple compressor or an EQ balancing processor, they would be a valuable addition to the existing archive of his work. Like much of the life that was Jackson C. Frank, they appear to have been lost to us forever.

Appendix Seven

Obituary of Judith Piepe, July 2, 2003
by Karl Dallas

The burgeoning Soho scene of the Sixties and Seventies, when soon-to-become famous young guitar geniuses and singer-songwriters could be heard for a few pence in folk cellars and church crypts, was presided over by Judith Piepe, a big, motherly German refugee whose speciality was ministering to the homeless.

Judith Maria Sternberg, social worker and songwriter: born 22 February 1920; married secondly Tony Piepe (one daughter), third 1981 Stephen Delft; died Levin, New Zealand 19 June 2003.

The burgeoning Soho scene of the Sixties and Seventies, when soon-to-become famous young guitar geniuses and singer-songwriters could be heard for a few pence in folk cellars and church crypts, was presided over by Judith Piepe, a big, motherly German refugee whose speciality was ministering to the homeless.

She befriended some who became big names, like Simon and Cat Stevens, but will also be remembered by the countless waifs and strays who flooded into London at that time, seeking their for-

tunes, but often finding only loneliness in its empty streets. Piepe always said her fondness for these lost ones came from having wandered through Europe as a stateless person in the years before her arrival in UK on the very eve of the Second World War. She kept open house at her home in Cable Street, East London, for almost any folkie who needed a place to crash.

Simon later recalled:

"They all came down to Judith's house. There was Sandy [Denny, singer with Fairport Convention], and Al Stewart. It was a really rich seam, and it's too bad it's never been documented, because it was really important. It had a big, big effect on a lot of people, and really influenced English pop. The Beatles were touched by it, and the Moody Blues and a whole lot of other big groups."

Piepe had heard Simon perform at the Flamingo club, usually a rhythm 'n' blues haunt, and worked hard to get him a daily spot on the BBC's Five to Ten religious slot in March 1965, which she introduced herself. As a result, he was offered a contract by CBS, for whom he recorded the rare Paul Simon Songbook, a one-hour session of solo acoustic recordings of songs that later hit the charts during his partnership with Art Garfunkel. Piepe wrote the notes on most of the songs, and also the foreword for a printed songbook of the same title, in which she said:

"I consider Paul Simon to be particularly significant because of the wide range of his songs, his intellectual and emotional approach give them an appeal to far more than just a narrow section of the population.
Paul Simon's songs are personal and individual, the expression of his own thoughts and feelings, hopes and fears, problems and frustrations of our time, of his generation. In speaking for his generation he says what others feel but cannot find the words to say, and in doing so has a liberating and healing effect."

Judith Piepe was a larger-than-life woman around whom legends accumulated. She was said to have driven ambulances for the Loyalists during the Spanish Civil War, yet when I knew her she said she couldn't drive. She was said to have worked for British political intelligence during the early days of the war, which might explain why she was able to obtain British citizenship when so many other anti-Nazi Germans were being interned as enemy aliens.

Even her birthplace was in doubt. She was very proud that she was a "Schlesian", born in Silesia, then part of Prussia, now Poland, in 1920. Yet she spoke German with a Berlin accent, and her daughter maintains she was born in the German capital. Her mother was said to be a French gypsy; not so, say others, she was a well-known Jewish intellectual and art dealer.

She said very little about her father, which was also strange, since he was Fritz Sternberg, an esteemed Marxist economist who had exchanged polemics with Trotsky and ended his days in the United States, where he became a member of Roosevelt's "kitchen cabinet" and was a respected contributor to learned journals like The Nation. She fell afoul of the Nazis as a teenager in Berlin and was arrested for a time by the Gestapo, escaping after three months in jail just before being tried in absentia and sentenced to death for high treason.

After acquiring British citizenship, she never lost her charming Mittel Europa accent. She married Tony Piepe (actually her second marriage, though she never spoke of the first) and mothered a daughter, Ariel. Though her father was Jewish and she was brought up an atheist, by the time I met her she had converted to Christianity and was associated with St. Anne's Church in Soho. In actual fact, by asking her musician and singer-songwriter friends to play there she created what was in effect one of the country's first folk clubs to have its own premises, though Russell Quaye's skiffle cellar and Les Cousins in Greek Street were probably already the main reasons so many youngsters flocked into

Soho.

However, not all her protégés remembered the time happily. Simon said some years later:

"One day I got caught in a downpour and I stepped inside St Anne's Cathedral [sic], which is on a little park in Soho. I was impressed with the sermon that I heard being delivered. What impressed me was that it didn't say anything, nothing.
When you walked out of there, it didn't make any difference whether you walked in, unless you dug stained-glass windows, you know. Because the meek are inheriting nothing, nothing and that's the basis of this song called "Blessed"."

Three members of the Soho crowd in those days, Peter Bellamy, Heather Wood and Royston Wood, under the name Young Tradition, recorded her song The Hungry Child on their album for Transatlantic So Cheerfully Round, in 1967.
In the winter of 1969, the St Anne's crypt became a regular night shelter for the homeless and developed into the charity Centrepoint, taking its name satirically from the nearby office tower block at the top of Charing Cross Road, whose owners found it more cost-effective to maintain it empty.
Judith met and became the partner of Stephen (later Simcha) Delft, a guitar builder and repairer. They married in the summer of 1981 and emigrated to New Zealand the following year. She became very frail in her later years and was taken into a rest home two years ago.

Karl Dallas

SONGS *by* JACKSON C. FRANK
Unreleased, unrecorded lyrics and the scribbles of a man

When Jackson passed away in 1999, his possessions came to me, as his heir and also as administrator and executor of his estate, a role set forth for me as part of my role as his legal guardian, and later reaffirmed when his mother discovered his will in a photo album in her home. He didn't have much more to his name when he died than he did when I first met him in Queens, New York in 1993. He had, besides his apartment furniture and his clothing, most of which he had outgrown, a pair of guitars, up one from 1993, a small television, a couple of notebooks and a couple of books. Inside the notebooks, which were mostly empty pages, were the lyrics to several songs, with one or two snippets of others included. What follows are transcripts of all of them, to the best of my ability, given his handwriting which, as Phil Ochs said of his own penmanship, "wouldn't have suffered much if his hands were webbed." There are no known melodies or chord progressions for any of them, with the exception of the first one, which is also the only one that I saw him perform, in the weeks prior to the 1994 session at UCCC. He tired at the session and never got around to recording the song, which is untitled.

This is in d modal on the fifth fret capoed:

The columns are rolling
But I am holding onto you
Just a soldier till it's over
Fighting world war two
They'll take us from the farmlands
From the assembly lines too
Where there's war upon the waters
They'll take the boys in blue
Chorus: Like a rose trellis in the wind of winter
Shaking out the dry petals to the ground
It takes a man from his woman to tear
The world destroyers down

If I take a train in Paris
If I'm running in a field
If the time to really care is
too sudden to conceal
I'll do my tour of duty
And god ain't it enough
There's home and all its beauty
We have to learn enough's enough
Chorus
The columns are rolling
But I am holding onto you
Just a soldier till it's over
Fighting world war two

Another untitled ditty:

I wonder who sent the raindrops
to fall upon my head
I wonder until the rain stops
then I go to bed

I was forty years old before now
I'll be fifty before the spring
Now diamond ring girls and the time on their curls
Gave me this song to sing
(Unintelligible) into motion
A tiger that danced the tune
Walked in off the ocean
In the mirror of the moon

The (unintelligible) came to incite me
And faded half on a throne

And I wonder who sent the raindrops
To fall upon my head
I wonder until the rain stops
Then I go to bed.

Another seemingly finished song, "Angel of Night." This one bears the notation, "D modal, 5th fret" but again, the chords and melody are missing.

Angel of night, in the garden of light
Where I dreamed you
Come closer to me then this melody can dream you
Please take my hands,
For then are the plans that might free you

First come the stars
Then come the scars
Over milkweed
The blind (unintelligible) their sight
Times perfect delight
In the same need

I have some secrets
Here all alone on the shelf
But talking to you has
Once again made me myself
Free though the stone
The puppeteer trying to own you
If not for me
Probably he would enthrone you
The temperature rises
The fire all through the day
While your lips crave the water
(Unintelligible) these things away.
Maybe baby you should review this lesson
Shake off the bonds
More magic wands for confession
Time has a way of hanging it all on a nail
Now is the time for your heart to set sail.

It is a tough task deciphering the scribbles of the man. Ironically, when he was younger his penmanship was impeccable, but as he got older, and more on the edge of his particular madness, or under certain medicines, his script was all but undecipherable, which makes one tend to make assumptions as to what he meant to say, etc. The following song is pretty direct, lamenting his being in a "house of the mad." It is probably called "The Prisoner." I know that he saw his body, with all its wounds and scars, as a prison from which he could never escape.

Tell me said the prisoner
In a voice so low and sad
How came I to be selected
To this house of the mad?

Do I dream of false conviction
In everything I do?
Is there a place for this burden
In the eyes of just a few?

Will there be no answer given?
Is perfect just a choice?
Do I see a stain in patience
All following a voice?

My heart says the prisoner
Was torn in parts enough
To go on with such a victory
Is painting (parting?) words enough

I never knew a friend here
Never passed a scale
And as the total victim
I judge the password failed

Tell me said the prisoner
In a voice so low and sad
How came I to be selected
To this house of the mad?

The following is one of two really complete and solid songs, all words legible and sensible, which is not always the case with anything written by hand.

Wasted by the sudden winds
Out on the street alone again
Can't get to you it's plain to see

Walking lame without a cane
Will the rainbow come again?
But here's what they did to me.

If only I could make a bet
That they ain't finished what they started yet
I'll leave and go back to my home
Walls of nightmares stolen fears
I've been in a prison made of years
They sail on a sea of stone.

Jenny cries at holes in shoes
Sarah has the simple blues
Time is willing not to go
Who is watching in this night
Who is wrong when it is right
Mumbling illusions forced to show

Faints in bands of purple hats
Blindness seeing this or that
I can't get to you, it's plain to see
I can't believe what they done to me.

Here is the one song that exists in recorded form:

"Juliette"

Hunted by sunlit stone animals deep in the forests of Eden
Juliette your love it amazes me I have no way of believing
You are the first one to know anything of my loving
You are the past one the present and the last one I'm learning
City speaks as evening streaks down the sidewalks of tomorrow
Dark waters turn in endless centuries between the neon and the

shadows
Cloud covered people come dance 'neath the steeples of wonder
Visions of horsemen crowd all the ceilings we're under
And I'm caught wondering how and why we know we both knew
what we were after
It's just like me to go on and on this way 'til I lose you but not
your laughter
Teaching me who tried to wake some sleeping pharaoh's daughter
Just as the crowds along the way release you when they find you
Teaching me it's just a way thru the troubled waters
As the seaside crawled away and let the sun surround you

And last of all, and possibly best of all is a song that might be called "Trying Harder to be a Man." I sense that this song, aside from Juliette, could be his unsung masterpiece, but then, I'm partial. I also invite the reader to make up your own tune for it. I have made up mine, and it seems to go nicely with the poetic rhythm of the piece. Any way you approach it, it is a fine piece of work.

I fight with my soul
For the hour is late
You took my life
And the pain is so great
Used to wake in the morning
Know just what to do
If I was younger I'd live without you
And I ain't even got a plan
Tryin' harder to be a man.

It ain't my intention
A lie should come true
The one I tell

To keep on lovin' you
It's too much,
The sadness it takes
It's too much
The madness it makes
And I ain't even got a plan
Tryin' harder to be a man

Soon I will own you
And no more I'll spend
These wicked days,
Trying to mend
Age will come to us
And drive us apart
Two broken people
With one broken heart
And I ain't even got a plan
Trying harder to be a man.

Once in a lifetime
You meet your sad end
Once in a lifetime
You ain't got a friend
Once in a lifetime
The times ain't that few
Once in a lifetime
I fell loving you
And I ain't even got a plan
Trying harder to be a man.

I fight with my soul
For the hour is late
You took my life
And the pain is so great
Used to wake in the morning

Know just what to do
If I was younger I'd live without you
And I ain't even got a plan
Tryin' harder to be a man.

It is certainly likely that there are more songs out there. Jackson could seemingly conjure them up quickly and in the early years that he was in Woodstock he must have written many, many more, a true lost treasure trove. Maybe the publication of this book will help bring them out of hiding, maybe not.

It is known that there are lost recordings out there, somewhere. One of these, and the most desirable, would be the session that Jackson recorded with his friend Richard Stanley, a year before the trip to England. According to Stanley, it was a high quality recording on reel-to-reel tape and contained many of the songs that later appeared on the 1965 LP. Although Jackson always liked to claim that he wrote all the songs in England, there are few bits of evidence, Richard Stanley's sharp memory that Jackson liked to change the facts around to enhance the legend being one of them, as it were. Mark Anderson also recalls a professional recording setup that a motel owner near Gettysburg College had in one of the rooms, where Jackson recorded a number of old traditional songs. Anderson also recently recovered a badly crumbling recording he made with Jackson at college, labeled "Mark and Jackson. Talkin' and Signifying," which has been restored to playability and Jackson's performances are scheduled for release in 2014.

A presumed video recording of a performance at Katz's Deli, in Woodstock, New York, in 1975 has not been located as of 2014. Several people recall it existing and being broadcast on public access TV in Woodstock but the recording, if it does still exist, was likely done on a defunct medium that might be troublesome when it comes to finding a machine to play it back, if it is ever found. All likely archives at the Woodstock Library have been searched, to no avail.

So, there you have it. If no more music appears, enjoy and appreciate what is out there. That it even was written and played is a minor miracle, since the fact that Jackson survived the cauldron at the Cleveland Hill School is itself a major miracle. Knowing him and being able to play a positive role in his life was the finest gift I have received, and I am proud to be able to share his story, and mine, with you here. Peace.

Jim Abbott